T0400296

ONE IDEA, MANY PLANS

Planners tend to promote formal plans as the only game in town while diverse efforts of urban actors shape our cities. Tracking the development of the American "neighborhood unit" concept in independent India's planning practice and literature—from the national level policies to on-the-ground applications in the city of Jaipur—Vidyarthi explains how a host of actors, including neighborhood residents, squatters, politicians and developers, made different kinds of plans that assimilated the design concept in line with their practical concerns and cultural preferences, creating unique variants of neighborhood urbanism over time. *One Idea, Many Plans* counters misguided characterization of these unforeseen efforts as "unauthorized" by state authorities. It shows how the frequently informal and tacit plans were neither arbitrary actions nor aimless subversions, but purposeful future-oriented efforts that shaped the envisaged sociality and spatiality of Indian cities in more meaningful ways than the official master plans promoting planned neighborhoods.

Carefully illustrating the different kinds of plans local actors use to guide incremental adaptation, improvement and investment, Vidyarthi offers insights about how we might improve formal plan-making. Scholars, students and professional practitioners interested in different regions of the global south would find these lessons useful as a new generation of city design ideas, like sustainability and new urbanism, gain traction in an increasingly globalized world.

Sanjeev Vidyarthi is an Associate Professor at the University of Illinois at Chicago, USA. Trained as an architect, urban designer and spatial planner, Sanjeev studies how to make better plans for places. His research interests include ideas and actions in the fields of planning theory and history, and globalization and development studies.

"This fascinating and important account of the impact of Clarence Perry's 'neighborhood unit' concept (first formulated for New York City in the 1920s) in postcolonial India is a model for the emerging field of global planning theory and practice. Through extensive research and interviews, Sanjeev Vidyarthi shows how an idea that initially represented an imported Western modernity was transformed and regenerated by the creative efforts of Indian planners, developers, and above all by the residents of the neighborhoods themselves."
—Robert Fishman, Professor of Urban Planning, Design and Architecture, University of Michigan, USA

"This well-written book is not just an important contribution to the story of urban development processes in India but also to planning history generally. It shows how planning concepts get re-worked in new situations and become embedded in norms and procedures. Centered round a detailed case study of the Indian city of Jaipur, it provides a well-researched longitudinal study of how urban development processes evolved and how planning ideas entered into these processes. It will be particularly valuable for those interested in the evolution and effects of postcolonial planning practices."
—Patsy Healey, Emeritus Professor, Town and Country Planning, Newcastle University, UK

"Vidyarthi has skillfully deciphered the DNA of almost every Indian town through his reading of development planning and by critically analyzing the idea of the neighborhood unit. His insightful mapping of on-the-ground effects of formal planning ideas and their subsequent mutations is what is crucial for us to understand the residential fabric of the urban Indian landscape—which in the coming decades will be home to at least 400 million people. A succinct and powerful contribution to the very thin literature on urban India."
—Rahul Mehrotra, Professor and Chair Department of Urban Planning and Design, Harvard University, USA

ONE IDEA, MANY PLANS

An American City Design Concept in Independent India

Sanjeev Vidyarthi

Routledge
Taylor & Francis Group

NEW YORK AND LONDON

First published 2015
by Routledge
711 Third Avenue, New York, NY 10017

and by Routledge
2 Park Square, Milton Park, Abingdon, Oxon OX14 4RN

Routledge is an imprint of the Taylor & Francis Group, an informa business

© 2015 Taylor & Francis

The right of Sanjeev Vidyarthi to be identified as author of this work has been asserted by him in accordance with sections 77 and 78 of the Copyright, Designs and Patents Act 1988.

All rights reserved. No part of this book may be reprinted or reproduced or utilized in any form or by any electronic, mechanical, or other means, now known or hereafter invented, including photocopying and recording, or in any information storage or retrieval system, without permission in writing from the publishers.

Trademark notice: Product or corporate names may be trademarks or registered trademarks, and are used only for identification and explanation without intent to infringe.

Library of Congress Cataloging in Publication Data
Vidyarthi, Sanjeev.
One idea, many plans : an American city design concept in independent India / Sanjeev Vidyarthi.
pages cm
1. City planning--India--American influences. 2. City planning--Social aspects--India--History--20th century. I. Title.
HT169.I5V53 2015
307.1'2160954--dc23
2014034574

ISBN: 9781138798113 (hbk)
ISBN: 9781138798120 (pbk)
ISBN: 9781315756745 (ebk)

Typeset in Bembo and Stone Sans
by Saxon Graphics Ltd, Derby

CONTENTS

PREFACE

The story of twentieth-century city planning in most of the world is told using the flip sides of the same argument: how the colonial and postcolonial elites imported and imposed development ideas from the West, and the manner in which expected beneficiaries and excluded actors contested and sabotaged their plans using whatever means available. Using that premise as a point of departure, I track the development of an American concept that served as the prototypical model for designing residential neighborhoods in post-independence India. My aim in doing so is to explore lessons that city builders—officials, planners, politicians, residents and developers—can use to make better plans and places.

I first encountered different kinds of planning and their effect on settlements while working as an architect in the Indian city of Jaipur during the 1990s. Benefitting from the upsurge in India's economy, my professional practice had grown rapidly and undertook a wide range of projects, including various forms of housing, institutional campuses, neighborhood facilities and even the master plan for an entire city. I worked hard and my days were long. Yet my colleagues, collaborators, clients and I often felt dissatisfied with the impact our efforts produced on the overall urban form; we were frankly frustrated with the manner in which Indian cities developed over time. For instance, unanticipated developments—such as informal settlements, unauthorized shrines and jerry-built shops—slowly yet surely would emerge in residential localities and areas set aside for open spaces, transforming the places that we designed with utmost care. I wondered why we planned the way we did and how we could do better.

I passionately grappled with these questions during the years that followed. I explored diverse literature, thought through theoretical traditions and analytical frameworks, conducted carefully conceptualized field-based research, reflected upon my personal experience, and synthesized knowledge and learning from some of the smartest people in academe. These influences are fundamental to the nature and disposition of my work.

Given the many commonalities between cities of the global south, readers in different parts of the world will find this book both pertinent and topical. Depending upon the reader's interest and orientation, this book can be read in several ways. Some readers will find it useful as a concise snapshot of India's city-planning trajectory during the second half of the twentieth century, while others may well enjoy the detailed explanation of different approaches to plan-making.

The book is organized in three conceptually distinct yet interrelated parts. The first part focuses upon the origin and purpose of the discursive planning concept, and India's planning agenda and practice in the decades immediately following the country's independence in 1947. The second and third part describe the concept's applications in Jaipur, widely perceived as India's indigenously planned city. The second part explains the interplay between the built spatiality and envisaged sociality of planned neighborhoods, and the wide variety of tacit and informal plans sponsored by neighborhood residents and users. The final part explains how real-estate developers interpreted the meaning of neighborhood planning according to various goals and purposes, while politicians, in line with the popular orientation of India's ever-deepening democracy, sought to reconcile the disparate efforts of different planning actors.

I gratefully acknowledge the many colleagues, well-wishers, and friends who made this project possible. I would not have made it to graduate school without the encouragement from Rohit Singh, Prof. Mohammad Hasan and Nihal Mathur. Research would have been difficult without generous financial support from the University of Michigan, American Institute for Indian Studies, Faculty Scholarship Support Program of the University of Illinois at Chicago (UIC), and the Department of Urban Planning and Policy at UIC. I thank the officials of the Government of Rajasthan, the Jaipur Development Authority, the Jaipur Municipal Corporation, the Town Planning Organization and the Rajasthan Housing Board for sharing their experiences and relevant plans and policy documents with me. Thanks are due also to the staff of the Indian Town Planning Institute, Town and Country Planning Organization and the School of Planning and Architecture, New Delhi, for their assistance with archival materials. I am indebted to members of the Indian planning profession who candidly shared their lifelong experience of city planning and development with me. I especially want to thank Narendra Rajbanshi, M. N. Joglekar, M. N. Deshpande, Mukul Singh, Muktiraj Chauhan, V. K. Soral, Y. K. Bhatt, R. K. Sharma, A. K. Gupta, B. G. Sharma, A. N. Purohit, K. N. Mathur, Sayed Shafi, B. G. Fernandes, R. L. Bawa, B. L. Mehra, H.S. Mathur and G. S. Nandiwal for their help and guidance. I also thank currently serving planners, many of whom wished to remain unnamed, for sharing their stories and insights about how urban India works.

I first became interested in the discipline of city planning while studying at the University of Leuven in Belgium with Professors Andre Loeckx, Louis

Albrechts, Jef Van Den Broeck and Han Verschure. Work on this project began at the University of Michigan, where I was again fortunate to have wonderful teachers and mentors, including Robert Fishman, Doug Kelbaugh, Jonathan Levine, Richard Norton, Joe Grengs and Scott Campbell. The dissertation committee left an indelible imprint on my way of thinking. Gavin Shatkin asked probing questions and taught me the ropes of research design, while Aseem Inam pushed me to think about the complexity of cities and the importance of purposeful planning interventions. Will Glover helped me in numerous ways on this project, not least by posing simple questions that frequently challenged my ostensible knowledge of Indian cities and forced me to think in broader ways.

I rewrote most of this book while working at the UIC in an intellectually stimulating environment with supportive department heads and wonderful colleagues. Charles Hoch has influenced me most. Through his own scholarly example, pragmatic reasoning and careful thinking about the field of planning, he not only helped iron out wrinkles in my approach but also coached me in meaningful ways. Charlie, Will and Marty Jaffe generously read portions of the manuscript and provided constructive criticism and valuable feedback. None, of course, are responsible for such errors of commission or omission that remain.

Friends from graduate schools are now spread far and wide but constitute a key part of my network. Khalid Bajwa, Ahmed Zaib Khan Mehsud, Sevin Yildiz, Chris Coutts, Carlton Basmajian, Anirban Adhya, Raju Mann, Elijah Davidian, Konstantina Soureli, Ashok and Priyam Das and Neha Sami continue to provide warmth, companionship, and intellectual sustenance. My partners—Shashikant Singhi, Kavindra Jain and Kiran Mahajani—and many close friends in Jaipur, including Ashok Pareek and Piyush Singh, consistently support, sustain and indulge me in innumerable ways. Friends in many other parts of the world have extended hospitality and generosity in ways that cannot ever be repaid. Martijn De Coster, Christoph Thijs, Toon Coenen, Ajay and Seema Godra, Narayan and Razia Pendse, and Rajan and Nandita Bhatt have made me feel at home in Leuven and Delhi. I am also grateful to Catalina Ortiz, Meng Sun, Marcela Lopez, Yang Yu, Marina Toneli and April Jackson for sharing the discoveries of their own emerging research projects with me.

Peers and senior colleagues provided encouragement and venues in which to present and polish my work. I wish to thank Chris Silver, Andre Sorensen, Tim Mennel, Amita Sinha, Robert Freestone, Richard Harris, Amrita Daniere, Rahul Mehrotra, Wlliam Mazzarella and Nihal Perera for helpful discussions and feedback on this project. Nicole Solano at Routledge has been an ideal editor. The confidence she placed in this project right from inception made the task of completing the manuscript that much easier. Judith Newlin provided invaluable clarifications and editorial support. Vanessa Mickan copy-edited the manuscript with utmost care and affection. Four anonymous reviewers enthusiastically supported the project and provided precise and detailed comments that helped improve the book. I simply could not have finished this project without the talented and good-natured assistance of Sushil Verma in Jaipur and Sarah Kellerman at UIC, both of whom helped me with the book's illustrations.

Finally, my family—including my wife, Priti, and our parents, siblings, cousins and their spouses—have been solid pillars of strength. Priti and my daughter, Anandita, have lived with this book since the very beginning. Without their love and affection, this project would not have been possible. I dedicate this book to them.

PERMISSIONS AND ACKNOWLEDGEMENTS

Chapter 1 is published in revised form from "Reimagining American Neighborhood Unit for India," in Patsy Healey and Richard Upton, eds. *Crossing Borders: International Exchange and Planning Practices* in Royal Town Planning Institute Library Series, London: Routledge (2010), pp. 73–93, reprinted with permission from Taylor & Francis Books (UK). Chapter 2 is reprinted in revised form from "Inappropriately Appropriated or Innovatively Indigenized? Neighborhood Unit Concept in Post-independence India," *Journal of Planning History* 9, no. 4 (2010): pp. 260–276, reprinted with permission from Sage publications. Portions of Chapters 3 and 4 are published in revised and expanded form from "Indianizing the Neighborhood Unit: The Jawahar Nagar Plan," in Nihal Perera and Wing-Shing Tang, eds. *Transforming Asian Cities: Intellectual Impasse, Asianizing Space, and Emerging Translocalities*, London: Routledge (2013), pp. 190–206, reprinted with permission from Taylor & Francis Books (UK).

The "neighborhood unit" diagram on the cover page is reproduced from Perry, C. 1929. *Regional Survey of New York and its Environs*. Vol. VII, p. 88, with permission from Regional Plan Association, New York.

Maps, photographs and drawings not otherwise credited were created by the author.

INTRODUCTION

Many people's positions and perspectives conflate the idea of planning with governance, even as different *kinds* of plans shape our cities. This book tracks some of the plans made around the "neighborhood unit," an American planning concept that became the prototypical model for designing residential neighborhoods in independent India. Offering a story about how plan-making works in different ways, I explain how a divergent range of plan-makers interpreted and adapted this design idea in line with their practical needs and cultural preferences. In order to distinguish between the various efforts, I use the terms "spatial plan" and "spatial planning" to describe purposeful future-oriented efforts that various actors (individuals, households, communities) make to anticipate and improve existing urban conditions.[1] In contrast, I use the terms "urban plan" and "urban planning" to refer to the formal plans prepared by professionals as technical advice, which include regulation and investment decisions for governance by public and corporate agencies.

The notion of urban planning in independent India stemmed from the liberal idea of development planning, whose practitioners believed that the State should employ its resources and legitimacy to pursue all-round improvement for people of all walks of life.[2] There is nothing particularly Indian about the idea itself; the premise that the State can and should play an active role in organizing and leading development has been a cornerstone of public policy in many parts of the world. However, the application of this tradition of state-sponsored development in the field of city planning and development during the decades immediately following India's independence in 1947 was distinctive in at least two important and interrelated ways.

First, inheriting power from the departing British, India's indigenous elites built a rhetoric that identified plans with explicit and predictable outcomes, ignoring the inherently provisional and contingent nature of planning work.[3]

Operating within the context of Prime Minister Jawahar Lal Nehru's distrust of the private sector and belief in centralized planning, the tiny group of new ruling elites—comprising political leaders, elected officials, technical experts and state bureaucrats—tasked itself with making and implementing an ambitious range of plans at an audacious scale in an uncharted territory. Second, the new ruling elites combined the institutional templates and routines the colonists had left behind with new ideas about development and planning. For instance, colonial agencies such as the Urban Improvement Trust, dominated by engineers and bureaucrats, continued to function even as the authorities adopted the new master-plan approach aimed at creating a comprehensively planned city comprising self-contained neighborhoods.

Thus, however inadvertently, the new profession of urban planning became a subordinate part of a postcolonial bureaucracy, which had not only survived the transition of power but also grown rapidly after India's independence.[4] However, the established cadres of state officials had very different conceptions of planning and development compared to the first generation of Indian planners, who joined the public sector upon returning from graduate schools in the United States and United Kingdom during the 1950s, as well as the great majority of people who lived in the new towns and neighborhoods but were excluded from the formal planning process. The combination of different positions and expectations provoked a range of plans centered around the idea of planned neighborhoods. While some plans pursued independent goals, many aimed to transform the official plans. I use the term "transformation" to denote a positive and significant change in form that alters the identity of something, just as a caterpillar turns into a butterfly. In this sense, and from the spatial planning perspective, meaningful change does not happen when actors respond to urban plans passively with indifference but when they engage actively by resisting, adapting, or appropriating different proposals.

Planned Neighborhoods

The idea of planned neighborhoods is central to the field of city design and embodies several important concerns of the modern planning movement. At its core, the concept (in all its avatars) combines a description of physical features (dwellings, infrastructure, amenities) with an account of social meaning (neighborliness, solidarity, civic pride) tied to place.[5] It posits that a specific kind of layout will generate proximate social effects. Although the meaning of the term "neighborhood" remains fuzzy and contentious, the concept's popularity draws upon a rich history and the influences I discuss below, which are critical to clarifying my own approach.

Central to the idea of planned neighborhoods, which emerged against the gloomy backdrop of the industrial city, was a belief in universal human progress inspired by the nineteenth-century reformist movement. Fundamental to this belief was the proposition that humans everywhere want and can pursue a better future, despite the ubiquity and variety of oppressions to which they are subjected. According to this line of thinking, it is as valid in New York as it is in New Delhi to provide carefully planned physical elements—such as well-provisioned dwellings, parks and open spaces—and supporting infrastructure—such as water supply and sewerage systems, schools and convenience shopping—that contribute to a safe and pleasing living environment. In a reflective essay contemplating India's city-planning experience, Ravi Kalia (2006) explains how the notions of social reform and universal progressivism propelled both the thoughts and actions of leaders as they embraced ideas such as political democracy, social equality and secular polity, while promoting an array of new towns and city-extensions across the recently independent nation.

The idea of progress, however, does not diminish the importance of cultural prerogatives. William Glover (2008) shows how cities are empirical as well as imagined entities. Biases and preferences of concerned actors actively, even if implicitly, shape the manner in which planned places are conceived, designed and developed. The preferences of planners and their sponsors, for example, were deeply imbued in design features such as single-family homes and residential-only land use of planned neighborhoods. On the one hand, the employment of these physical elements reflected the prevalent belief in the ability of the material quality of cities to affect society. On the other hand, in the context of postcolonial India, the disciplined layout and ordered geometry of the planning concept made immense sense to the indigenous elites, who, like the colonial British, perceived Indian cities as chaotic and wanted to reform them along modern lines using state-centered initiatives such as statutory master plans.

However, the most significant boost to the popularity of planned neighborhoods came from the practical need to organize city growth. The straightforward design principles of the planned-neighborhood concept not only offered ease and fit for professional use but also helped relevant actors such as subdividers and civic and elected officials make practical judgments about organizing urban land for residential purposes, which constitute the largest land use in human settlements. In this respect, the planned-neighborhood concept's perceived ability to tackle the complexities of the real world helps the idea persist and even flourish as a new generation of practitioners search for feasible and attractive ideas. This is perhaps most evident in the fact that the idea of planned neighborhoods not only continues to play an important role in contemporary planning literature and practice in different parts of the world but has recently been offered a fresh lease of life by the influential Congress of New Urbanism (CNU).[6]

The Organization of this Book

In line with my focus on different kinds of plans, each chapter of this book describes a planning effort centered on the neighborhood unit concept. I pay particular attention to the progressive aspects of the planning idea as well as to the practical needs and cultural preferences of concerned urban actors. Chapter 1 introduces the neighborhood-unit concept and explains how the pioneering planners Otto Koenigsberger and Albert Mayer made discursive plans adapting the concept in line with the cause and context of Indian spatial planning. Analyzing planning efforts from the 1950s, the chapter describes how the pioneering planners construed the planning concept as an instrument of modernization and development, substituting the original American concerns and values that had shaped the concept. Such an interpretation of the concept by pioneering planners reflected the priorities of their clients, who saw the idea of the planned neighborhood through the lens of developmentalism, imagining that its application in India would produce a different set of outcomes than originally intended.

Chapter 2 explains how the neighborhood unit's institutionalization in planning parameters facilitated its assimilation in Indian professional practice to the extent that planners stopped questioning its foreign credentials and started using it as the prototypical model for neighborhood design. The chapter begins by explaining how the first generation of Indian planners had to reconcile the tensions between the perceived foreignness of the neighborhood unit, which violated the nationalistic fervor of the times, and its imagined potential for urban development. Based on examples from a variety of planning documents—including the Delhi Master Plan (DMP), the first Indian city plan with legal standing and formative influence upon the profession during the 1960s—I argue that planners solved this dilemma by appropriating the concept through a series of actions, including schematic tabulation of the neighborhood unit's design principles. These actions not only effaced the idea's American ancestry but also produced a template of stripped-down modernism that practitioners could use as scaffolding for local adaptations. Once broken down in such a manner, the concept was easy to internalize and deploy using parameter plans that provided the legitimacy of rational precision and fit with the procedural nature of formal planning practice.

Chapter 3 argues that local planning histories and practices shape the framing and implementation of formal urban plans in more significant ways than planners usually imagine. It begins by describing Jaipur, a princely city that was ruled by a local monarch, planned in the seventeenth century, and popularly perceived as an exemplar of indigenous planning and design traditions. I argue that while the officers of the new state of Rajasthan, of which Jaipur became the capital, superseded the princely era officials, the modes of governance and development from the princely period continued to provide a useful framework (and frequently the actual personnel) for post-independence urban institutions. I then describe planners' attempts to transition to a comprehensive planning approach during the late 1960s, in line with national trends. These efforts centered upon the city's first master plan, which employed the DMP protocol recommending outward-focused development using compulsorily acquired peripheral lands. Describing the designing and building of Jaipur's first two planned expansions based upon the neighborhood unit and carried out by the public sector during the 1970s, I show how national planning policies interacted with local dynamics to shape the domains of city planning and development.

Chapter 4 explains user plans. It shows how, notwithstanding their exclusion from the formal planning process, neighborhood residents and service providers transformed the built environment in line with their practical concerns and cultural expectations. Seeking amenities and a good residential environment, which had catalyzed the conception of the neighborhood unit in the first place, user plans aimed to adapt the built spatiality both at the plot and neighborhood level, following a different approach to moral economy than the one anticipated by officials. The chapter describes two examples that involved informal collaboration among neighbors for constructing extra bedrooms on mandatory open space, and comparatively better-organized collective efforts to build extra-legal temples in public parks and open spaces during the 1980s. The second part of the chapter describes how neighborhood workers and aspiring entrepreneurs saw economic opportunity in residents' requirements for maids, servants, gardeners, handymen, laundries and dairies supplying fresh milk, and chose nearby rural settlements and adjacent parcels of unoccupied government land as suitable locations from which to supply these services. As a result, small clusters of jerry-built huts gradually became productive informal settlements that not only grew concurrently with the adjacent planned neighborhoods but also acquired political patronage and utilities during the 1980s and 1990s.

Chapter 5 explains how princely practices and established typologies continued to cast their influence even after their ostensible substitution by independent India's new planning approach. The chapter begins by explaining how developers' plans promoting subdivision development constituted a larger shift from the pre-independence mode of land regulation and development administered by state bureaucrats and engineers to the post-independence planning approach premised upon comprehensive urban plans prepared by professional planners. Proceeding slowly and strenuously, the transition created a unique situation, characterized by old-guard reluctance to relinquish control over land administration, housing shortages and a lack of regulatory frameworks and oversight matching the new planning approach. Developers addressed the opportunity by relying upon familiar routines and customary business practices. These included the older template of bungalow-oriented, inward-looking colonial–style plotted development and the traditional social and familial connections they utilized for buying, partitioning and selling agricultural land on the urban edge. The chapter concludes by illustrating how developers' plans steadily took form even as they subverted formal plans and catalyzed ungoverned land grabs.

Chapter 6 analyzes the effect of interaction between different kinds of plans in shaping the city's form and organization. It begins by discussing how diverse plans centered on the idea of planned neighborhoods began to crystallize in Jaipur during the late 1980s. The collective impact was clearest at the often-overlooked intermediate spatial and policy scales—between the city-level master plan and planned neighborhoods, and the top-down planning approach and bottom-up adaptation efforts—that rendered Jaipur's post-independence quarters like a patchwork quilt of differently planned areas juxtaposing each other. Here, many rural and informal settlements abutted their formally planned conjoined twins, which had dramatically changed from within, while a jumble of private subdivisions surrounded them all. Catalyzed by the growing public demands for utilities and civic amenities, Jaipur's politicians enacted a slew of populist measures, including the piecemeal regularization of unauthorized subdivisions and incremental legalization of many informal settlements—a process that continues even today.

Notes

1   This definition is in line with Robert Fishman's broad conception of planning as collective action for common good. See the introduction to *The American Planning Tradition: Culture and Policy*. However, my understanding of spatial planning allows the possibility that different institutions and actors might pursue their own plans.
2   For a first-hand account of the influence of the idea of development in the years immediately following India's independence see, Bowles, *Promises to Keep: My Years in Public Life*. Also see, Merrill, *Bread and the Ballot*.
3   The mismatch between the anticipated and actual outcomes of planned projects is described brilliantly in Hirschman, *Development Projects Observed*.
4   Subramanian, *Journeys through Babudom and Netaland*.
5   See, Rohe, "From Local to Global."
6   See, Talen, *New Urbanism and American Planning*.

PART I

1

DISCURSIVE PLANS

Conceiving Planning Ideas

The conviction that we can build better places is a powerful one. It not only motivates various actors—such as residents, homeowners and officials—to anticipate and improve existing urban conditions, it also catalyzes the conception and adoption of formal urban plans. Central to the development of twentieth-century planning thought and practice is the view that professionally prepared plans can help guide progressive efforts to provide improved amenities, mobility and propriety, helping to bridge many historical divisions, regional differences and social challenges.[1] Exemplifying this approach, planners have employed the idea of the neighborhood unit in diverse contexts, including the United Kingdom, United States, Ghana, India and China.[2]

In the first part of this chapter, I describe the American social anxieties, theoretical influences and practical concerns that shaped the origin of the idea of the neighborhood unit in the 1920s. My aim is to explain the manner in which the contemporary reformist movement influenced the neighborhood unit's conceptualization as a physical planning instrument intended to address a particular set of urban and social concerns. Combining a description of physical features with an account of social meaning tied to place, the concept posits that a specific kind of layout will generate proximate social effects. In the second part of this chapter, I describe the concept's introduction to India. Here, my objective is to highlight a different set of concerns, such as national development and modernization, which underpinned pioneering planners' belief that the neighborhood unit suited the Indian context, just as well as it suited the American context.

By explaining how planners modified and repositioned the discursive concept in line with their comprehension of the local context, I highlight how the neighborhood unit's meaning and purpose in India was markedly different from that in the United States. But, not discounting the importance of clients' cultural preferences and practical requirements, the idea ultimately symbolized progressive impulses in both places. When seen through this lens, the presumed "universal" significance of the notion of a well-provisioned, place-based community was in itself the most significant attribute of the neighborhood unit concept.

Clarence Perry and the Neighborhood Unit

The origin and applications of the neighborhood unit concept are well documented.[3] In this section, my focus is on highlighting the influence of the contemporary American context on the conception of the neighborhood unit. The expression "neighborhood unit" was first employed by New York planner Clarence Perry in the 1920s to refer to his proposed physical planning concept for designing neighborhoods. In suggesting this concept, Perry drew upon several sources of knowledge, such as his own professional and personal experiences, recent theoretical advancements and his association with other like-minded individuals concerned with the design and planning of cities. An understanding of these influences is important, because it helps us comprehend how the social and civic concerns of the times served as a wellspring for Perry's imagination.

Clarence Perry spent most of his professional life at the Russell Sage Foundation in New York, where he worked from 1909 to 1937. The Sage Foundation was a leading philanthropic organization of the time, founded in 1907 to work in the areas of social and civic reforms. Concerns about how to improve American urban communities were emerging in contemporary social sciences and the humanities, motivating turn-of-the-century reformist thinking. For example, the American intellectual elites were concerned that the speeding up of urbanization ruptured the traditional ties between the individual, household and place. While some commentators were deeply pessimistic about the future of modern cities (for example, White and White 1962), some reformists approached the developing metropolis with a combination of pragmatism and optimism, believing that a restoration of the links between family, neighborhood and community might offer a possible solution. Jane Addams, who founded a settlement house, and the influential pragmatic philosopher John Dewey subscribed to this view. The basic tenet of these social reformers was not to defy or ignore the city but to work toward promoting community and social communication, and inculcating neighborliness in the seemingly inchoate and hostile urban environment.[4]

These concerns were probably best articulated in the literature that came out of the new field of urban sociology. Louis Wirth, the Chicago School sociologist, laid out the primary characteristics of the contemporary metropolis in his seminal essay *Urbanism as a Way of Life* (1938). Here the grimmer side of his argument raised the specters of "anomie" and "alienation" in an imagined "mass society," and the brighter side evoked the prospect of a new, progressive era of urbanity, tolerance and cosmopolitanism. Perry was exposed to this emerging literature, and at various times in his career acknowledged the influence of Professors Charles Cooley, Robert Park and Herbert Miller, who emphasized the importance of neighborhood institutions to social welfare.[5] In his 1909 book *Social Organization*, Cooley argued that neighborhoods were the nurseries of "primary ideals," which he identified as loyalty, truth, service and kindness. Park and Miller's works were underpinned by similar concerns and influenced Perry:

> It is only in an organized group—in the home, the neighborhood, the trade union, the co-operative society—where he is a power and an influence, in some region where he has a status and represents something, that man can maintain a stable responsibility. There is only one kind of neighborhood having no representative citizen ... the slum; a world where men cease to be persons because they represent nothing.[6]

Such influences catalyzed Perry's belief that in ever-growing and increasingly differentiated cities, citizens needed a comprehensible and accessible focal point, such as a neighborhood school, around which to base their daily activities. He also imagined that the school's centrality would be further strengthened if the neighborhood, with the school at its heart, became the basic unit for planning, and if the logical definition for a neighborhood derived from the distance a child could easily walk to school.

A second set of influences on the neighborhood unit concept came from Perry's interest in physical planning. He lived in the planned community of Forest Hills Gardens, a spacious suburban development sponsored by the Sage Foundation, and subscribed to the prevalent notion that physical changes in the urban fabric could improve social life and enhance the spirit of citizenship. In advocating the use of neighborhood schools as a focal point to foster a spirit of civic community, Perry was also influenced by the 1907 St. Louis Plan.[7] This was one of many plans prepared following the Columbian Exposition of 1893, most of which copied the "city beautiful" ideas of the Burnham Plan of Chicago in their focus on centralized civic centers.[8] The St. Louis Plan, however, was unique in that it suggested the construction of half a dozen civic centers in different parts of the city. These civic centers were envisaged as a combination of facilities around a common center, such as a park.

In addition to his personal experiences and exposure to recent theoretical advancement, a third distinctive set of influences shaped Perry's imagination: interactions and collaborations with other like-minded individuals who were concerned with the design and planning of cities. Perry's technical milieu provided him with an opportunity not only to learn from other scholars and professionals but also to showcase his work within diverse institutional networks. For instance, Perry collaborated with Clarence Stein and Henry Wright in the design of the planned community of Radburn.[9] He also worked as a team member of the Regional Plan Association of America (RPAA) alongside Lewis Mumford and Catherine Bauer, who had written in support of the neighborhood unit concept.[10] Additionally, Perry's presentations in a variety of institutional settings helped him accommodate wider concerns into his argument in favor of neighborhood units. Perry presented the outlines of his concept, tentatively named the "community unit," at the National Conference of Social Work in 1924, where he argued that the neighborhood:

> With its physical demarcation, its planned recreational facilities, its accessible shopping centers, and its convenient circulatory system—all integrated and harmonized by artistic designing—would furnish the kind of environment where vigorous health, a rich social life, civic efficiency, and a progressive community consciousness would spontaneously develop and permanently flourish.[11]

Here, Perry explicitly linked the contemporary social concerns that preoccupied his audience with spatial means that could address those concerns, in accordance with the popular belief that appropriate urban planning could reinvigorate and sustain the links between the individual, family and community. He was also offering a unique imagined program for how those relationships could be restored in practice, through place-based features such as distinct neighborhood boundaries, road networks and parks. These initial arguments, in an improved format and accommodating a broader range of concerns, matured into the neighborhood unit concept, which Perry presented in the *Regional Survey of New York and its Environs* in 1929.

As evident in Figure 1.1, Perry's proposal for the neighborhood unit was strictly residential in character, in line with the zoning principle, and pivoted around a centrally placed community open space that reinforced civic pride because it contained the school. The public school was, he wrote, in a real sense "a civic institution." He went on, "It flies the national flag ... is found in every local community ... and deserves a dignified site."[12] Along with the school, which occupied the heart of the neighborhood unit, Perry's concept contained three other basic design elements: small parks and playgrounds, small stores and a hierarchal configuration of streets that allowed all public facilities to be accessed safely by pedestrians. To define the relationship between these design elements, Perry prescribed six simple planning principles in detail:

- Size: a residential unit development should provide housing for that population for which one elementary school is ordinarily required, its actual area depending upon population density.
- Boundaries: the unit should be bounded on all sides by arterial streets, sufficiently wide to facilitate bypassing through traffic.
- Open spaces: a system of small parks and recreation spaces, planned to meet the needs of the particular neighborhood, should be provided.
- Institution site: sites for the school and other institutions having service spheres coinciding with the limits of the units should be suitably grouped about a central point.

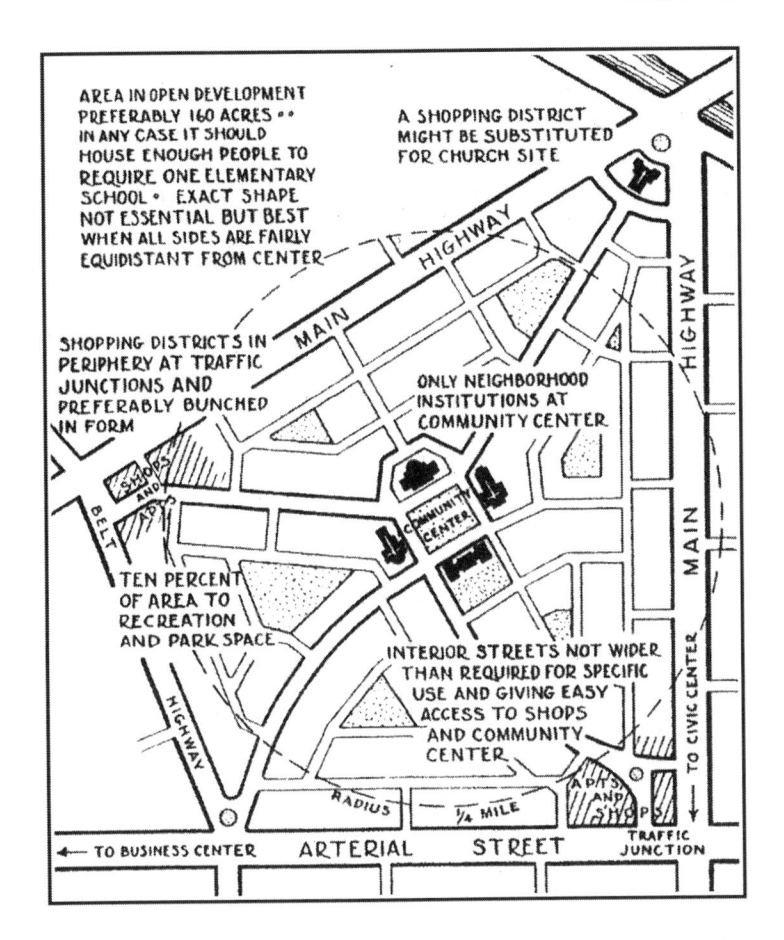

FIGURE 1.1   Clarence Perry's neighborhood unit concept
Source: Perry, C. 1929. *Regional Survey of New York and its Environs.* Vol VII, p. 88.

- Local shops: one or more shopping districts, adequate for the population to be served, should be laid out in the circumference of the unit, preferably at traffic junctions and adjacent to similar districts of adjoining neighborhoods.
- Internal street system: the unit should be provided with a special street system, each highway being proportioned to its probable traffic load, and the street net as a whole being designed to facilitate circulation within the unit and to discourage its use by through traffic.[13]

Perry's concept made its way into the American planning profession within a couple of years of publication, and his design principles quickly became general guidelines for neighborhood planning.[14] The neighborhood unit concept achieved special prominence at President Hoover's 1931 National Conference on Home Building and Home Ownership, where it was cited as a potential solution by each of the four committees formed at the conference, which focused on city planning and zoning, subdivision layout, large-scale building and development, and housing and community.[15] Over the following years, the concept was not only one of the most "widely discussed urban planning ideas" but also became the "stock planning item" for designing neighborhoods in the postwar years.[16] Tridib Banerjee and William Baer acknowledged this when they wrote of the neighborhood unit: "Even when not specifically invoked, its premises and constructs have guided residential planning and design. Its credentials are impeccable, its position preeminent, and its use ubiquitous."[17]

However, the establishment of the neighborhood unit concept as the leading physical planning model in America did not occur without it receiving some criticism. The concept was attacked on two principal grounds. First, some scholars argued that it was predicated on a notion of physical determinism, attempting to force interaction and congeniality upon neighborhood residents. Jane Jacobs (1961) contended that multi-use, unplanned and diverse neighborhoods are instilled with vitality, in contrast to Perry's conception of a static and exclusively residential community. Herbert Gans (1968) argued that "spatial units" were not a prerequisite for "social units," and people's lives were not influenced by their physical environments to the extent posited by Perry.[18] Second, and perhaps more seriously, the concept was accused of encouraging neighborhoods as a means of social division. This criticism stemmed from Perry's labeling of neighborhood units as "self-contained," which Christopher Silver later identified as a code word for the enforcing of social boundaries between neighborhoods, while encouraging homogeneity within them: "The neighborhood unit plan sought to insulate affluent city residents from the disruptive influence of forced interaction with supposedly incompatible social groups."[19]

Indeed, Perry had experienced what he would refer to as the "benefits" of homogenization first-hand while living in the successful suburb of Forest Hills Gardens, which "attracted people with similar tastes and living standards."[20] He was convinced that neighborhoods required high levels of social capital. He envisaged the formation of a kind of club of people with similar tastes. He considered this desirable because the whole neighborhood body would "acquire a homogeneity that would facilitate living together and make possible the enjoyment of many benefits not otherwise obtainable."[21] Chicago-based prominent planner and community activist Reginald Isaacs denounced Perry's model because it sought to obliterate his own ideal of heterogeneous neighborhoods.[22] Isaacs believed that heterogeneity was one of the most important characteristics of successful neighborhoods. Philadelphia planning consultant Henry Churchill seconded Isaacs' critique. In his view, the neighborhood unit was not a natural urban form, and the planner's role should be to control, not obliterate, "the urban pattern of confusion."[23]

After the publication of his idea in 1929, Perry grew more confident about its feasibility, and in his 1939 work, *Housing for the Machine Age*, he repositioned the concept as "The Neighborhood Unit Formula." This formula offered "principles and standards in definite, objective terms which the professional planner could apply in preparing a plan suited to the topography and other characteristics of a particular site."[24] The tone of this work is strikingly different in comparison to his 1929 essay. By now, he stood convinced that the new neighborhood units needed to be planned and executed comprehensively. Perry therefore devoted an entire chapter of the book to urging local governments to start compulsory acquisition of private property rights for assembling land in order to plan new neighborhood units.[25] However, Perry retired from the Russell Sage Foundation in 1937, and by the time this later text was published, his direct influence was waning.[26] He died a few years later, before seeing the widespread influence of his idea in other parts of the world, including India. The overseas popularity of the neighborhood unit would have probably surprised him, because he had come up with the concept primarily as a remedy for the perceived ills of contemporary American cities. The next section describes how a different set of concerns influenced pioneering planners in faraway India.

Introducing the Neighborhood Unit to India

In India, the imaginations of pioneering planners were inspired by a totally different set of concerns about national development and modernization. To elucidate the relationship between contemporary Indian concerns and the ideas of pioneering planners, I will focus on an empirical analysis of the ways in which these planners adapted the neighborhood unit concept. Before I do so, an understanding of the role of Indian elites and their influence on the contemporary development and planning agenda is important. The modernizing aspirations of these elites were not only pivotal to the development agenda of independent India, but they also critically informed the belief of pioneering planners that the neighborhood unit was an appropriate model for independent India.

Indigenous Elites and the National Planning Agenda

Under British colonial rule in India, new indigenous elites had arisen. They were unconnected to historical sources of authority, such as the feudal order, and were committed to social reforms, modernization and development. These elites were largely metropolitan in education and orientation, and they were employed in modernized occupations such as teaching, law and medicine. Their ambitions fueled the emergent idea of modern India, which, although constrained by the colonial order, matched the aspirations of Indians, rather than colonial designs of what a modern India ought to be. Recent scholarship has pointed out that these elites, who had played important roles in the struggle for independence, inherited formal national power when the British departed.[27] Many of these elites did not own landed property and thus lacked close connections with village society, which, in their view, needed to be reformed and modernized quickly in order for India to progress. They imagined a modern society to be wealthy, just, democratic, orderly and in full control of its own affairs—in short, akin to those found in Western Europe and North America. In contrast, they perceived India, especially its villages and the historical parts of its cities, to be a traditional society: poor, inequitable, repressive, violent and dependent.

Development, in this schema, was seen as a process of moving from the latter type of society to the former, and became the prime index for measuring efforts toward modernization.[28] Mainstream development theory, which emerged in the period immediately following India's independence in 1947, argued that development was a social, political, economic, cultural and physical process. New physical contexts were needed, such as the ones produced by the neighborhood unit concept. Also needed were new political institutions (such as legislatures and courts), cultural mores (individualism and self-orientation) and social structures (nuclear family and a casteless society). Pioneering planners and their elite clients in India saw in the neighborhood unit an appropriate instrument to advance this development agenda, which had quickly emerged as the "most powerful influence structuring social and economic transformations in the non-Western world" in the twentieth century.[29]

None other than Prime Minister Jawahar Lal Nehru spearheaded the formulation and advancement of the national development agenda. Planning, as is well documented, played an important part in Nehru's scheme for India. It would be no exaggeration to describe Nehru as a planner's planner, as was exemplified when the Institute of Town Planners, India (ITPI) voted him its first ever unqualified fellow in 1958.[30] At one point, Nehru had exclaimed: "You know how attached I am to the concept of planning."[31] As early as 1938, a good nine years before India's independence, the National Planning Committee, chaired by Nehru, had defined the concept of planning: "Planning under a democratic system may be defined as the technical co-ordination by disinterested experts, of consumption, production, investment, trade, and income distribution in accordance with social objectives set by bodies representative of the State."[32]

Thus, in recommending tools such as the neighborhood unit, the planner was essentially a "disinterested expert" merely facilitating "technical coordination," and his or her recommendations were strictly outside the domain of politics, because the plans were presented to bodies staffed by technical experts, not public representatives.[33] This implied that planners, because of their technical expertise, could be trusted to select the right tools, such as the neighborhood unit, for achieving the desired objectives, and the merits of such a decision were not open to discussion in a political forum. Nehru believed that "under modern conditions we must have experts. If we want to utilize them to the full we must allow them a free hand and there should be as little interference as possible with their work."[34]

The processes used to design and carry out such a planning agenda were facilitated by the State. Sunil Khilnani has identified that the key success of

Nehru's premiership was the "establishment of the State at the core of Indian society."[35] In Nehru's India, the State aimed to be the final articulator of what constituted a good life for its citizens. In the field of urban development, this meant commissioning the preparation of formal plans; Nehru commented: "what I should like in regard to every city is a clear plan of what a city will be like, say, 20 or 30 years later."[36] To realize these plans, it was acceptable for the State and local governments to use police power to acquire private property rights in order to facilitate the planning and construction of new cities and city-extensions. Nehru justified this strategy with statements such as: "In the India of today, the growth of cities, big and small is quite anarchic. It is ugly, it is horrible, in fact, it is painful to see. I am surprised at how it is tolerated by large corporations and city municipalities."[37] The land acquired in this way was to be used for housing a civic and happy community of citizens through the deployment of expert-recommended tools, such as the neighborhood unit. Nehru considered a happy community to be vital for the mission of building a secular and casteless society, as part of the wider project of building an independent nation-state. While laying the foundation stone in 1948 for Bhubaneswar, the new capital city of Orissa state, he was glad to note: "The architect and the chief engineer have thought of this future city in terms not of a few palatial buildings but of a happy community."[38]

The acceptance of the neighborhood unit was aided by the fact that the concept shared several characteristics with the established typology of Civil Lines and also promised to improve its perceived shortcomings. British colonists had developed the Civil Lines, a euphemism for the sequestered European quarters in South Asian cities, during the nineteenth century. They were typically residential settlements of broad and regular streets with bungalows set among vast lots, occupied by the families of expatriate civilian officials. The introduction of the Civil Lines was a significant event in the narrative of Indian cities, as it represented a decisive break from the indigenous city, which was seen by the colonial British as unhygienic, chaotic and incomprehensible.[39] Importantly, the Civil Lines typology had permeated the aspirations of the indigenous elites, who, by the early twentieth century, had begun to plan their own residential areas emulating the landscape of Civil Lines.[40] Nehru, however, subscribed to more egalitarian ideals and had once sarcastically remarked: "Nearly all the Big Noises and Little Noises live in the Civil Lines."[41] Thus, the use of the neighborhood unit in India represented a compromise between the aspirations of the elites and Nehru's vision of a modern socialist state for the mass of the people.

Making it easier for the elites to see the potential of the neighborhood unit was the fact that it shared several design features with the colonial Civil Lines, such as setback of building lines, regular and wide roads, parks and open spaces, and a certain spatial discipline and order that created a tidy appearance. These similarities meant that the neighborhood unit typology did not revolt outright against the aspirations of the indigenous elites, who, like the colonial British, continued to harbor a fear of the indigenous city.[42] A booklet published by the

Town Planning Organization of the state of Uttar Pradesh expressed the elites' fears crisply: "Today, one has an opportunity to choose between planning and no planning, slums and ill-ventilated colonies on the one hand and well-planned and ventilated ones with wide roads, playgrounds and other public amenities, etc., on the other."[43] Thus, in accordance with Anthony King's assertion that the Civil Lines and its bungalows were not just a spatial form but also an attitude of the mind, which persisted long after colonial rule, the modern neighborhood unit promised to fit neatly into the post-independence elitist space vacated by the colonial Civil Lines.[44]

The neighborhood unit concept, especially after its adaptation by pioneering planners, contained several design features that promised to improve the perceived shortcomings of colonial Civil Lines. The neighborhood unit's much smaller lots were more economically viable than the vast lots of the Civil Lines. They also promoted the high-density development deemed helpful in preserving "valuable agricultural land in the interest of the nation."[45] The concept fitted well with Nehru's secular prerogatives, since Indians of all religions would live together in the new neighborhood units, rather than being segregated, as was the case in traditional quarters of Indian cities. The neighborhood unit also appealed to Nehru's progressive and nationalistic sentiments, because it promised to house the school in the center, with the nation's flag flying high.

In the following section, I explain how pioneering planners such as Otto Koenigsberger and Albert Mayer repurposed the neighborhood unit concept, adjusting its original American concerns and anticipated outcomes to address the developmental and modernist concerns of their Indian clients.

Repositioning the Neighborhood Unit

Otto H. Koenigsberger's convictions and design philosophy, which made him amenable to the neighborhood unit, were a reflection of his formal training in the enlightened and modernist traditions of the Weimar Republic.[46] At his alma mater—the Technische Hochschule, Berlin—his mentor was the reputed Weimar architect Ernst May, who was famous for designing public housing in Frankfurt am Main. May's architectural education had included study in Britain, where he worked with Raymond Unwin, absorbing the lessons and principles of the garden city movement. May's portfolio was thus ahead of its time, including features such as semi-independent houses well equipped with community elements such as playgrounds, schools and common washing areas. These facilities also featured in the neighborhood unit concept. May's influence on Koenigsberger was profound and lasting, as is evident in the latter's writings on his works in India.

Koenigsberger's activities in India reflect two major convictions that underpinned his planning philosophy, and both are evident in his sustained faith in the neighborhood unit. The first was a belief in the universalist dimension of modern architecture and planning, which could transcend boundaries and be equally valid in all locales.[47] The second tenet was an extension and reinforcement of the first. Koenigsberger believed that nonsectarian and standardized solutions, such as the neighborhood unit, could swiftly alleviate religious–political strife and the tensions around the scarcity of housing in post-independence India.[48] These beliefs are most evident in his partially successful effort to set up a factory at Delhi for producing prefabricated housing units. These houses were to be erected quickly across India, along the lines of the privately built suburb of Levittown, New York, constructed in the early 1950s.[49]

In 1944, Koenigsberger moved from his planning position in the princely state of Mysore, one of the many regions ruled by local kings, to the government of India as the director of housing, in the Ministry of Health. The next seven years saw him working feverishly, supervising the planning of several new towns to accommodate refugees migrating from the newly created Pakistan, and designing Bhubaneswar.[50] Designed in 1948 as the new capital for the state of Orissa, Bhubaneswar was Koenigsberger's most prestigious assignment in India. For him, as would be the case a little later for Albert Mayer, designing a brand new capital city from scratch was an unrivaled professional milestone.

In designing Bhubaneswar, Koenigsberger assumed that the neighborhood unit was an appropriate fit with the planning concerns of post-independence India (as Mayer would for Chandigarh). In his mind, the concept's origins in the United States did not matter at all because it was universally applicable modern typology, especially suitable for the development agenda of newly independent nations. This position is made explicit in his assertion that the neighborhood unit had a "special appeal to the people of under-developed countries" and, with some adaptations, fit the Indian context well because it extended India's ancient tradition of rural self-government (the so-called "village *panchayats*") into the modern age: "The neighborhood units of the new towns form the best possible links with the type of community life they [Indians] know from their villages."[51]

However, Koenigsberger adapted the neighborhood unit in line with the modernist and nationalist agenda of his elite clients. For instance, he extended Perry's original objective of creating social capital into an attempt to inculcate secularism and castelessness. This becomes evident in the plan of Bhubaneswar, where Koenigsberger adapted the neighborhood concept in two ways. The first was groundbreaking for India: he repositioned the neighborhood unit as a means to produce a secular and casteless society, anticipating by several years the suggestion of the Interim General Plan for Delhi to use neighborhood units to prevent "ghetto-formation."[52] Koenigsberger believed that, given the caste traditions of India, there was a real threat that neighborhood units could become insular pockets, each populated by single socioeconomic or religious groups. The solution, in his view, lay in "the attempt to provide in each neighborhood a cross-section of the population, taking good care to have each social and professional group represented in it roughly in accordance with the relative strength in the whole community."[53]

Koenigsberger's adaptation of the concept in order to dissolve caste barriers is instructive because it stood in contrast to Perry's advocacy for socially similar neighborhood units. While Perry's claims about the virtues of homogeneity had eventually led in the United States to the branding of the neighborhood unit concept as an instrument for segregation, Koenigsberger's argument that neighborhood units could create mixed communities was largely accepted in India. Despite occasionally successful resistance from the hierarchal Indian bureaucracy—which desired homogeneity, in accordance with seniority among officials—Koenigsberger's approach was largely adopted in Indian cities, as is evident in the plans of administrative cities such as Bhubaneswar and industrial cities such as Bhilai. Most city-extensions across urban India planned after the 1960s aimed at mixing up different economic strata of society. Later, the Housing and Urban Development Corporation (HUDCO) played a major role by institutionalizing this idea.[54]

The suggestion that the neighborhood unit should create casteless and secular neighborhoods was drastic, given that caste and religion in India historically served as the main criteria for organizing residential quarters. Koenigsberger's proposition appears daring and somewhat counter-intuitive in hindsight; but in accord with the aspirations of his clients, he substituted the secular and modern concept of the nation for caste and religious affiliations as the social "glue."

The idea that each neighborhood unit should house different class, religious and caste groups also demonstrates the belief of pioneering planners and their clients that neighborhood units would have a civilizing effect on the residents, a majority of whom were recent immigrants from villages or the historical quarters of Indian cities. This marks a second major difference between the application of the neighborhood unit concept in the American and Indian contexts. In India, the elites who signed up to Nehru's vision visualized the disciplined spatiality of neighborhood units as a crucial design feature that would reduce the enormous cultural gap between the educated and civilized few, and the illiterate and uncivilized many, once they began to live together. This belief in the power of the physical environment to exert a civilizing impact comes alive in this quote from Nehru:

> You should not accept or tolerate ugliness anywhere, in your life, in your activities, in your buildings. The worst type of ugliness of course is ugly behavior of individuals and groups. But to some extent, the environment reflects itself in the behavior of the individual, as a beautiful environment helps in developing a sense of beauty in the people who live there. It is desirable, therefore, that what we build, however simple and humble it may be, should have some artistic value. And mind you, do not connect artistic value with money.[55]

This quote highlights Nehru's belief that the spatial environment can improve ugly behavior among individuals and groups, while emphasizing the role of a certain type of aesthetics that is not achieved by large or expensive features, such as big bungalows or ostentatious settings, but comes about by building a well-provisioned but simple and disciplined physical environment such as that of the neighborhood unit.[56] Nehru was once again articulating a relationship between the spatial aspects and the social outcomes of a physical environment: ugly and uncivilized behaviors can be controlled, and even obliterated, by the spatiality and constituent design features of a residential environment. The neighborhood unit, in this scheme, was imagined as a vehicle that promised deliverance by hauling the "uncivilized" into a planned realm, whose envisaged spatiality also served an auxiliary pedagogical purpose.[57]

Koenigsberger was not the first to imagine that the neighborhood unit concept could be employed to house a cross-section of society. In his native Germany, a housing estate had been planned in the early 1940s to reflect the National Socialist Party's ideology of *Volk ohne Raum*, which meant breaking the class barrier and uniting the workers and farmers as "one people." Koenigsberger might have been familiar with this project. The plan for this estate, catering to a population of 7,000, resembled Perry's concept closely, but the German planners insisted that the idea was inherently a German solution.[58] It is perhaps ironic that Koenigsberger, himself a Jew persecuted by the Nazis, imagined that the same idea could dissolve caste and religious barriers in India.

Koenigsberger's second major adaptation, which he called the "band-town" formation, used the scalability feature of the concept to arrange a single row of neighborhood units, not more than half a mile in depth, on both sides of a motorized traffic artery.[59] He found these "chains of neighborhoods strung to an arterial road, like pearls on a string" a sensible arrangement for two reasons.[60] First, it ensured that all units were designed with walking distances in mind, which was appropriate as most residents lacked cars and would therefore use public transport. Second, this arrangement consolidated the small and scattered open spaces within the units into a compact space, which was desirable because scattered pieces of parkland were difficult to maintain in India's dry climatic conditions, easily becoming "brown patches of dusty desert."[61] The consolidation of these areas was intended as a way to refashion Perry's small central square on a grander scale, embellished with a "monument, fountain or other ornamental feature," to be used for community activities.[62] This large focal space could be used for civic and nationalistic functions such as the new nation's Independence Day (August 15) or Republic Day (January 26). In combination with their intention to represent a cross-section of society in the new neighborhoods, this underlined the fact that the pioneering planners and their elite Indian patrons not only imagined the neighborhood units to be compatible with their project of nation building but also visualized them as a microcosm of the nation.

Thus, Koenigsberger's adaptations of the neighborhood unit reflected many aspirations of his most important patron, Prime Minister Nehru, who unequivocally endorsed Koenigsberger's plan and commended it while laying the foundation stone of Bhubaneswar, once again emphasizing its role in reinforcing the new national identity among its residents:

> The new town will be grouped in self-contained neighborhood units, each comprising about 850 families. This will enable the town to grow without losing its community and neighborly character. In each area residential houses will surround the schools and shopping centers and will be near to open fields and recreation grounds. In the center of the town will be a group of public buildings with a Gandhi memorial pillar symbolizing the life and teachings of Gandhiji.[63]

Nehru, however, was aware of the inherent contradiction of deploying Western models in the post-independence context. On the one hand, these models fitted well with the ideals of a secular, modern and democratic polity, and therefore appeared necessary to ensure the progress of the nation. On the other hand, they violated the nationalistic concerns of the indigenous elites, who wished to see a confident and self-reliant nation purged of both colonial legacies and Western influences—a theme I pick up in the next chapter. Nehru tried to balance both demands. For instance, while inviting the American planner Albert Mayer to "build up community life on a higher scale without breaking up the old foundations" in 1946, and asking him to utilize Western ideas, he cautioned that it was not "an easy matter, for the resources are limited at present and the conditions are often very different from those in Western countries."[64] Nehru's cautionary advice implicitly encouraged planners to both employ Western models and carefully combine them with local cultural and social practices.

Albert Mayer and his assistant Matthew Nowicki took Nehru's advice seriously, as evident in their report entitled "Supplementary Notes to the Architectural Study of Superblock L-37," prepared in 1950. Here Nowicki's detailing of the neighborhood plan exhibits a conscious effort to adapt the neighborhood unit to Indian conditions, in accordance with Nehru's comments. The houses were designed around courtyards to provide an internal space that was private and sensitive to the climate, and they also had a provision for terraces to enable the residents to sleep outdoors during the summer nights. Most important, the plan tried to capture the essence of the heart of an Indian urban quarter: the bazaar.[65]

Albert Mayer, like many other Westerners, was fascinated with the oriental bazaar and believed that the bazaar's modern avatar, the shopping center, could preserve and encourage "as far as we can in a reasonably orderly way do so ... the marvelous excitement and gaiety of the bazaar, the people in their sociable pre-occupation with shopping and visiting undisturbed by traffic."[66] This belief is evident in Nowicki's detailed plan of the shopping center, which provided for everyday local practices such as shopping and negotiating while sitting on the floor. Nowicki also incorporated the possibility of installing a seasonal canvas roof, an idea borrowed from the thatch overhangs in indigenous bazaars, to protect the merchandise and provide shade to the pedestrians. He also proposed including a separate area for street hawkers.

Mayer's works in India, like Koenigsberger's, reveal his ideological moorings. His employment of the neighborhood unit in the master plans of Kanpur and Mumbai, which he completed before planning the iconic Chandigarh, reflected his past experiences in the field of what is now called community planning and development.[67] Mayer had gained insights into community housing through a decade of planning experience. In the late 1920s and the early 1930s, he worked for and collaborated with leading architects and planners of the times, including such stalwarts as Clarence Stein and Henry Wright, both of whom made use of the neighborhood unit concept. As a member of a team along with Henry Wright, Allen Kamstra and Henry Churchill, he designed the planned community of Greenbrook, New Jersey during President Franklin D. Roosevelt's second administration, and this experience had also prepared him for planning new towns and neighborhoods. These prior experiences and the modernist development agenda of India's elites informed Mayer's idea that the neighborhood unit suited the Indian context even better than its place of origin, for reasons he summed up to a gathering of planners in Washington, D.C., in October 1950: "However useful the neighborhood concept is here, it is more valid in India, where most people are still villagers and small-community people at heart, and fairly recently by origin."[68]

Such generous advocacy of the neighborhood unit, and the quick employment of it in iconic projects such as Chandigarh, Bhubaneswar and Gandhi Nagar, helped it become institutionalized into Indian planning practice.[69] In India, as in the United States, the neighborhood unit concept eventually became the prototype for designing city-extensions and new towns. Its penetration and popularity can be gauged from the fact that, in 1966, M. C. Krishna Swamy reported about fifty such new towns in an article for the *Journal of the Institute of Town Planners, India*. Krishna Swamy commented that "irrespective of the developing agency the main concept and the basic planning principle dominant in these new towns is the self-contained neighborhood unit."[70] This brings us to a suitable point to recapitulate the two sets of imaginations that enabled the neighborhood unit concept to become the recurrent theme of plans for new towns and city-extensions in both the United States and India.

Conclusion

During my research, I found not even one reference in Koenigsberger's or Mayer's Indian publications to the American urban context in which the concept of the neighborhood unit originated, or to the social anxieties that had prompted its invention. The focus of these documents, rather, was oriented solely toward the planning concerns of the new nation and the development agenda of the planners' clients. I believe the pioneering planners did not evoke the American social concerns and urban context for two reasons. First, similar to their perception of other liberal conceptions, such as a casteless society and secular polity, they believed that the neighborhood idea was universally valid and did not have a monogenic allegiance to any particular locale, including the one in which it was produced. To them, the discursive concept could be customized for particular contexts and its design principles adapted to specific needs, but the basic notion of a well-provisioned place-based community that the neighborhood unit espoused made sense across different cultural settings.

Second, Indians focused on the progressive aspects of the neighborhood unit, perceiving the concept as modern and not specifically American, and thus the pioneering planners did not need to be concerned about its U.S. origins. In line with the ideals of "high modernism" (Scott 1998), Mayer and Koenigsberger believed that planning ideas such as the neighborhood unit were justly transferable, and cities such as Chandigarh, Bhubaneswar and Brasilia could be built anywhere in the world. However, Mayer and Koenigsberger had to reconcile a remarkable contradiction in order to facilitate the neighborhood unit's introduction to India. On the one hand, they imagined the neighborhood unit as an appropriate physical model for producing modern citizens who, for instance, would be secular and caste neutral. On the other hand, they imaginatively linked the concept with a romantic vision of India's historical villages in order to satisfy the nationalistic concerns of the indigenous elites. To Koenigsberger, this latter perspective was self-evident in the fact that the neighborhood unit extended the ancient tradition of self-government in India's villages into the future. To Mayer, the concept was a better fit in India compared even with its place of origin, because Indians were "still villagers and small-community people at heart."[71]

However, pioneering planners mainly worked on high-profile planning efforts and signature urban projects sponsored by the highest echelons of the new nation's leadership. In contrast, lower rungs of the postcolonial bureaucracy conceived and pursued the bulk of the formal planning interventions. State officials and planners in India, as in many other parts of the world, relied upon a regulatory, land-use-centered approach and intrinsically mundane parameters such as neighborhood standards and subdivision codes in order to operationalize the abstract concepts and progressive ideas characterizing this kind of liberal development planning. That is the focus of the next two chapters.

Notes

1 The progressive roots and liberal aspects of the modern city-planning movement are well documented. See, for instance, Fishman, *Urban Utopias in the Twentieth Century*; and Ward, *Planning the Twentieth-Century City*.
2 See, for example, Dahir, *The Neighborhood Unit Plan*; Kirchherr, "Tema 1951–1962"; Hicks, "Rebuilt Agadir"; and Lu, "Traveling Urban Form."
3 Perry, *The Neighborhood Unit*; Perry, *Housing for the Machine Age*; Silver, "Neighborhood Planning in Historical Perspective"; Johnson, "Origin of the Neighborhood Unit"; Patricios, "The Neighborhood Concept"; and Lawhon, "The Neighborhood Unit."
4 Banerjee and Baer, *Beyond the Neighborhood Unit*.
5 Perry, *The Neighborhood Unit*, 126.

6 Ibid., 127.

7 Gillette, "The Evolution of Neighborhood Planning."

8 Smith, *The Plan of Chicago*.

9 Mumford, "The Neighborhood and the Neighborhood Unit."

10 Mumford, "The Planned Community"; Bauer, *Modern Housing*.

11 Perry, "Planning a City Neighborhood from the Social Point of View," 421.

12 Perry, *The Neighborhood Unit*, 72.

13 Ibid., 34.

14 Gillette, "The Evolution of Neighborhood Planning," 427.

15 Banerjee and Baer, *Beyond the Neighborhood Unit*, 24.

16 Silver, "Neighborhood Planning in Historical Perspective," 165–170.

17 Banerjee and Baer, *Beyond the Neighborhood Unit*, 3.

18 However, Gans himself employed neighborhood units as the basic building blocks when working with the consulting team that planned the new city of Columbia, Maryland, during the mid-1960s. See Forsyth, *Reforming Suburbia*, 116.

19 Silver, "Neighborhood Planning in Historical Perspective," 166.

20 Perry, *The Neighborhood Unit*, 110.

21 Ibid.

22 Isaacs also denounced the neighborhood unit as "a fad picked up by technicians who have not yet reached the maturity of the well-rounded planners." Isaacs, "The 'Neighborhood Unit' is an Instrument for Segregation," 219.

23 Cited in Silver, "Neighborhood Planning in Historical Perspective," 169.

24 Perry, *Housing for the Machine Age*, 49.

25 Ibid., 159.

26 Gillette, "The Evolution of Neighborhood Planning," 432.

27 See, for instance, Chakrabarty, *Habitations of Modernity*; and Chatterjee, *The Politics of the Governed*.

28 Huntington, "The Goals of Development"; and Gusfield, "Political Community and Group Interests in Modern India."

29 Sivaramakrishnan and Agrawal, *Regional Modernities*, 2.

30 The significance of this accolade can be gauged from the fact that in its almost fifty years of history, ITPI has elected only three unqualified fellows. Another was Bhagwan Das, who was involved in the first master plan of Delhi and was later a Lieutenant Governor of Delhi.

31 NIUA, *Jawahar Lal Nehru on Building a New India*, 52. A greater emphasis is generally placed on the economical and technological aspects of Nehruvian planning. However, for Nehru, planning was a tool to encourage progress in all fields of national life. He wrote that India's problems called for "planning on a national scale, encompassing all aspects of economic and social life, for efforts to mobilize resources, to determine priorities and goals and to create a widespread outlook of change and technological progress." Ibid., 50.

32 Cited in Prakash, *Another Reason*, 198.

33 Chatterjee, *The Nation and Its Fragments*, 202.

34 NIUA, *Jawahar Lal Nehru on Building a New India*, 71.

35 Khilnani, *The Idea of India*, 41.

36 NIUA, *Jawahar Lal Nehru on Building a New India*, 116.

37 Ibid., 26.

38 Ibid., 117.

39 Hosagrahar, "Mansions to Margins."

40 Khan, "Cultural Transfers."

41 NIUA, *Jawahar Lal Nehru on Building a New India*, 102.

42 Dipesh Chakrabarty has succinctly described this phenomenon: "It would be unfair … to think of this perception as simply Western. What it speaks is the language of modernity, of civic consciousness and public health, even of certain ideas of beauty related to management of public space and interests, an order of aesthetics from which

the ideals of public health and hygiene can not be separated. It is the language of modern governments, both colonial and postcolonial, and, for that reason, it is the language, not only of imperialist officials, but of modernist nationalists as well." Chakrabarty, *Habitations of Modernity*, 66.

43 UPTPO, *Progressive Uttar Pradesh*, 4.

44 King, *Colonial Urban Development*.

45 ITPI, "Autumn Planning Seminar and State Planning Officials' Conference at Lucknow," 23.

46 Koenigsberger's career is described in Aldhous et al., "Otto Koenigsberger," and a brief biographical note by the Development Planning Unit at University College London. Development Planning Unit, University College, London. (No date). Accessed at www.ucl.ac.uk/dpu/Otto%20Koenigsberger/OHK.htm, viewed on March 23, 2006.

47 See Koenigsberger, "New Towns in India."

48 Liscombe, "In-dependence."

49 The failure of this production project and the subsequent political fallout was a principal reason for Koenigsberger's departure from India. However, the factory was taken over and renamed by the Government of India in 1953, and continues to function today. Accessed at www.hindprefab.com/english/memories.html, viewed on February 9, 2006.

50 Koenigsberger's article "New Towns in India" describes nine such new town projects. Some, such as Bhadravati and Bhubaneswar, were designed by him. For some towns, such as Faridabad and Rajpura, he collaborated with various planners. Other towns, such as Nilokheri and Kalyani, were designed by other planners under his supervision.

51 Koenigsberger, "New Towns in India," 105.

52 TPO, *Interim General Plan for Greater Delhi*, 18.

53 Koenigsberger, "New Towns in India," 107.

54 Interview with a senior HUDCO official on April 24, 2006.

55 NIUA, *Jawahar Lal Nehru on Building a New India*, 30.

56 The idea that material objects and spatial arrangements could reshape urban society was central to nineteenth-century reform across the Anglo-European world. See Glover, *Making Lahore Modern*, xxi.

57 The civilizing mission included neighborhood-wide bodies called *Vikas Mandal* (Development Councils) that were intended to sensitize and "educate" the local population in accordance with the neighborhood unit's civic aims. See Clinard and Chaterjee, "Urban Community Development." See Bijlani, "Urban Social Facilities," for how the mission did not work.

58 Schubert, "Origins of the Neighborhood Units Idea in Great Britain and Germany," 34.

59 Grenell, "Planning for Invisible People," 101.

60 Koenigsberger, "New Towns in India," 109.

61 Ibid.

62 Perry, *The Neighborhood Unit*, 40.

63 NIUA, *Jawahar Lal Nehru on Building a New India*, 118.

64 Kalia, *Chandigarh*, 47.

65 Ibid., 68.

66 Mayer, "The New Capital of Punjab," 174. British planner A. E. S. Alcock expressed similar sentiments while explaining the employment of the neighborhood unit in the plan of Tema, Ghana. He highlighted the inclusion of "Palaver ground," a traditional African-type market and open-air meeting place: "One of the reasons why [neighborhood] units of this size may be successful in recreating feelings of belonging is the West African custom, when people seek others' company in the evening, of walking up and down the principal streets near their homes, meeting, greeting and gossiping ... the small trading area and the open-air meeting place ... will recreate the social atmosphere of the village." Alcock, "A New Town in the Gold Coast," 52.

67 Kalia, *Chandigarh*, 53.
68 Mayer, "The New Capital of Punjab," 174.
69 See Kalia, *Bhubaneswar*; and Kalia, *Gandhi Nagar*.
70 Swamy, "New Towns in India," 42.
71 Mayer, "The New Capital of Punjab," 174.

2

PARAMETER PLANS

Operationalizing Concepts

Serving Jaipur city's statutory development agency since its inception in 1982, Ms. Varshney had risen diligently through the ranks to become a senior town planner. During the course of my research for this book, I visited her often, seeking information and clarification, while a noisy bank of phones and an incessant flow of visitors and official files competed for her attention. Normally amicable, her manner stiffened swiftly, betraying bureaucratic confidence and slight impatience, when she fended off favor-seeking politicians, developers, and fellow officials. Boldly taking on persistent enquirers, she used well-rehearsed gestures to point them upstairs to the offices of higher authorities. She remembered the neighborhood unit from graduate course work but believed that abstract concepts had little to do with everyday planning work and official routines.[1] Nonetheless, she showed hints of idealism as she deftly deployed her intimate knowledge of bureaucratic parameters and neighborhood standards to navigate the treacherous terrain of postcolonial planning.

This chapter describes how the neighborhood unit concept became an indistinguishable part of Indian planning practice. Outside the field of urbanism, scholars in a range of disciplines—such as cultural studies, historiography, and anthropology—have argued that indigenous actors gradually transform alien ideas and typologies. Gyan Prakash, a historian of colonial science and modern India, posits these transformations as "a realignment of power, a renegotiation of the unequal relationship between Western and indigenous languages."[2] And Arjun Appadurai, leading scholar of cultural dimensions of globalization, sees these transformations as processes leading to indigenization: "As rapidly as forces from various metropolises are brought into new societies they tend to become indiginized in one or other way."[3] In this chapter, I employ these approaches to transformations in order to explain how post-independence Indian planners dealt with the concept of the neighborhood unit over time.

On the whole, Indian planners' response to the neighborhood unit comprised three distinct acts, which largely conform to notions that guide the study of postcolonial planning: co-optation, displacement, and assimilation. I focus on assimilation, and discuss co-optation and displacement when pertinent. As explained in Chapter 1, pioneering planners such as Koenigsberger and Mayer had positioned the concept of the neighborhood unit to suit the post-independence environment, with the hope that the planned spatiality of built units would co-opt the residents into a particular mode of civic life and help create a modern citizenry. In this respect, the building of neighborhood units attempted to displace the indigenous styles of living and attendant patterns of urban form. However, the first generation of Indian planners had to constantly negotiate the tensions between the foreign origins of the neighborhood unit concept, which violated the nationalistic fervor of the times, and its perceived modernity, which they considered vital for the country's development. This contention encouraged them to engage in discursive appropriations that eventually led to the assimilation of the concept into planning practice. These events did not take place in chronological order; they overlapped and also ran parallel at times. However, the following discussion is arranged sequentially in order to present a coherent narrative.

The Neighborhood Unit in Independent India

As described in the previous chapter, the neighborhood unit fitted well with independent India's initial planning agenda, which was deeply influenced by the elites' developmental concerns, perhaps best articulated in the domain of urban public affairs by the recommendations of the Health Survey and Development Committee.[4] The recommendations not only "set the line of thinking at the government level" but also reflected the prevalent view among the departing British and the new political elites that India's human settlements needed a robust dose of planning:[5]

> Most of the populated rural and urban centers in the country have grown up in the past without due regard to the principles of planning ... It is, therefore, essential to regulate the growth of towns in accordance with the principles of sound planning, to make a determined effort to eradicate existing slums and to prevent conditions in which they can grow again and thrive.[6]

However, there were few planners in India at the time of independence, in 1947. In fact, only eight planners assembled in October 1949 to initiate the Indian Board of Town Planners, the precursor to the Indian Town Planning Institute (ITPI).[7] Chaired by Koenigsberger, the board quickly resolved to enhance its membership by admitting qualified architects, engineers, legal practitioners, and economists.[8] The ITPI was constituted in 1951, and the annual autumn Town and Country Planning seminar was inaugurated a year later. By 1958, the planning community was well organized and 108 delegates participated in its annual conference, held at Jaipur. The proceedings of these seminars and conferences are a crucial window into the contemporary networks and milieus where new practices and ideas were formed, debated, refined, and publicized.[9]

Many of the seminar proceedings and speeches suggest the building of a double rhetoric. On the one hand, planners are called upon to contribute to the "new age" that is dawning in India. On the other hand, participants propagate a certain perception of desired urbanity. For instance, while inaugurating the fourth ITPI conference, at Lucknow in 1955, the governor of the largest Indian province, Uttar Pradesh, K. M. Munshi, exhorted the planners that "the unscientific growth of town and villages has become a menace in the atomic age and the town planner has to fight it." A leading nationalist and scholar in his own right, Munshi articulated the way forward in his keynote address:

> Worst feature of modern town is the lack of demarcation between the factory and the residential area. This creates a tremendous problem, all kind of vehicles are mixed up on the roads … and all this is happening in India 100 years after Georges Haussmann pushed his magnificent boulevards through the slums of Paris and 50 years after the [British-made] Sandhurst road eliminated the slums in the most populous part of the Mumbai city.[10]

In turn, planners' contributions to the rhetoric centered upon two issues. Similarly to members of any professional association, planners solicited the State's patronage by underscoring the significance of their own trade: "Planning is necessary not only for the sake of our physical environment but also to build our nation, to put in the citizens of the state that spirit, health, and outlook which free citizens must have."[11] Toward this, planners called for a comprehensive land-use planning policy that required the "setting up of a suitable planning machinery at all levels [of governance]."[12] Second, planners, who often themselves came from elite backgrounds, used this occasion to beseech the consent of the larger society by associating planning with high moral principles such as public service, spatial discipline, and nation building.[13]

In interviews I conducted with planners who were active at the time, they were unanimous in saying that they made a conscious effort to create a new urban environment conducive to development in the national interest.[14] These planners were driven by what they perceived as the moral and intellectual superiority of their endeavor, and they believed in their own formally recognized expertise. They also, almost wholeheartedly, subscribed to Prime Minister Jawahar Lal Nehru's dream of creating a modern, developed, and self-reliant India. However, in retrospect, they were probably imprudent, because there were so few of them to carry out even a small part of such an overwhelming mission, if it was at all possible. Solace was to be found in Nehru's attitude of noblesse oblige, which led him to speak approvingly of such endeavors by dominant groups among the indigenous elites: "A creative minority is always small in numbers, but if it is in tune with the majority, it is always trying to pull up the latter … Without a creative minority, a civilization must inevitably decay."[15]

Some planners recounted the type of residential urbanity they sought to create: predominant residential land use, houses or walk-up apartments with foliage or lawns in setbacks, wide and clean roads with walkways, and social infrastructure such as schools and convenience shopping—characteristic design features of the neighborhood unit. As discussed in the previous chapter, the neighborhood unit shared many of these spatial features with the colonial typology of Civil Lines, which it eventually displaced. In this respect, the neighborhood unit concept did not violate the aspirations of the indigenous elites, who, by the early twentieth century, had begun to plan their own residential areas emulating the landscape of Civil Lines.[16] Unlike the Civil Lines, the new neighborhoods were not sequestered from the city but promised equality by virtue of being identical to other cells of the city. Finally, and perhaps of most importance, the neighborhood unit in India was not envisaged as an exclusive and expansive abode of the privileged class but as an egalitarian model that promised to house all income and social groups in a spatially disciplined environment—a clever way to co-opt the working class and other marginal groups in the project of nation making.

The idea of housing diverse social groups in the new neighborhoods was important for several reasons. First, many planners I interviewed believed that the built spatiality of planned neighborhoods provided an appropriate incubator for the grooming and sustaining of a modern citizenry. This was crucial because the many uneducated people, who had migrated from rural areas or the historic quarters of Indian cities, could be expected to learn from the educated residents and participate fully in the democratic affairs of the new nation. Second, the tacit pedagogical mission was also expected to spread civic virtues, such as cleanliness and cooperation, among diverse sections of the population.[17] Third, the disciplined spatiality of new neighborhood units was not only expected to negate the exclusivity of the Civil Lines but also the squalor and associational life of working-class communities, which were often politically charged and could be expected to carry over antiestablishment feelings, however residual, from the colonial period.[18] However, these veiled agendas, neither articulated clearly by the planners nor anticipated by the residents, didn't matter at a certain level, because planners perceived and positioned the concept as an instrument for moving independent India from "old to new" in line with Nehru's exhortation to the free nation—a call that dominated the climate of opinion at the time.[19]

Breaking Down the Neighborhood Unit Concept

The planning fraternity formally accepted the concept of the neighborhood unit at the fourth conference of ITPI, held at Lucknow in 1955, when it derived "Planning standards for community services and facilities" from the tenets of the neighborhood unit. Planning standards, the conference cautioned, should eventually be worked out on a regional basis, because given India's vastness, uniform standards would not do justice to the inherent climatic, social, and economic differences between places. The conference recommended that until regional standards evolved, it would be useful to adopt a few "workable standards" based on their "experience and the experience gained in other progressive countries."[20] In reality, the lack of trained planners and an ever-increasing workload meant that region-specific standards were never prepared and the "workable standards" filled in whenever needed. For example, in 1960, H. K. Mewada, author of the first master plan for the city of Guwahati, in the northeastern tropical state of Assam, reported that the "planning standards adopted for the Master Plan have been based on the recommendations made by the ITPI, India, at its Lucknow Seminar" and that the "development of new areas [of Guwahati] shall be on the basis of neighborhood principles."[21]

In order to ensure that the standards were usable in a variety of contexts, they were presented in the form of a table containing the types and percentages of different land uses needed to plan a generic neighborhood for 10,000 residents. The advantage of this format (Table 2.1) lies in the fact that, apart from knowledge of Perry's six design principles, the planner needs only two magical numbers— desired density of persons per acre and the available land area for the proposed neighborhood—to arrive at the "correct" breakup of acreages of land uses required to "design" a neighborhood unit:

TABLE 2.1 Land use table recommended by the ITPI at its Lucknow Seminar

Land use table for a residential neighborhood of 10,000 population					
Gross density (persons/acre)	20	30	40	50	60
Net density (persons/acre) excluding all major open spaces, viz. secondary schools with play fields, shops, public buildings, car parks etc.	30	56	90	100	120
Residential area (in acres)	333	178	111	104	84
Primary schools with playgrounds (3 to 4 in number, each not more than 400 students)	20	20	20	20	20
Secondary schools with play fields (one each for boys and girls, each not more than 400 students)	24	24	24	24*	24*
Open spaces, viz. children's play area, parkways, or connecting greens and organized games area excluding school playing fields (4 acres/1,000 minimum)	76	74	63	51	40
Public buildings, shops, car parks etc.	31	25	20	17	15
Total area (in acres)	434	321	238	218	183

* Primary schools and their playgrounds should form a part of a neighborhood. In the case of central areas of existing towns where high density becomes necessary to be adopted, the secondary schools and their playing fields may be provided outside the neighborhood, but within a walking distance of not more than one mile.

Source: Proceeding of the Autumn Planning Seminar and State Planning Officials' conference held at Lucknow, India in October 1955, reported in the November 1955 issue of the *Journal of the Institute of Town Planners*, India.

The table accomplished several crucial tasks. First, it provided planners with the legitimacy of rational precision. Second, by collapsing the design concept into a mathematical formulation, it offered a template of stripped-down modernism that practitioners could use as scaffolding for local adaptations. Finally, and perhaps most important, the tabulation blurred the concept's American ancestry by breaking the linkages between what Tridib Banerjee and William Baer termed the contextual, manifest, and tacit values of the neighborhood unit.[22]

Because this was a crucial step toward the neighborhood unit concept's eventual internalization by Indian planners, a brief review of Banerjee and Baer's viewpoint is needed. They suggest that the neighborhood unit concept combines three important clusters of values. The first cluster, *contextual values*, represents the intellectual concerns and thinking of the turn-of-the-century American reformist movement, such as a perceived need to strengthen the traditional links between the individual, the place, and the community, which had weakened due to an amorphous social and moral order. The second cluster, *manifest values*, is the embodied performance of the design principles of the neighborhood unit concept. These values capture the practitioners' concerns about creating a physical place that provides opportunities for leisure, recreation, and social interaction, and an environment that is safe, protected, pleasing, and secure. Banerjee and Baer recognize the third cluster as *tacit values*. These are unstated values based on pragmatic social and economic considerations, such as Perry's presumption of social homogeneity to protect owner-occupancy appeal, territorial integrity, and the impermeability of a particular social group. The tacit values facilitate the endorsement of developers, municipalities, and lending institutions.[23]

By rupturing the linkages between the three value clusters, the table enabled the amusing and real possibility of a planner in a one-cow Indian town, spatially and spiritually removed from Perry's conception, to design a city-extension with the aid of an elementary slide rule. The table also made the concept appear simple to Indian planners: they could now design neighborhood units, or the thin modernist infrastructure and parcel organization, because they were easy to conceive when they were abstracted from the social context in an uncomplicated mathematical table. Finally, the table opened up the possibilities of appropriation through the translation and internalizing of the concept.

The appropriation of the neighborhood unit by Indian planners through the processes of adaptation, translation, and internalization becomes more understandable when viewed through two lenses: first, the ruptured linkages between the contextual, manifest, and tacit values of the neighborhood unit concept make sense in light of Appadurai's notion of "soft" cultural forms.[24] When studying exogenous phenomena and ideas in host societies, Appadurai recommends making a distinction between "soft" and "hard" cultural forms. He defines hard cultural forms as "those that come with a set of links between value, meaning, and embodied practice that are difficult to break and hard to transform."[25] For instance, he calls the sport of cricket a hard cultural form, because it transforms the players more easily than it is itself transformed. The neighborhood unit, in contrast, is a soft cultural form, "which permits relatively easy separation of embodied performance from meaning and value, and relatively easy transformation at each level."[26]

Second, Gyan Prakash, in his text *Another Reason: Science and the Imagination of Modern India*, traced the relationship between science, colonialism, and the modern nation. His central thesis is that science in the colonial world simultaneously served the paradoxical role of an instrument of the empire and a symbol of liberty, freedom, and universal progress. The indigenous elites seized upon this ambiguous role of science and attempted to do several things: adapt it, through legitimizing the role of science by creating a hybrid form that combined Western ideas with local cultural and social practices; translate it, by confronting and renegotiating the unequal relationship between Western and indigenous languages; and internalize it by breaking it down so that while its Western origins could be criticized, its program of modernization could be absorbed. These acts were not only a kind of cultural co-optation but also a clever way to adopt many of the practical benefits of scientific inquiry.

Appropriating the Neighborhood Unit

Appropriations of the neighborhood unit started as soon as it was introduced in Indian planning practice with adaptations. Kevin Lynch has described a well-adapted place as "one in which function and form are well fitted to each other."[27] It could be achieved in many permutations by adaptation of the neighborhood unit to local practices or vice versa, and also by a mutual adaptation. For example, planners facilitated the constitution of neighborhood-wide *Vikas Mandal* (development councils) in the late 1950s to sensitize and "educate" the residents to the civic aims of the neighborhood unit.[28] Planners believed that such institutions could be used for instilling a collective sense of belonging in neighborhood residents and purging traditional influences such as caste. At the other end of the spectrum, pioneering planners in India such as Albert Mayer and Otto Koenigsberger imagined that adapting the spatial features of the neighborhood unit would enable the concept to fit with local conditions.

In accordance with Appadurai's notion of soft cultural forms, such adaptations, in a similar way to the mathematical table, separated the original contextual values of the neighborhood unit from the act of its employment (or the manifest values) and impregnated the concept with new contextual values, such as the envisaged purge of traditional practices. Similarly, the tacit values of the concept—which in the United States were implicit in the endorsement of developers, municipalities, and lending institutions—were substituted in India with the approval of political leadership and the planning fraternity. Not surprisingly, these initial adaptations were seen favorably by Indian planners, who employed adapted versions of the neighborhood unit concept to plan new cities—such as Faridabad, near Delhi—and to prepare master plans, such as for the city of Nagpur.[29]

However, unlike the German Koenigsberger and the American Mayer—who, owing to their universalist worldview did not give any credence to the fact that the neighborhood unit concept had foreign origins—Indian planners, notwithstanding adaptations, soon began to express the difficulties they faced in reconciling the concept's foreign origins. K. N. Mishra, village and town planner to the Government of Uttar Pradesh and the author of the Master Plan for Allahabad, prepared during the mid-1950s, expressed the sentiment thus:

> In recommending the adoption of this neighborhood principle … for future residential areas, it has been constantly borne in mind, that a pattern of life which is foreign to the nature of people of Allahabad may not be imposed upon them. Planning and housing policy should keep in step with the traditional domestic habits of the community and concentrate on improving and developing that environment which is best thought to lead to a happy and healthy life.[30]

Despite such a candid expression of reservation, the master plan for Allahabad recommended the neighborhood unit be adopted for future extensions of the city.[31] This dichotomy reveals the tension that Indian planners in the post-independence period had to constantly negotiate between their imaginations of the good life that the neighborhood unit purportedly would deliver and their intellectual sensitivities about using a concept of foreign origin. Moreover, planners were not yet sure about the usefulness of the neighborhood unit in solving the problems of indigenous parts of Indian cities, which constituted the bulk of urban India. These tensions eventually forced Indian planners to do two things. First, they attempted to translate the neighborhood unit; and second, they extended the translated concept to the indigenous Indian city. The forum for both of these tasks was the Delhi Master Plan (DMP), published by the Delhi Development Authority in 1962, which is the focus of the next section.

Translating the Neighborhood Unit

The trigger for commissioning the preparation of the DMP in 1955 was the problems caused by the large-scale migration of refugees into Delhi following the partition of India and Pakistan in 1947. The initiation of the DMP also fit well with the recommendation in the national government's second five-year plan (1956–60) that master plans be prepared for all important towns.[32]

The DMP was the first major planning exercise for the first-generation planners of independent India, most of whom had just returned home after attending graduate schools in the United States and United Kingdom.[33] They collaborated with a group of experienced American planners, who were sponsored by the Ford Foundation following a request from the government of

India in 1958.[34] Although essentially a conventional master plan in the sense that it focused on the physical city, the overarching contribution of the DMP was to introduce the "comprehensive" paradigm to Indian planning practice, which replaced the colonial urban infrastructure improvement model.[35]

It is interesting to see the final shape of the DMP, which, in contrast to the standard American practice, addressed both land use and zoning issues. The first section of the DMP focused on land-use analyses and proposals, while the second contained the subdivision regulations and zoning code.[36] Moreover, unlike the master plans for American cities, which are usually advisory in nature, the DMP had legal standing. By combining land-use proposals with subdivision regulations, the DMP aimed to "guide the development of the new areas in accordance with the Land Use Plan. As long as this is done along sound planning principles with adequate space standards, the future of the city is assured."[37] The space standards were similar to the table formulated at ITPI's Lucknow seminar (Table 2.1) in 1955.[38]

One of the frequently used phrases in the DMP is "self-contained." Borrowing from Perry, the DMP applied the notion of self-sufficiency at various geographical scales (Figure 2.1). At the highest hierarchal level and geographical scale, the city was divided into "eight planning divisions which are self-contained in the matter of employment, residential places, recreational areas, shopping and other requirements."[39] The city of Delhi was to be surrounded by "six Ring Towns, self-contained in matters of work and residential places."[40] At the other extreme, the lowest hierarchal level and geographical scale, the plan split the neighborhood unit into self-contained "housing clusters."

URBAN DELHI

↓

Eight Planning Divisions (Each 300,000 to 750,000 population)

↓

3 Central Business Districts and 15 District Centres (Each District Centre serves 150,000 to 250,000 population)

↓

Community Centre for 40,000 to 50,000 population

↓

Residential Planning Areas (Each 12,000 to 15,000 population)

↓

Residential Units (Each 3,500 to 5,000 population)

↓

Housing Clusters (Each 750 to 1,000 population)

FIGURE 2.1 Urban hierarchy in Delhi Master Plan
Source: Derived from Delhi Master Plan, 1962.

The housing cluster was the lowest self-contained tier in the planning hierarchy "conceived from the bottom upwards."[41] It was envisaged for a population of 750 to 1000 people and, in the view of the DMP team, roughly corresponded to "traditional 'Mohallas' and 'Kuchas' [typology of indigenous settlements] in the Old City of Delhi and, in fact, are found in its rudimentary form in almost all of the Indian cities and towns."[42] Four to six such housing clusters were grouped around a primary school and convenience stores with a small park, and together these comprised what the DMP called the "residential unit." Apparently the DMP was attempting to split Perry's neighborhood unit into sub-units by employing an analogy from the indigenous part of Indian cities, *Mohallas*, and figuratively it was trying to translate the Western concept into indigenous language; but probably of greatest importance, the DMP was aiming to translocate the origin of the idea itself into India's traditions to claim equivalent ownership.

Such an effort was important for two reasons. First, the translocated concept, demonstrable as a part of indigenous patrimony, would cease to violate the intellectual sensibilities of Indian planners; and second, it could also be used as an alibi to contest claims that this form was simply mimicking the West. Gyan Prakash has described the role of indigenous elites as to not "appear as a copy of the original, but as a ghostly double that resists identification as a copy by asserting difference."[43] Thus, by renaming the "neighborhood unit" as the "residential unit," which was composed of traditional "*Mohallas*," planners were not only attempting to translate the idea but were also already discounting potential claims of copying by asserting the difference between their formulation and Perry's conception.

Once the concept appeared translated, planners perused Perry's often-overlooked suggestion that the neighborhood unit was extendable to the existing city—in this case, *Mohallas* and *Kuchas* of Delhi's historic quarters.[44] The DMP team conducted a series of what it called "work-studies" to devise and illustrate a methodology for extending the neighborhood unit concept to the indigenous parts of Delhi. Planners intended to demonstrate that the *Mohallas* and *Kuchas* of old Delhi, which "appear as a sprawling mass of structures of varying size, shapes and construction, criss-crossed by narrow streets and lanes," could be redeveloped as "residential units."[45] A total of six examples were worked out, and the smallest planning unit in each of them was what the planners called the "Mohalla Unit": "Each 'Mohalla unit' contains a local sub-shopping centre, usually located near the primary school and easily accessible from its catchment area ... with six to twelve shops for supplying odds and ends and will be a great help to the house-wife."[46] The Mohalla Unit was a "ghostly double" form that imitated the original but resisted identification as a copy by asserting difference.

Internalizing the Neighborhood Unit

That the neighborhood unit concept had been internalized into the Indian planning practice became evident during interviews with planners of later generations.[47] Their answers can be broadly divided into two categories and bear an interesting correlation with the age of respondents. The first category of answers was mostly given by senior planners who frequently evoked indigenous parallels to the neighborhood unit such as *Mohallas, Kuchas, Vadas,* and *Poles,* found in Indian cities among different regions. This group of respondents can be called the translators. One senior planner, aged about 70 years, said:

> Yes, I was exposed to Clarence Perry's neighborhood unit as a graduate student. But while working as a planner, I never felt that this idea had foreign origins. You know, it could have gone there from here! See, we had forms of neighborhoods probably not definable by Western spatial norms, but tell me, were these *Mohallas* and *Katras* neighborhoods or something else?[48]

The second category of answers typically came from junior planners, who can be called the internalizers. They were aware of Perry's neighborhood unit, courtesy of planning pedagogy, but did not discern any relationship between it and the present neighborhood planning standards in India. Moreover, this group of respondents frequently insisted that a Western concept would probably never work in the Indian context. Ms. Varshney, who is in her late forties and can be called an internalizer, said:

> See, you know that foreign ideas do not work here. They might appear fancy in the beginning, but no, no they can't work here. Perry and his ideas might have been used by earlier planners, but now things are different. See, I studied the neighborhood unit—in Planning Theory? Yeah, but for my present work, we use our own norms.[49]

Gyan Prakash might call this a good example of internalization. In his argument, such a phenomenon would happen because the translation of Perry's idea to Mohalla Unit not only enabled the Indian planners to continue questioning the feasibility of employing a Western idea in the Indian context but also permitted them to continue using the modernity of the neighborhood unit to sustain their own imaginations of the "good urban life." In Prakash's own words:

> This nation's past was at once enabling and disabling. If its philosophical and scientific heritage and its traditions of renunciation and collective life poised India to advance the spirit of the present age, the widespread inequality, poverty, undeveloped resources, and religious divisions hobbled its progress ... [However] the past was not dead but alive, open to the modern age and ready to give moral direction to science and technology. The beauty of this formation was that it located the nation as a space for the critique of Western modernity while internalizing the program of modernization.[50]

Therefore, by internalizing the neighborhood unit, planners not only left open the possibility of criticizing its Western modernity but also retained its stripped-down program of modernization. This program was to be carried out using the indigenous "Mohalla Unit," which had already rendered redundant any allegations of copying. As a result, Perry's concept stood, depending upon the viewer's gaze, inappropriately appropriated or innovatively indigenized; impregnated with adapted manifest values, new contextual values, and altered tacit values. This facilitated the concept's institutionalization as the prototypical proviso for neighborhood planning and design in India.

Institutionalization of the Neighborhood Unit

The institutionalization of the neighborhood unit in Indian planning practice is perhaps most evident in planning parameters and official rules such as those governing subdivision of urban lands. The concept's inscription in official regulations was facilitated by the dispersal of DMP planners and graduating students who were exposed to the neighborhood unit in planning school and later took up jobs in public-sector organizations across various states of India. These factors are described below.

Human Agency

The dispersal across the country of Indian members of the DMP team following the DMP's completion facilitated the subsequent deployment of the DMP's prescriptions in the master plans of many new and existing Indian cities.[51] The dispersal was accelerated by a countrywide shortage of planners, which meant that the young Indian DMP team members had numerous opportunities and subsequent professional mobility.[52] The shortage of planners occurred because many new public-sector organizations were being set up, and the publication of the DMP had jump-started the preparation of master plans across urban India. These preparations gained further encouragement when the third five-year plan (1961–66) of the Government of India promised to provide full financial aid to the states for preparation of master plans of important cities.[53] Two conditions further entrenching planning practice in the state's apparatus were attached to the federal aid: suitable town and country planning legislation enabling enforcement of the master plans was to be in place, and the recipient state was to have established a town planning organization with an adequate number of trained personnel.[54] Many of the DMP's prescriptions, such as the norms for neighborhood planning, were enshrined in procedures and master plans when the DMP planners rapidly rose through the ranks to head these public-sector planning organizations.

The institutionalization of the neighborhood unit was also aided by its spread in planning pedagogy. Several 1960s planning theses at the leading planning college—the School of Planning and Architecture (SPA), in New Delhi—either documented a new town based on the neighborhood unit, such as the city of Bhubaneswar, with the students reporting the status and progress of the city-building project; or they were proposals in which students proposed a planning intervention, again based on the neighborhood unit, for existing cities such as Mangalore.[55] A few more ambitious theses proposed plans for a new capital city, yet again based on the neighborhood unit.[56] Such theses ensured an ongoing and deepening exposure of the students to the neighborhood unit, as the students constantly attended and discussed one another's presentations.

In addition, planning students were also exposed to new towns under construction across India through site visits, which were a mandatory part of the academic curricula, and publications, including journal articles.[57] Apart from the influential Chandigarh and Bhubaneswar, there was an abundance of potential sites to be visited, as a large number of new towns were being constructed across India. Koenigsberger, in an article entitled "New Towns in India," published in 1952, mentioned ten such new towns under construction. Fourteen years later, M. C. Krishna Swamy reported about fifty such new towns that were either already commissioned or were being constructed across India. He also mentioned that "irrespective of the developing agency the main concept and the basic planning principle dominant in these new towns is the self-contained neighborhood unit."[58]

Agency of Planning Procedures

Subdivision norms, especially those formulated during the 1960s and 1970s, perhaps bear the strongest testimony to the institutionalization of the appropriated neighborhood unit. For instance, in the newly created state of Rajasthan, the first-ever rules for subdivision of urban lands were enacted in 1964, titled the "Rajasthan Urban Areas (subdivision, reconstitution and improvement of plots) Rules." Gopal Singh Nandiwal, a University of Manchester–trained planner, used Lewis Keeble's chapter on the neighborhood unit in the standard planning text at the time, *Principles and Practice of Town and Country Planning*, as the point of reference in creating these rules.[59] Accordingly, the uniform rules for all the urban areas of Rajasthan state, which completely ignored the presence of long-existing local customs and traditional usages of lands, stipulated that 10 percent of the new neighborhoods must be open space and in no case more than 66 percent of the total scheme area should be plotted. The rules also required the layout plans to incorporate Perry's design principles, such as hierarchal road widths, single-family houses, and schools.

In 1975, following the preparation of the master plan for Jaipur—which had prescribed the internalized version of the concept, or the "planning unit"—these subdivision rules were further elaborated according to the DMP's recommendations. The subdivision rules now specified physical sizes for tot-lots (playgrounds), parks, schools, and shops to be provided in a neighborhood. The regulatory ceiling of 66 percent plotted area in a residential scheme was maintained, though in practice the government agencies provided more open space than the minimum stipulated 10 percent, and consequently the plotted area rarely exceeded the range of 50–55 percent preferred by Perry. Seen another way, these subdivision rules were, in fact, paraphrasing the area relations between different land uses in a typical neighborhood unit as suggested by Perry (Table 2.2).

Such paraphrasing was not an isolated phenomenon; similar exercises were carried out in other states and at the federal level. In the mid-1960s the Committee on Plan Projects constituted by the Government of India published the *Report on Industrial Townships*. It laid down uniform guidelines for "land-use structure and densities for future planning of townships under the public sector to ensure unity in the level of service and amenity, safety and efficiency combined with economy in construction and maintenance of townships."[60] The suggested land-use structure in the new townships of a "residential sector," a moniker for the neighborhood unit that became popular in Indian planning practice after the employment of the term in Chandigarh, was stipulated in a similar format (Table 2.3).

Originally conceived to provide planners with a benchmark for designing neighborhoods, these tables gradually became planning conventions with

TABLE 2.2 Area relations of the plan

Complete Unit	160 acres	100 percent
Dwelling-house lots	86.5	54.0
Apartment-house lots	3.4	2.1
Business blocks	6.5	4.1
Market squares	1.2	0.8
School and church sites	1.6	1.0
Parks and playgrounds	13.8	8.6
Greens and circles	3.2	2.0
Streets	43.8	27.4

Source: Derived from C. A. Perry, "The Neighborhood Unit, a Scheme of Arrangement for the Family-Life Community." *Regional Plan of New York and its Environs* (New York: Committee on Regional Plan of New York and Its Environs, 1929), p. 3.

TABLE 2.3 Land use table for a sector

Uses	Percentage of developed area
a. Residential plots	45 to 50%
b. Roads and streets	15 to 20%
c. Schools (including playgrounds)	12 to 15%
d. Parks and open spaces	8 to 10%
e. Shopping	2 to 4%
Other uses	Balance
Total	100%

Source: Derived from M. C. Krishna Swamy. 1966. "New Towns in India." *Journal of Indian Town Planning Institute*, Vol. 49–50, p. 46.

obscure origins and ancestry. In this respect, these tables signify a successful assimilation of the appropriated neighborhood unit concept in Indian planning practice.

However, planners' acts of appropriating and assimilating the exogenous planning concept of the neighborhood unit were not carried out in isolation; they corresponded well with the overall response of the host society. As explained in the following chapters, a multitude of actors made their own plans, appropriating the built neighborhoods to the point where they represented a distinct form of urbanism. The envisaged residential land use became mixed; open spaces and recreational parks housed temples; building setbacks were built over; and floors above the legally permissible height increased the envisaged density. The rich, vibrant, and diverse reality stands further in relief when compared to Perry's rather staid prescriptions and practitioners' mundane parameters for neighborhood design. Perhaps of most importance, a large number of residents favored their appropriated neighborhoods over other available options, including the newly developed neighborhoods.[61] This shows that while planners focused on the discursive concept, the larger society gradually assimilated the built neighborhood units.

Conclusion

As I have shown in this chapter, post-independence Indian planners picked up the concept of the neighborhood unit right from where the pioneering planners left off. On the one hand, they continued to produce adapted variations of the neighborhood unit that were perceived as contextually sensitive; on the other hand, they disseminated the concept widely in line with the new nation's modernist planning agenda. Toward this end, they used professional milieus, such as planning conferences and seminars, that helped in broadening planning clientele and achieving the consent of other elite groups. Most important, and promoting the procedural nature of formal planning practice, they derived planning parameters and neighborhood standards from the design principles of the neighborhood unit—a step that not only blurred the concept's American ancestry but also broke the linkages between its constituent contextual, manifest, and tacit values.

However, over the next decade, they had to constantly negotiate between their own imaginations of a "good urban life," which the neighborhood unit purportedly provided, and their intellectual sensitivities about using a concept of foreign origin. Planners were also not sure about the usefulness of the neighborhood unit in solving the problems of indigenous quarters of Indian cities. They attempted to solve these conundrums by translating the concept in two ways: linguistically and figuratively. This enabled them to argue that similar spatial configurations also existed in indigenous quarters of Indian cities and therefore not only did the concept have roots in indigenous patrimony but the tenets of the neighborhood unit could be employed to regenerate historical quarters. Once translated, the concept was easy to internalize because it no longer appeared foreign, and this paved the way for its spread across Indian states and cities through the 1960s and 1970s. In the next chapter, I explain how local planning practices and city-building traditions did not disappear with India's independence, however, and significantly shaped the manner in which planners used design ideas and planning parameters to make formal urban plans.

Notes

1 Her observation, in this respect, is in line with Bish Sanyal's assertion (based on a survey) that many planning practitioners did not find planning theory—or, indeed, any theory—useful. See Sanyal, "Globalization, Ethical Compromise and Planning Theory." Also see a powerful rebuttal in Friedmann, "Why Do Planning Theory?"
2 Prakash, *Another Reason*, 50.
3 Appadurai, *Modernity at Large*, 32.
4 Chaired by Sir Joseph Bhore of the Indian Civil Service, the committee was constituted by the colonial government in 1943 and submitted its report in 1946. See Health Survey and Development (Bhore) Committee, *Final Report*. 4 Vols.
5 TCPO, *Urban and Regional Planning and Development in India*, 22.
6 Ibid., 21.
7 Kalia, *Chandigarh*, 25.
8 Koenigsberger was a director in the Ministry of Health, Government of India, and also the senior-most planner in the country at the time. See ITPI, *Silver Jubilee Year Book,* 102.
9 Ward, *Planning the Twentieth-Century City*, 8.
10 Ibid.
11 UPTPO, *Progressive Uttar Pradesh*, 4. Such an effort was also important to justify the role of planners themselves. In the same speech, Governor K. M. Munshi had expressed sympathy for planners because in a newly independent and developing country, "many people looked upon the town planner as a kind of nuisance … [Engineers of] the Public Works Department looked upon him as an enemy and it was common for government departments to look upon a town planner as a kind of white elephant." ITPI, "Autumn Planning Seminar and State Planning Officials' Conference at Lucknow," 8.
12 ITPI, "Autumn Planning Seminar and State Planning Officials' Conference at Lucknow," 9. This call was important because planners in many parts of the world generally derive legitimacy in bureaucratic arenas by using their expertise to inform land-use decisions. Thomas Reiner highlights the connection between the design of planned neighborhoods and planning's land-use orientation in the following words: "Urban planning has a land use basis and bias and planners have been most successful in developing techniques of control and effectuation, and of symbolism and communication, in this portion of the field." Reiner, *The Place of the Ideal Community in Urban Planning*, 124.
13 Many contemporary publications highlight these themes. For example, see UPTPO, *Progressive Uttar Pradesh*, 3.
14 Six senior and now-retired planners were interviewed by the author in semi-structured and open-ended format. Barring one who was in his late eighties, others were in their mid- to late seventies and had attended graduate school in the United Kingdom or United States in the late 1940s or early 1950s. On average, the interviews lasted about 90 minutes. Two of the planners were interviewed twice.
15 NIUA, *Jawahar Lal Nehru on Building a New India*, 57.
16 Khan, "Cultural Transfers."

17 The elitist bent behind educating poor residents stands out in many later writings as well. For instance, as late as the mid-1980s, Mr. H. U. Bijlani, an erstwhile chairman of the Housing and Urban Development Corporation (HUDCO), while writing on urban social facilities, argued that resources must be set aside for educational programs "which tell the citizens, especially belonging to the economically weaker sections as to how to maintain and look after the physical facilities and personal hygiene." Bijlani, "Urban Social Facilities."

18 See Chakrabarty, *Rethinking Working-Class History*.

19 Two respondents mentioned the phrase "moving from old to new" to refer to the dominance of the contemporary climate of opinion. Nehru originally, and rather famously, used the phrase in his independence eve address to the constituent assembly. Accessed at www.harappa.com/sounds/nehru.html, viewed on May 14, 2006.

20 ITPI, "Autumn Planning Seminar and State Planning Officials' Conference at Lucknow," 23.

21 Mewada, "Master Plan for Gauhati (sic)." Like many of his colleagues, Mewada had attended graduate school in the United States. He studied architecture at Cornell University and city planning at the University of Illinois in 1950. Ravi Kalia has documented Mewada's employment of the neighborhood unit concept to plan Gandhi Nagar, the new capital city for the state of Gujarat, and believes that Mewada was exposed to Perry's neighborhood unit in graduate school. See Kalia, *Gandhi Nagar*.

22 Banerjee and Baer, *Beyond the Neighborhood Unit*, 20.

23 Ibid.

24 Appadurai, *Modernity at Large*, 90.

25 Ibid.

26 Ibid.

27 Lynch, *Good City Form*, 167.

28 Clinard and Chatterjee, "Urban Community Development."

29 Vagale et al., "Faridabad—A Critical Study"; and Nagpur Improvement Trust, *Nagpur Master Plan*.

30 Mishra, *The Development of Allahabad*, 16.

31 Ibid.

32 TCPO, *Urban and Regional Planning and Development in India*, 23.

33 Young Indian planners who worked on the DMP were: Sayed S. Shafi and Banarsi Das Kambo, who had attended Massachusetts Institute of Technology; B. N. Rahalkar, who attended Harvard University; R. L. Bawa, who attended University College, London; Sri Manohar, who attended the University of North Carolina; Madan Malik, who attended the University of Southern California; P. B. Rai, who attended Georgia Tech; and B. G. Fernandes, who attended the University of California, Berkeley.

34 The American planning team comprised: Gerald Breese, a sociologist who is Professor Emeritus, Department of Sociology at Princeton University; Bert Hoselitz, a development theorist from the University of Chicago; Britton Harris, a geographer who was Professor Emeritus of City and Regional Planning at the University of Pennsylvania; Edward Echeverria, a physical and land-use planner; Walter Hedden, a transportation expert who had worked with the New York Port Authority; Arch Doston, an international development planner who recently was Professor Emeritus of Governance at Cornell University; and George Goetschius, a sociologist. Albert Mayer led the team. See Staples, *Forty Years*, 52.

35 Banerjee, "Understanding Planning Cultures: The Kolkata Paradox." Also see Sundaram, *Pirate Modernity*. However, the DMP's notion of comprehensiveness differed substantially from the meaning of the term in standard American usage. For example, a new public-sector agency called the Delhi Development Authority (DDA)—which had dominant control over Delhi's urban development, including the planning, building, and selling of housing units in the new neighborhoods—was set

up to implement the DMP. Headed by politically appointed civil servants, not locally elected representatives, the DDA undertook large-scale acquisition of privately owned peripheral lands to implement the DMP. In these respects, the DDA's implementation of the DMP marked the initiation of the State's near-monopoly over the development of new neighborhoods and housing—a trend that gradually spread to many other parts of India.

36 DDA, *Master Plan for Delhi*, 5.
37 Ibid., 64.
38 Ibid., table 8.
39 Ibid., 7.
40 Ibid., 1.
41 Ibid., 64.
42 Ibid.
43 Prakash, *Another Reason*, 51.
44 Perry, "The Neighborhood Unit, a Scheme of Arrangement for the Family-Life Community," 106.
45 DDA, *Master Plan for Delhi*, Volume II, 24.
46 Ibid., 14.
47 The author interviewed a total of 18 planners in the cities of Delhi, Jaipur, Bangalore, and Nagpur. All were junior to first-generation planners both in age and government service, and, in contrast to first-generation planners trained abroad, had attended graduate school in India.
48 Interview conducted in January 2006.
49 Interview conducted in May 2006.
50 Prakash, *Another Reason*, 213.
51 Ansari, "Evolution of Town Planning Practice and System of Urban Government in India."
52 Young Indian planners dispersed widely after the publication of the DMP. For instance, R. L. Bawa went to the Delhi Municipal Corporation in the early 1960s and then left in the mid-1960s to become the chief town planner of the state of Bihar. In the 1980s, he became a regional chief in the Housing and Urban Development Corporation (HUDCO). B. D. Kambo left Delhi in the early 1960s for Bihar, and in 1967 he went to Rajasthan as the chief town planner and architectural advisor to the state government.
53 TCPO, *Urban and Regional Planning and Development in India*, 24.
54 Ibid.
55 See, for instance, Kamilia, *A Study of Bhubaneswar*; Gowda, *Planning Proposal for Mangalore*; Mehta, *Udaipur: A Planning Study*.
56 Bansal, *The Aspect of Urban Design for a State Capital in India*.
57 Several planners mentioned the importance attached to site visits and study trips in the syllabi at the time. Moreover, many journal articles of the time mention the employment of the neighborhood unit concept in different parts of India. See, for instance, Khambatta, "Master Plan of Township at Vikroli."
58 Swamy, "New Towns in India," 42.
59 Interview with Mr. G. S. Nandiwal, March 2006. Professor Keeble had incidentally taught at Mr. Nandiwal's alma mater, the University of Manchester.
60 Swamy, "New Towns in India," 46.
61 Thirty-four residents of three neighborhoods planned during the 1970s were interviewed by the author in semi-structured and open-ended format during the summer of 2006.

PART II

3

FORMAL PLANS

Making Official Attempts

Received wisdom holds that post-independence planning policy and practice turned its back on India's past. The adoption of the comprehensive planning model for the building of new towns such as Chandigarh and the pursuit of outward-oriented development in existing cities such as Delhi epitomized both a rejection of provincial sentimentalism about the history and heritage of urban India and the use of state power to translate Nehru's modern vision on the ground.[1] Overall, the approach was in line with the ideology of the ruling elites, who envisioned India's future in the image of liberal democracies such as those found in Western Europe and North America. They posited development as the index by which efforts toward modernization were to be measured, and the State's primary task.[2] Thus, even when paying lip service to the historical narratives and regional identities for nationalistic causes, such as those evident in the colorful tableaux of Delhi's Republic Day parade and the state pavilions of *Pragati Maidan,* permanent exhibition grounds showcasing national progress, Indian planners faced forward and not backward.[3] So, how did planners make urban plans in places beyond the familiar Chandigarh and Delhi? What role did the neighborhood unit concept play in these efforts?

About 175 miles southwest of Delhi, the city of Jaipur combines India's princely past and post-independence urban change. Symbolizing ancient city-planning traditions in the popular imagination, Jaipur has long been perceived as India's indigenously planned city. The colonial British never directly ruled Jaipur, which, along with about two-fifths of South Asia, remained a part of princely India until the country's independence (Figure 3.1). A lack of direct British intervention meant that Jaipur did not experience a range of colonial urban phenomena such as racial segregation between "white" and "native" localities. Similar to many other Indian cities, Jaipur has both grown quickly after independence, from a population of about 300,000 in 1951 to a population of about 3 million in 2011, and witnessed the application of stock planning instruments, such as master plans and planned neighborhoods. Thus, Jaipur's recent expansions may be more broadly representative of urban change in the post-independence period than entirely new cities, such as Chandigarh, or those of British India, such as Kolkata and Mumbai, despite the prominence of those cities in the literature on urban India.

This chapter introduces Jaipur and explains the manner in which the city's context shaped the making of post-independence urban plans. Three distinct but interrelated subplots frame the story. First, the royal administration planned and governed the city of Jaipur more comprehensively than the post-independence Indian state. Land acquisition and official coordination required to build development projects and new city-extensions, for instance, were not an issue under the king's authoritarian rule. As in other high-ranking princely states— such as Hyderabad, Baroda, Bhopal and Mysore—hereditary monarchs took pride in Jaipur's distinctive civic identity and up-to-date infrastructure. The city was known for impressive palaces and monuments as much as for its piped water supply, street lighting and trash removal.

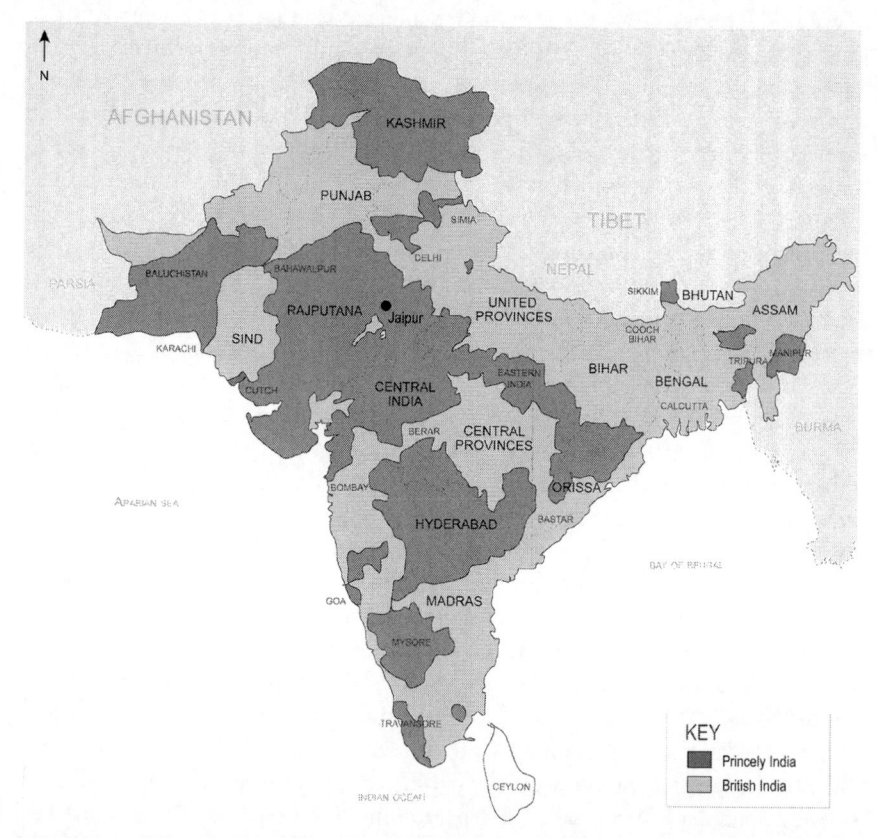

FIGURE 3.1   Jaipur in Princely India before the country's independence in 1947

Second, the city of Jaipur was no stranger to modernization, with a series of urban improvements taking place over at least a century before India's independence, even though the society's overall disposition remained comparatively conservative. Princely Jaipur boasted several schools, movie halls, parks, hospitals and new bungalow-oriented residential areas, even as the *purdah* system (segregation of sexes) was widespread and the education of girls was not very common.[4] Occupational communities and identity-based social groups typically inhabited specific localities and patronized particular shrines, while the urban economy was largely centered upon the local bazaars. In these respects, and however ambiguously, Jaipur's king-led and elite-supported "indigenous modernity" bridged society's conservative and progressive impulses in deeply symbolic and tangible ways that were critical to the city's spatial organization and social functioning.[5]

Third, in pursuing the ideal of a comprehensively planned city comprising self-contained neighborhoods, post-independence planners hoped to tap the legitimacy and historic role of state power in Jaipur's design and development. But facing pressing concerns on multiple fronts, the newly created Rajasthan state, of which Jaipur became the capital, had little focus on cities and their issues. Modes of governance and development from the princely period continued to provide a useful framework (and frequently the actual personnel) for post-independence urban institutions, while the local elites disliked Jaipur's rapid urbanization. Even as professional planners made formal plans promoting the progressive aims of a new planning approach, such as the mixing of different populations in residential neighborhoods, and sought to create their own space and standing in the rapidly expanding postcolonial bureaucracy, they did not overlook the priorities of local elites, including their characteristic inclination to control and regulate city growth. More important, and as I show in the following chapters, local cultural preferences and established patterns of city living featuring temples, bazaars, domestic maids and helpers, never disappeared and, in fact, actively anticipated the manner in which diverse non-state actors eventually transformed the intended outcomes of formal plans. The kind of planning efforts that the government and state institutions made was significant in its own right and mattered in important ways, but not to the extent public-sector planners projected and not in the manner Nehruvian elites anticipated.

The first part of this chapter provides an overview of Jaipur's pre-independence planning and development trajectory. In the second part, I describe how national planning policies interacted with local dynamics to shape the domains of urban governance and development after India's independence. Focusing upon the city's first master plan, which employed the DMP protocol, and the designing of Jaipur's earliest planned expansions based upon the tenets of the neighborhood unit, the latter section describes the nature and scope of formal urban plans made by the public sector.

Princely Modern

Architecture and urban historians have documented the nature and scope of colonial and postcolonial interventions in a variety of contexts.[6] My aim in this section is to provide a brief overview of the manner in which planning efforts led by the princely state shaped Jaipur's design and development over time. An appreciation of the city's planning trajectory not only helps us to understand regionally prominent notions about civic identity and pride but also helps us to comprehend the aspirations and priorities of the local gentry.

Comparatively a recent city by South Asian standards, Jaipur was founded by Maharaja Sawai Jai Singh in 1727, about sixty years before L'Enfant started planning Washington, D.C. Jaipur's plan demonstrates a formally conceived regularity with distinct spatial features, such as the division of the city into nine squares, a gridiron pattern with hierarchal and wide roads, and Cartesian orientation. The plan's regularity attracted the attention of colonial visitors, who reported its deviance from the "chaotic" layout of other Indian cities and identified Jaipur as a superlative example of city building in this part of the world. Among the earliest British visitors to the city was James Tod, who was an amateur historian and from 1818 to 1823 was a political agent to western states of the Rajputana region, which is almost contiguous to the present state of Rajasthan. He posited that the layout's regularity stemmed from the founder's predilections for astronomy and scientific pursuit:

> The character of Sawai Jai Singh is worthy of an ample delineation, which would correct our opinion of the genius and capacity of the princes of Rajputana, of whom we are apt to form too low an estimate … Jaipur [not only] became the seat of science and art … [but also the] only city in India based upon a regular plan with streets bisecting each other at right angles. Almost all the Rajput princes have a smattering of astronomy, or rather of its spurious relation, astrology; but Jai Singh went deep, not only into the theory, but the practice of the science.[7]

In contrast, many later observers, while mentioning Jai Singh's interest in astronomy, assert that Hindu scriptures informed Jaipur's planning.[8] Pursued more vigorously in recent times, this line of argument advances the thesis that the plan, its proportions and orientation, and the layout of major buildings are based upon the treatises on *Vastu Vidya*, or the traditional knowledge about city building and architecture.[9] Notwithstanding the debate's merit, the "discovery" and writings about India's indigenously planned city attracted further attention and a range of visitors. Some came looking for an authentic royal experience in planned settings, while others wanted to see the built example of natives' ancient intellect.[10] Thus, within a relatively short period in a city's long life, Jaipur came to exemplify India's old wisdom; satisfying a diverse range of romantic and inquisitive gazes, including those we might recognize as Orientalist today.[11]

However, the founder himself probably possessed a global outlook, as he is reported to have consulted Portuguese Jesuits and plans of Chinese cities during the building of Jaipur.[12] Anticipating the need for a robust economic base, Jai Singh invited artisans and traders from other regions, who helped establish Jaipur as an important node of business networks. The *Imperial Gazetteer of India* described Jaipur as the equivalent of London's Lombard Street for all of Rajputana, highlighting the city's importance as a major banking center and money market. It also noted the expertise of the city's artisans in dyeing, marble carving, pottery and brass work, and the resulting trade with large parts of British India.[13]

Specialized crafts such as *Meenakari*, or the making of intricately enameled jewelry, and exclusive goods like locally hand-printed fabrics distinguished Jaipur among Indian cities of comparable size and princely standing. They also provided the mercantile classes with a significant identity and sizable income. In the city's guidebook, the British resident—the representative of the viceroy (the colonial governor)—who was posted at Jaipur in the early twentieth century noted the names, addresses and specialties of leading businesses, implicitly assuring visitors and sightseers of a fair deal, and observing that the "wealth of the city must be enormous."[14] Although there is no known estimate of the personal wealth of the city's residents at the time, it is hard to imagine that the city economy was not dual—that is, marked by a few privileged and many poor. The nature and scope of civic improvements, discussed below, provide a reasonable idea of the state's investment in Jaipur's upkeep, which might have contributed to the resident's observation. However, it is important to note that *lagaan* (agricultural taxes) of various types on the peasants, constituting approximately two-thirds of the state's total income, largely funded Jaipur's civic improvements.[15]

After the planned layout, two major interventions shaped Jaipur's long-term development. The first comprised a sequence of standalone but frequently interrelated civic projects broadly conceptualized along the lines of the colonial urban infrastructure improvement model employed in British Indian cities.[16] Implemented during the reign of three kings over approximately eighty years, these projects contributed to the gradual modernization of Jaipur's urban infrastructure. The second and more radical intervention took place during Mirza Ismail's premiership (1942–46). He instituted new practices, such as the large-scale building of planned neighborhoods and commercial districts beyond the city's walls, and by doing so, shifted the foci away from the historical quarters. These two developments influenced the nature and scope of planning practice, and also shaped elites' aspirations and preferences in fundamental ways.

Sawai Ram Singh, who ruled Jaipur from 1835 to 1880, first patronized the building of modern public works.[17] Superintended by the prolific colonial engineer Swinton Jacob, the newly founded Public Works Department (PWD) organized all the different types of civil works, including architectural and planning services.[18] Jaipur's civic projects were evidently comparable, and perhaps even better in some aspects, to those undertaken in British India's cities.[19] These included road paving, municipal lighting, waste collection, water supply systems, and the construction of schools, parks and a museum and a hospital.[20] Ram Singh also ordered the city painted uniformly, strengthening Jaipur's distinctiveness and earning it the sobriquet of India's "Pink City." It is said that he took the rather idiosyncratic step of having the city painted to welcome Edward VII. Rudyard Kipling provides a vivid description of contemporary urbanity in his distinctive prose:

> How much Colonel Jacob has done for Jaipur will never be known because the officer in question is one of the not small class [British colonial officials] that resolutely refuse to talk about their own work. The result of the good work is that the old and the new, the rampantly raw and the sullenly old, stand cheek-by-jowl in startling contrast. Thus, the branded bull trips over the rails of a steel tramway which brings out the city rubbish; that lacquered and painted *Rath* [ceremonial cart], behind the two stag like trotting bullocks, catches its primitive wheels in the cast-iron gas-lamp post with the brass nozzle a-top, and all Rajputana, gaily-clad small-turbaned swaggering Rajputana, circulates along the magnificent pavements.[21]

Although Kipling's account certainly reinforced the city's romantic image, it omitted key differences between contemporaneous developments in Jaipur and British India's cities. First, the royal treasury routinely paid for Jaipur's civic improvements in addition to all of the municipal expenses.[22] Second, no major demolitions took place in order to carry out these civic improvements.[23] Both were in sharp contrast with the cities under direct British rule—such as Ahemdabad, where officials routinely imposed additional tax burdens on residents to expand municipal services, and Kolkata, where the colonial British regularly demolished buildings in native quarters to make way for civic improvements.[24] At some level, the situation in Jaipur was in line with the public largesse native kings routinely exhibited toward their subjects. For example, the rulers commonly granted state servants cash awards and lands for faithful and loyal service, and land titles to the poor, who built dwellings on unoccupied and marginal locations.[25]

Moreover, unlike British India, where a range of urban actors were increasingly involved in local governance and the shaping of public culture, in Jaipur, the king, his courtiers and a handful of British or British-trained officials controlled civic and public affairs.[26] Apart from the ex-officio city engineer and health official, the royal court nominated all twenty-six members of the municipality's executive council.[27] They came almost exclusively from the minuscule gentry comprising merchants, professionals and *Jagirdars,* or nobles.[28] The *Jagirdars* often had kinship ties with the king and frequently held important administrative positions in the court. The emergent professional class—comprising teachers, lawyers and doctors—was largely employed by the state, while the merchants depended on the state for business and protection.[29] Further, given the lack of modern industry until the 1940s, Jaipur did not have a significant number of industrialists or organized working-class people, who were increasingly playing important roles in the local politics of cities in British India such as Kanpur, Mumbai and Kolkata.[30]

The nature and scope of public works changed when Jaipur's first anglicized king—Sawai Man Singh, who was trained under the British residents' watchful eye—came to the throne in 1922.[31] Unlike his predecessors, Man Singh openly professed loyalty to the empire; routinely spent the summers in London; did not mind, and perhaps enjoyed, his philanderer's reputation; and famously headed Jaipur's polo team.[32] Fittingly, within a few years of kingship, he chose to live outside the city walls in a refurbished garden palace, ostensibly fashioned after Versailles, and appointed career officials as *Dewans*, or prime ministers, to take care of administration during his prolonged absences.[33]

Mirza Ismail, prime minister from 1942 to 1946, took a keen interest in urban issues. The elites' perception of Jaipur's desired urbanity was deeply influenced by his patronage of interrelated notions about large-scale planned development and his aversion for the unplanned, along with notions about Jaipur's spatial distinctiveness and unique urban legacy, which had matured over several decades.

Mirza Ismail had served as Mysore state's *Dewan* for fifteen years, overseeing the building of modern industries, a hydroelectric power station and civic amenities.[34] He had also worked closely with Otto Koenigsberger, whom he had appointed as the chief architect and planner of Mysore in 1939. Koenigsberger introduced Mirza to modern planning ideas such as master plans and planned neighborhoods when he planned a residential extension for Mysore state's steel plant in the town of Bhadravati.[35] Not surprisingly, Mirza encouraged the development of the first commercial district and major thoroughfare outside the city's perimeter wall—later named M.I. Road in his honor—and the establishment of the University of Rajputana at Jaipur. He also commissioned the planning and development of new bungalow-style residential extensions—which were fast replacing vernacular typologies such as *Havelies*, the traditional courtyard houses, as the preferred choice of elites in other Indian cities.[36] Jaipur's first extension, aptly named New Colony, had been developed in 1932. Mirza's tenure witnessed the rapid development of several new neighborhoods, such as Bani Park and C-scheme, which were promptly patronized by local elites, who had been migrating from the historical quarters, following the Maharaja's own example.[37]

Mirza shifted the developmental focus away from the city's historical quarters and, perhaps of more importance, also attempted to organize and clean them. He encouraged the formulation of the first-ever building bylaws that sought to control building activity and usage in the walled city.[38] Mirza also undertook demolition drives, attempting to remove what he perceived as incongruous additions. He called "cleaning the city, which was in a most deplorable condition" the proudest achievement of his rather short stay in Jaipur.[39] Herbert Matthews, a field reporter for the *New York Times*, compared Mirza's mission with that of the indomitable Robert Moses. With a certain élan, in his autobiography Mirza quotes Matthews's dispatches filed in October 1942:

> When the stream of American tourist flows back to this famed "Pink City" after the [Second World] war, they are going to find it more thoroughly transformed and improved than New York after Robert Moses got through with it … For every tree I cut down I will plant a hundred, said Premier Ismail when he was driving me around the city to see the improvements. [He also said] When I tear down a man's house I want him to leave it smiling and knowing that he is going to a new and better one.[40]

Mirza Ismail left in 1946 for Hyderabad, just a few years before Jaipur merged with independent India. From the seat of a relatively small princely state, Jaipur became the capital of India's second largest state, Rajasthan, which came into existence in 1950. The next section describes the developments in Jaipur in the post-independence period.

Planning Post-Independence Jaipur

The impact of independence on urban India has not been well documented. The old country's violent partition and the large-scale movement of people accompanying that momentous event altered the social fabric and future trajectories of many cities. In a recent essay, William Glover has described the massive housing shortages in Delhi that resulted from the historic rupture, and people's desperate attempts to find places of their own—attempts that, at some level, have continued to define the urban situation ever since.[41] Rajasthan shares a long border with the new country of Pakistan and received a large number of refugees.[42] In addition, a range of pressing concerns—such as the unification of former princely states, the formation of basic administrative structures and the transition to democracy—meant that the newly formed state government had little attention and few resources to deal with other issues.[43] On the one hand, given the emergent resource constraints and restricted attention on urban affairs, the government largely permitted, and even co-opted, many practices from the pre-independence period.[44] On the other hand, it focused on reconciling and streamlining administrative procedures for the previously princely entities, and creating standardized organizations in line with those of postcolonial India.

For instance, the state government did not alter the organizational structure or function of Jaipur's main urban development agency, the City Improvement Board (CIB), which was formed in 1942, during Mirza Ismail's premiership. Depending upon the PWD's practices and seconded personnel, the CIB was a civil-engineering-oriented organization that took a utilitarian approach to city design and development.[45] The CIB continued to develop new bungalow-oriented city-extensions, conceptualized during Mirza Ismail's tenure, until its amalgamation with the Urban Improvement Trust (UIT) in 1961. Post-independence neighborhoods—modeled after the colonial Civil Lines, however paradoxically—were named Bapu Nagar and Gandhi Nagar, after the new nation's father, in line with the contemporary climate of opinion.[46] The PWD's influence continued unabated when the state government created urban improvement trusts in major cities, beginning in Jaipur, to undertake the improvement of existing areas and the development of urban extensions.

The genesis of urban improvement trusts in India dated back to the turn of the nineteenth century, when the colonial government first set up improvement trusts in cities under their direct control, including Mumbai in 1898 and Kolkata in 1911.[47] The idea was to administer urban development activities by controlling them at the executive—rather than the municipal—level, because popularly elected Indian nationalists were increasingly gaining power in the latter.[48] Headed by government appointees and staffed largely by engineers and technical overseers, Rajasthan's urban improvement trusts, like their counterparts in other Indian states, focused upon prestigious and remunerative activities, such as the development of new areas and urban infrastructure, while mundane yet tricky functions, such as public hygiene and cleanliness, remained the responsibility of elected municipalities.[49] Along similar lines, and following national trends, new public-sector agencies emerged gradually in the field of urban development in Jaipur. The organizational setup and scope of the Delhi Development Authority (DDA) influenced both the formation of the Jaipur Development Authority (JDA), which replaced the UIT in 1982, and the Rajasthan Housing Board (RHB), which came into existence in 1970 and focused upon comprehensive development of planned neighborhoods comprising ready-built dwellings.[50]

Against this background of institutional continuity and incremental change, professional planners found a toehold in the state bureaucracy when the government initiated a town-planning section within the PWD in the early 1950s. The new cadre of town planners succeeded in delineating its own domain in 1959, when the state enacted the Urban Improvement (UI) Act, enabling legislation for public-sector-led planning activities, including the preparation of master plans.[51] Shortly afterward, the planning section separated from the PWD as a statutory department of the state, and it was rechristened the Town Planning Organization in 1963.

Despite the administrative advances, planners still needed to validate their professional expertise in the engineering-dominated worldview of the urban development officials and agencies, which traced their lineage to the venerable PWD.[52] Not surprisingly, the Nehruvian trend of turning away from past practices and toward an ostensibly modern future was helpful, as was the importance of making new types of comprehensive plans using the latest techniques and purportedly rational parameters. I describe below how the planners used the DMP protocol to make formal plans at the city and neighborhood level, emphasizing the break from the princely past while accounting for the sensitivities and preferences of the local elites.

Banarasi Dass Kambo led the efforts for the first Master Plan of Jaipur (MPJ) and the earliest planned city-extensions based upon the tenets of the neighborhood unit. By all accounts, Kambo was both a highly committed professional planner and socially intelligent state official. He arrived in Rajasthan as the chief town planner and architectural advisor to the state government in 1967. Several of his coworkers recalled his liking for the DMP, which he often quoted verbatim and employed as a point of reference for planning norms, while a close colleague fondly described him as a "tough character" who was "better kept on your side" if you needed his support or consent in official meetings.[53] Kambo's authoritative stance on planning matters stemmed partly from the self-pride he took in his professional attainments. After working as a member of the DMP team in the late 1950s, he had supervised the design of the Bokaro Steel Plant's township in Eastern India; both employed the neighborhood unit concept.[54] Kambo had a degree in architecture from the Delhi Polytechnic, precursor to the prestigious School of Planning and Architecture (SPA), and a graduate degree in urban planning from the Massachusetts Institute of Technology.

The MPJ clearly carries the imprint of Kambo's DMP experience. Led by state planners, the plan-makers—comprising expert groups of leading officials from relevant departments—rendered technical input and advice on aspects such as traffic and transport, industry and business, utilities, environment and housing. Collective authorship not only enhanced the plan's legitimacy but also helped the town planners boost their status among their bureaucratic peers. The plan-making process followed the DMP protocol as well. After the government's sanction, planners conducted a civic survey, collecting diverse information about socioeconomic phenomena and existing land uses; analyzed this data, making projections for the horizon year (in this case, 1991); and then recommended land-use allocations and pertinent projects. After inviting comments from the public, but not requiring their actual involvement at any stage, the expert collective fine-tuned and submitted the draft master plan to the state government, which enacted it, according to bureaucratic convenience and political expediency, about five years later, in 1976.

Similarly to the DMP, the MPJ innately assumed (and repeatedly emphasized) the state's central role in organizing and leading outward-focused urban development, acquiring private lands as and when required. It also followed the DMP in highlighting the imperative of efficiency, by balancing different types of land uses and undertaking the development of self-contained planned areas at different spatial scales.[55] Just like the well-theorized comprehensive planning model, the MPJ unequivocally promoted the primacy of the professional expert in centralized planning. For example, ignoring the city's unique urban tissue, which featured a gridded road network and courtyard-based *Havelies*, the MPJ recommended the following for future residential areas:

> Philosophy of planning encompasses the total urban complex i.e. the entire city comprising of a number of relatively self-contained communities,

which at the lowest tier have a "housing cluster." Such a cluster may comprise of 150 to 200 families in order to promote intimacy, neighborliness, personal and family contacts. A number of clusters grouped together around some focal point such as a primary school and convenient shops with a small park shall form a planning unit—containing population between 4,000 to 5,000.[56]

This quote exhibits a certain self-assuredness rooted in the successful translation and internalization of the neighborhood unit, and the tone suggests an awareness of Perry's concept, though no reference is made to it. However, the MPJ justifies itself as a statutory requirement or state-sponsored development effort and also, by invoking the popular sentiment about Jaipur's distinctiveness, justifies the elites' historical impulse to control city growth, and the concomitant fear of unplanned urbanization:

The recent building activity has kept little regard for the traditional architectural and civic design aspects of the city with the result that there is a positive threat to the city's beauty, symmetry and design for which it has been so famous. All is not well the way Jaipur is expanding and some "order and system" is required to be brought in. It became imperative that adequate attention must be immediately paid to these problems and to avoid haphazard growth taking place almost everywhere. Need for a long-range comprehensive plan or a master plan was thus felt urgent to guide its future development.[57]

The strategy of addressing local sensitivities and priorities while pursuing the modernist agenda and emphasizing the break from the past also shaped the manner in which planners conceived the new neighborhoods. This is the focus of the next section.

Planning the New Neighborhoods

In the interviews I conducted, like any other group of professionals, planners implicitly emphasized their superior skills by criticizing the work of non-planners. Several called the layout of residential areas designed by PWD engineers and technicians as a "draftsman" mode of planning, because it followed these preset sequential steps. First, the outer boundary of the land was drawn on a blank sheet of paper. Second, a series of roads to provide access to all parts of the land were drawn. Third, the plots were demarcated alongside the roads. Finally, the residual open spaces within the blocks of plots were labeled as parks, open spaces, or schools, depending upon what the draftsman or his supervisor thought was most pertinent. Often concerned with maximizing the plotted area, this method had scant regard for neighborhood planning standards, which are described in Chapter 2, and hence they earned the depreciatory name of "draftsman planning."[58] In contrast, professional planners explained, they designed new neighborhoods using the latest features of the DMP and the Chandigarh plan. Examples are Jaipur's earliest two neighborhoods, Jawahar Nagar and Malviya Nagar, which were developed in the early 1970s by the RHB and UIT respectively.[59]

The influence of the DMP on Jawahar Nagar and Malviya Nagar is subtler than that of Chandigarh, because it came via planning parameters, which by then had percolated into the planning system across the country. Chandigarh's influence, which came via the reproduction of physical planning patterns, is more clearly visible in these neighborhoods. For example, the Jawahar Nagar plan contains a sequence of open spaces and parks so arranged that residents can walk through the entire locality, traveling both east–west and north–south, without negotiating vehicular traffic. In addition, Jawahar Nagar's plan comprises "sectors," an appellation that became popular in Indian planning after the creation of Chandigarh's famous neighborhoods, employing the tenets of the neighborhood unit, including arterial roads on all the sides, a hierarchal network of internal roads, predominantly residential land use, single-family houses, and open spaces and parks.

However, the plans of Jawahar Nagar and Malviya Nagar differed from Clarence Perry's idea of the neighborhood unit in two crucial ways. First, they did not provide schools at the core of each sector. Second, they provided convenience shops not at the neighborhood edge but in a central area denoted "commercial," segregated from the dwellings, or in a standalone block of shops. These were key digressions, as Perry's design principles posited the school as the neighborhood's central pivot and a few nearby shops as a prerequisite for self-sufficiency. The changes were not arbitrary but were deliberate acts of planners responding to long-available evidence that centrally placed schools did not really work in Indian cities, and shops adjoining houses attracted the opposite of well-to-do residents.[60]

In contrast to the education system in the United States, in most Indian cities, including Jaipur, the provision of schools is a state, not a municipal, function. The states usually lacked school building funds, and in many instances the lots earmarked for schools became dumping grounds. Rather than sending their children to the inexpensive but usually dreary schools run by the state's education department, most well-to-do and aspiring middle-class parents preferred sending them to the more expensive "English medium" schools, popularly called convents, managed by Christian missionaries and usually located in colonial-era neighborhoods. Even when convent schools could be persuaded to open branches in new neighborhoods, they usually provided complete education from elementary to high-school level, contradicting the planning idea of providing a hierarchy of primary, middle and secondary schools within quarter-, half- and one-mile radii of walking distance. The new neighborhoods offered too small a catchment area to attract the necessary enrollments. Thus, by the early 1970s, planners still provided school sites, but their positioning and combination (or separation) of elementary, middle and secondary levels did not carry much weight for Indian planners.[61] This is evident in the plans of Jawahar Nagar and Malviya Nagar.

Perry's idea of providing a few shops at the edge of a neighborhood was never attractive in Jaipur and many other Indian cities. For well-to-do residents, having shops close to houses worked against their imagined ideal residential environment. In fact, it appeared appalling to them, as it evoked the imagery of the indigenous bazaar and its associated cacophony, squalor and disorderliness. In contrast to the native city, the colonial typology of Civil Lines, characterized by broad and regular streets with bungalows set among vast lots, often set the benchmark for how the Indian elites imagined the ideal residential environment in the post-independence period.[62] Many planners came from similar backgrounds and, for the most part, they feared that the proximity of shops might encourage the owners of adjoining lots to convert their houses into shops. Thus, they usually located shops in a segregated block close to houses or in a separate area abutting the neighborhood.

Moreover, planners conceived Jawahar Nagar and Malviya Nagar as spacious, with less plotted area and more open and green spaces than Perry's. By the 1970s, local elites had begun to vociferously express their unhappiness with increasing congestion in Jaipur, which had been commonly perceived as a commodious city. A contemporary commentator noted that "the walled city of Jaipur is in a very bad state, with a crowd of people living unhygienically (sic) in crumbling houses. Besides, the once architectural consistency of the city is marred by the recent heterogeneous constructions."[63] The fact that land came free of cost from the government helped the planners in promoting parks and open spaces. One senior town planner noted: "You know the cost of land was nothing—it came free—and people wanted a very lavish thing, so we designed Jawahar Nagar this way."[64] Accordingly, only about 48 percent of Jawahar Nagar's original land use was residential, comprising mostly single-family residences, with about 4 percent earmarked for multifamily residences. Since the funds to maintain public spaces in Indian cities do not come simply through taxes paid by the owners of private lots, which would have pressured planners to minimize public land and maximize private land, the rest of Jawahar Nagar's land (52 percent) was planned as open space, comprising roads, schools, parks and public facilities. This made the neighborhood more spacious than Perry's and the DMP's recommendations to use 52–54 percent of a neighborhood for housing lots.[65]

But even as public-sector planners sought to address local sensitivities, there is little doubt that formal urban plans were essentially progressive and modern in nature.[66] Take, for example, the new neighborhoods' residents, who came from a range of social and economic backgrounds. Following a national policy decision adopted in the late 1960s, officials divided the population into five income groups using criteria that determined the housing they could afford.[67] Based on figures for expendable household income, officials calculated affordable plot sizes and built-up areas of houses for each income group. In order to keep costs within the predetermined affordability limits, engineers used low-cost building materials, such as locally available stone and cost-saving construction techniques, such as the use of prefabricated fixtures (see Figure 3.2). Attempting to address India's complex economic and social make-up, the allotment of units or lots followed both an affirmative action policy and an open lottery system within each income group.

Across all economic categories, 20 percent of housing was reserved for lower castes, called scheduled castes and tribes; ex-servicemen; freedom fighters who had fought for India's independence; and the employees of the state and national governments. The majority of housing was constructed for lower- and middle-income groups, with subsidies built into the housing finance model.[68] Out of the total 4,149 housing units in Jawahar Nagar, housing for the Economic Weaker Section (EWS) and Low Income Group (LIG) comprised 1,962 units; the Middle Income Groups (MIG-I and MIG-II) had access to 1,825 units; and the RHB built 362 units for the High Income Group (HIG). This was a significant shift, because in the inner quarters of Jaipur and many other Indian cities, deep-seated biases based on birth and much other discrimination had customarily decided people's social and spatial locations.

FIGURE 3.2 A ready-made middle-income group (MIG) house in Jawahar Nagar

Although important in their own right, Jawahar Nagar and Malviya Nagar were essentially two small neighborhoods in a large urban area. The newly established state of Rajasthan had many pressing concerns beyond the cities and their issues. Planners' illusion of using state power for city design and development did not translate into reality. The state government failed to live up to the central role envisaged by the MPJ and, unlike Delhi's decision-makers, did not even employ eminent domain to acquire vast tracts of the urban periphery for controlling Jaipur's future. Given their small numbers, limited power and statewide jurisdiction over rapidly growing urban areas, planners could not produce the detailed sub-city-level plans that would be required for follow-through of the MPJ. As explained in Chapter 5, the difficult transition from varying princely practices prevalent among different regions to a democratic polity and post-independence institutions resulted in slow development of supporting frameworks for the new planning approach. In twenty-one years of existence (1961 to 1982), Jaipur's UIT developed only one major city-extension—Malviya Nagar—while the housing shortages continued to grow unabated.[69] Thus, the government efforts were accompanied by appropriations, speculations and ungoverned land grabs, which continue to characterize Jaipur's growth even today.[70]

Conclusion

It is clear that established practices and preferences shaped the nature and framing of formal urban plans in Jaipur in more significant ways than planners usually imagine. As I have shown in this chapter, the break with Jaipur's pre-independence past was neither clean nor complete. Even if they so wished, professional planners could not simply turn their backs on local expectations and traditions while pursuing the new approach to urban planning. Adopting a practical approach, they attempted to balance the ambitious demands of the national elites, who set an ideologically progressive agenda, and the aspirations of local patrons, who rightfully took pride in Jaipur's distinctive identity while seeking to establish their own professional standing within the dynamic of regime shift and institutional change. The planners' efforts were indeed significant but not to the extent the plan documents promised, and not in the manner their patrons anticipated. More important, and as I explain in the following chapters, the implementation—or lack of implementation—of formal urban plans prompted a host of non-state actors to make their own spatial plans, which gradually transformed the governments' efforts in a range of meaningful ways.

Notes

1   Ravi Kalia's trilogy provides an overview of urban planning's ideology and trajectory in the decades immediately following the independence of India. See Kalia, *Gandhi Nagar*, *Bhubaneswar* and *Chandigarh*.

2 For a succinct overview of the evolution of the idea of development in India's polity, see the introduction in Sivaramakrishnan and Agrawal, *Regional Modernities*.

3 Many scholars have highlighted the Janus-faced nature of the indigenous Indian elite. For example, Gyan Prakash in *Another Reason* describes how the elite derived deep inspiration (and pride) from India's past even while fancying careers in future-oriented fields such as engineering, medicine and business.

4 Maharani Gayatri Devi, the charming and beautiful princess of Cooch Behar and later the third and youngest wife of Jaipur's last reigning ruler, pioneered the education of girls by promoting the first girls' education centers (named MGD school and Maharani college in her honor) at Jaipur during the early 1940s. Her autobiography, *A Princess Remembers: The Memoirs of the Maharani of Jaipur*, provides an insightful account of changes in Jaipur during the second half of the twentieth century.

5 Several scholars have posited that there is not a singular modernity, and divergent locales interpret and modify the constitutive concepts and phenomena in different forms. See Hosagrahar, *Indigenous Modernities*; and Nair, *Mysore Modern*. For the collaborative nature of the colonial modernity project in the context of early twentieth-century urban India, see Chopra, *A Joint Enterprise*.

6 See, for instance, Kusno, *Behind the Postcolonial*; Al Sayyad, *Hybrid Urbanism*; and Perera, "Indigenizing the Colonial City."

7 Tod, *Annals and Antiquities of Rajasthan*, Vol. 3, 1342.

8 See, for instance, Havell, *Indian Architecture*; and Volwahsen, *Architecture of the World*.

9 Sachdev and Tillotson, *Building Jaipur*. Also see Chakrabarti, *Indian Architectural Theory*.

10 See, for example, Arnold, *India Revisited*; and Caine, *Picturesque India*.

11 Said, *Orientalism*.

12 Anand, "An Epistle Dedicatory to the Master-builder Sawai Jai Singh."

13 *Imperial Gazetteer of India*, Vol. XIII, 401.

14 Showers, *Notes on Jaipur*, 17.

15 *Imperial Gazetteer of India*, Vol. XIII, 395.

16 Banerjee, "Understanding Planning Cultures."

17 Sarkar, *A History of Jaipur*.

18 For an account of Jacob's work, see Chapter 4 in Sachdev and Tillotson, *Building Jaipur*.

19 For a concise overview of British colonial interventions in urban contexts, see Home, *Of Planting and Planning*. For a description of architectural projects commissioned by Jaipur and other princely states, see Tillotson, *The Tradition of Indian Architecture*; and Metcalf, *An Imperial Vision*.

20 Roy, *History of the Jaipur City*.

21 Kipling, *Out of India*, 17.

22 *Imperial Gazetteer of India*, Vol. XIII, 400.

23 Roy, *History of the Jaipur City*.

24 Raychaudhuri, "Colonialism, Indigenous Elites and the Transformation of Cities in the Non-Western World." Also see Geddes, *Barra Bazaar Improvement*.

25 Customarily, Jaipur state overlooked the poor living on empty lands and periodically granted titles to the occupiers. Jaipur's earliest physical survey, undertaken in Samvat 1925 (1868), which nowadays serves as the quasi-official property register for historical quarters, records such properties as *Kooncha upaad*. Literally, the term *Kooncha upaad* means "pulling out the seasonal weed to clear the ground for building." The actual meaning, in official parlance, refers to such lands that were not formally allotted by the state but quietly occupied by common people. It is said that once the princely administration had demarcated the original plan on the ground and laid out the city's major roads and districts, they realized that the population of Amber—the nearby original capital of Dhoondhar state, which Jaipur replaced—had fallen way short of the capacity of the new city. Thus, they let it be known that the state would not mind if residents and newcomers occupied the available inner lots. Subsequently, the inner lots

of several districts—such as Chaukri Ramchandra Ji, Chaukri Ganga Pole and Purani Basti—were inhabited in this manner. Interestingly, the central district, Topkhana Hazuri, which houses the royal palaces, also has lots marked as *Kooncha upaad*.

26 Haynes, *Rhetoric and Ritual in Colonial India.*
27 *Imperial Gazetteer of India,* Vol. XIII, 400.
28 Rudolph and Rudolph, *Essays on Rajputana.*
29 Roy, *History of the Jaipur City,* 104.
30 Chakrabarty, *Rethinking Working-Class History.*
31 At the death of Madho Singh—who, like his predecessor Sawai Ram Singh, maintained a traditional lifestyle and avoided personal interactions with colonial officials—the British instituted a "modernizing" regency for the minor king Sawai Man Singh in 1922. Man Singh asserted his independence only in 1942, when he appointed Mirza Ismail as the prime minister. Robert Stern observes that Mirza's biggest success in Jaipur was to establish good relations with business classes and pro-nationalist movements, paving the way for an easy transition in 1947. Stern, *The Cat and the Lion.*
32 Crewe, *The Last Maharaja.*
33 Roy, *History of the Jaipur City,* 110. A patron of the imperial "Indo-Saracenic" style invented by colonial architects, Sawai Man Singh also sponsored the building of his house at New Delhi in a similar fashion. See Tillotson, "CG Blomfield Last Architect of the Raj."
34 Mirza, *My Public Life,* 81.
35 Liscombe, "In-dependence."
36 Khan, "Cultural Transfers."
37 Sealey, *Planned Cities in India.* Beginning in the 1880s, planned suburban developments took place in many cities. For an account of the process in Delhi, see Hosagrahar, *Indigenous Modernities,* 122–132.
38 Jaipur City Municipal Council, *Building Bye Laws.* In this respect, Mirza's approach echoed the actions of indigenous elites in other parts of the country, who, working closely with colonial authorities, sought to improve existing quarters and build city extensions modeled after their perceptions of desired urbanity. See Chopra, *A Joint Enterprise.*
39 Mirza, *My Public Life,* 81.
40 Ibid., 82.
41 Glover, *A Place of One's Own.*
42 Jaipur was no exception and registered a massive decadal population growth rate of 65 percent in the 1951 census.
43 The only exception was the centrally funded development of resettlement colonies for partition refugees in many cities of Rajasthan, including Jaipur, Ajmer, Udaipur, Jodhpur and Sri Ganganagar. Interview with a senior town planner at Jaipur, May 26, 2006.
44 The trend was not peculiar to Jaipur but prevalent among other parts of India as well. Fahim, *Local Government in India Still Carries Characteristics of Its Colonial Heritage.*
45 For the seminal significance of PWD's worldview and practices, see Scriver, "Empire-building and Thinking in the Public Works Department of British India." Also see Scriver, *Rationalization, Standardization, and Control in Design.*
46 Interview with a senior town planner at Jaipur, May 26, 2006.
47 TCPO, *Town and Country Planning in India,* 30. Following their establishment in Bombay and Calcutta, improvement trusts were created in several cities, including Hyderabad (1912), Lucknow, Kanpur, Delhi and Allahabad (1919–22); and Nagpur (1937), which is still in existence. See Kopardekar and Diwan, *Urban and Regional Planning,* 38.
48 Rosser, *Urbanization in India,* 80.
49 Singh, *Urban Planning in India.*

50 The RHB represented the state-controlled housing finance and delivery system the Government of India began developing in the late 1960s, following the recommendations of a report sponsored by the Ford Foundation. The report recommended the creation of housing boards, resembling "Public Housing Authorities in hundreds of American cities but [with] a wider range of responsibilities," crowned by an apex organization at the national level (The Housing Team *Report to Ford Foundation*, part one, 11). Consequently, the central government created HUDCO at the national level, with the aim of raising cheap loans through government bonds, insurance companies, banks and other public financial intermediaries in order to finance and provide technical expertise to state- and city-level public housing organizations such as the RHB. The "Housing Team" that prepared the report comprised: Dr. Louis Winnick, of the Ford Foundation; Mr. Uriel Manhiem, housing consultant, New York; Mr. Glen Beyer, Professor of Housing and Design, Cornell University; Mr. Robert Colwell, Director, Program Division, Federal Housing Authority; and Dr. Ernst M. Fisher, Professor Emeritus, Housing and Urban Land Use, Columbia University. The team visited India in 1964 and 1965.

51 It certainly helped that the national Autumn Planning Seminar and State Planning Officials' Conference was held in Jaipur in 1958, and the organizers used the event to lobby the state's decision makers. One of the recommendations of the conference exhorted the state government to set up a "properly staffed full-fledged state town-planning department," as other progressive states had done; the institute of town planners promised to provide all the necessary help.

52 The first generation of post-independence architects also faced a similar situation. See Menon, "The Contemporary Architecture of Delhi."

53 Interviews on February 14, 2006, and May 29, 2006.

54 TCPO, *Town and Country Planning in India,* 85.

55 Chief Town Planner and Architectural Advisor, *Master Plan for Jaipur,* 12.

56 Ibid., 37.

57 Ibid., 3.

58 Interview with a senior town planner on April 25, 2006. The draftsmen constituted the subordinate ranks of the PWD. They were trained in, and thus made drawings according to, the efficiency-oriented engineering tradition. For the impact of the PWD's practices on technical education, see Kumar, "Colonial Requirements and Engineering Education."

59 These two neighborhoods not only established the benchmark for the development of subsequent neighborhoods but also showcased many design ideas from the formal plan documents on the ground in Jaipur for the first time.

60 Interview with a senior town planner, February 14, 2006.

61 Interview with a retired planner, January 27, 2006. As a young planner in the 1960s, he had worked on neighborhood planning with the Delhi Development Authority, and he then moved to Nagpur, in Central India. In the 1990s he retired as the professor and chair of the Architecture and Planning Department of the Visvesvaraya National Institute of Technology.

62 Interview with the retired chief town planner of the national Town and Country Planning Organization (TCPO) on May 28, 2006.

63 Arora et al., *Jaipur,* 18. The authors describe an "anti-encroachment" drive at the time in the following words: "The campaign proved to be a pioneering attempt in the 'city beautiful' movement … On the very first day 111 *tharies* [jerry-built kiosks] were pulled down in the main bazaars, and within a month 800 were removed and several unauthorized constructions pulled down. Such beautifying and cleanliness drives should be perpetuated continually and the achievements should not wither away on the account of indifference or negligence." Arora et al., *Jaipur,* 83.

64 Interview with a senior town planner on April 25, 2006.

65 Perry, *The Neighborhood Unit*, 3; and Delhi Development Authority, *Master Plan for Delhi*, Table 8.
66 William Glover's articulation of the notion of spatial modernity in urban contexts informs my understanding and usage of the concept in fundamental ways. See *Making Lahore Modern*, 200.
67 Interview with a senior planner from HUDCO, April 24, 2006.
68 It is important to note that housing loans were unusually difficult to obtain before the liberalization of India's economy in the 1990s. Public-sector housing agencies, such as the RHB, provided ready-built units on monthly installments with variable repayment periods and cross-subsidy of interest rates among various income groups. In Jawahar Nagar, for example, the RHB offered the terms shown in Table 3.1.

TABLE 3.1 Table showing interest rates and repayment periods for different income groups in Jawahar Nagar

Economic Groups	Applicable Interest Rate (%)	Repayment Period
Economically Weaker Section (EWS)	7	18
Lower Income Group (LIG)	9	13
Middle Income Group – I (MIG-I)	12	10
Middle Income Group – II (MIG-II)	13	10
Higher Income Group	14	10

Source: Derived from Brochure for Jawahar Nagar published by Rajasthan Housing Board, 1981.

69 Compared to the authoritarian but efficient practices of the princely era, the process of land assembly became rather difficult in the post-independence period. Public-sector agencies such as the UIT undertook the development of planned neighborhoods according to progressive stages, which were fairly consistent in many parts of urban India, as described in the UI Act of 1959. First, the UIT would identify and frame a "residential scheme," or a proposed neighborhood, in its jurisdiction. This entailed scouting for a sizable parcel of state-owned land in order to avoid the cumbersome and large-scale acquisition of private lands. The process of framing the scheme meant marking the proposed neighborhood on the revenue map in order to identify adjoining private lands that needed to be acquired through eminent domain. Second, the UIT would seek the state government's permission to proceed with the proposed scheme and request the transfer of state-owned land in its name. Third, the UIT would acquire the identified private lands according to procedures described in the Land Acquisition Act of 1894. In the fourth stage, the UIT would ideally both possess the legal title and have physical control over the desired land, and make detailed development plans. Obstacles could, and often did, arise at each of these steps, including lack of coordination between different officials, legal interventions and political interference.
70 The authors of Jaipur's second master plan, adopted in 1998, acknowledged the massive subversion of the preceding plan:

> The proposals of bulk acquisition of land, in many cases, have been unsuccessful and invited legal wrangles. Housing cooperative societies have usurped almost all land in the urbanizable area thus restricting the Jaipur Development Authority (JDA) from taking up urban development programs envisaged in the master plan ... Rampant illegal construction of buildings took place throughout and Katchi Bastis [informal settlements] have emerged upon large tracts of land.
> Jaipur Develoment Authority, *Master Development Plan 2011,* 1

4

USER PLANS

Leveraging Unforeseen Opportunities

Young and recently married, Mr. and Mrs. Gupta moved to the newly inaugurated Jawahar Nagar in 1973. I interviewed them almost thirty-three years later, in the summer of 2006, when Mr. Gupta had recently retired as a professor from the University of Rajasthan. Using the South Asian expression "colony" for neighborhood, he summarized their lifetime experience of Jawahar Nagar: "This colony changed dramatically in front of our eyes. When we arrived, this place was barren (*Ujaad*) with no amenities, no shopping facilities, not even helpers, sweepers, and milk suppliers. Gradually everything became available and now we think—and you can ask anybody—this is one of Jaipur's best neighborhoods."[1] Their long-serving maid, who was setting up chai to mark the end of our formal interview, nodded in agreement. The maid knows the area well, said Mrs. Gupta, because she lives in the informal settlement across the street.

Many interviewees echoed Mr. Gupta's sentiment about Jaipur's planned neighborhoods, even as several qualified his generous endorsement with crucial detail.[2] Some explained that, given the authorities' trademark apathy, the residents often look after the parks and civic amenities themselves. A few described their unhappiness with free riders from the informal settlements, while the ceaseless construction and rebuilding activity bothered others. Some complained that their neighborhood has changed too much. Single-family houses have been converted into multifamily units and shops, changing the assigned land use; and floors have been added beyond permissible height, increasing the envisaged density. Indeed, today it takes a sharp eye to decipher the characteristic features of the neighborhood unit concept, such as residential-only land use, a network of parks and open spaces and centrally placed schools. So, what happened? How did the planned neighborhoods change so significantly, both from within and without?

This chapter examines two planning efforts at the heart of this transformation. In the first part, I explain how the residents leveraged the physical planning features of the infrastructure and dwellings—such as the setbacks around the building footprints, and parks and open spaces—to adapt the planned neighborhoods to suit their practical needs and cultural preferences. I also describe how the process of adaptation occurred largely through incremental and tacit plans that targeted the neighborhood's envisaged spatiality and sociality and changed it over time. In the second part of this chapter, I turn attention to the adjacent informal settlements housing a range of services and workers. By focusing upon the emergence and growth of these settlements, I describe how their builders pursued their own plans by capitalizing on the few inadvertent and marginal opportunities the planned developments created. The neighborhood workers and service providers, who were not factored into the formal plans, cleverly combined diverse resources, while seeking livelihood and shelter at relevant locations.

It is important to note that the actions of neighborhood residents and users are, rather ironically, driven by concerns similar to the ones that had catalyzed Perry's conception and the adoption of the neighborhood unit in Indian planning practice. These include concerns about creating a residential environment that is safe, supporting and protected; and a physical place that provides culturally appropriate opportunities for work, leisure, recreation and social interaction. Although distinguished by significant differences, such as the nature of sponsors and access to resources, the two planning efforts centered upon planned neighborhoods and informal settlements share a few other similarities. As explained in preceding chapters, India's centralized planning framework provides little formal space for non-state actors and their plans. Formal plans in India are legal documents that are difficult to modify and take on a life of their own in the labyrinth of postcolonial paperwork.[3] Thus, notwithstanding their rather innocuous nature, many of the planning efforts are unauthorized simply by default and hence are susceptible to punitive action and demolition by civic authorities. But given the ubiquity of such planning efforts across urban India, they have obviously continued to operate and proliferate in a tacit manner.

From the spatial planning perspective, the significance of user plans lies in the spontaneous emergence and provisional development of constituent actions. These actions signify a range of intelligent judgments actors make as they reconcile cultural and social prerogatives with city living, and the painstaking and purposeful efforts of diverse households to reduce privation and improve living conditions. Visualized another way, these actions encapsulate a multitude of people's planning efforts in the pursuit of progressive improvement and fine-grained development. Historically, that is how we have conceived and built the bulk of our settlements. Lewis Mumford, marveling at the long-term development of the medieval Italian city of Siena, called this kind of spatial planning "organic planning." He describes how the interactive effects of these incremental acts shape cities over time:

> In organic planning one thing leads to another, and what began as the seizure of an accidental advantage may prompt a strong element in a design,

> which an a priori plan could not anticipate, and in all probabilities would overlook or rule out … Organic planning does not begin with a preconceived goal: it moves from need to need, from opportunity to opportunity, in a series of adaptations that themselves become increasingly coherent and purposeful, so that they generate a complex, final design, hardly less unified than a pre-formed geometric pattern.[4]

The discussion below illustrates how neighborhood users in Jaipur engaged and transformed the formal plans even though they were not invited to participate in the state-sponsored planning process. In doing so, they created an urbanism that bound together the planned neighborhoods and informal settlements.

Planned Neighborhoods: Understanding the Envisaged Environment

In line with the national shift toward a state-centered model of urban development, as described in Chapter 2, new public-sector agencies emerged in the field of city development and housing in Jaipur. The comprehensive design and development of planned neighborhoods was a key component of their mandate. The UIT and its successor, the JDA, with which it amalgamated in 1982, developed neighborhoods comprising lots on which homeowners built their own dwellings per stipulated building norms. The RHB, which came into existence in 1970, developed neighborhoods comprising ready-built dwellings. As explained in Chapter 3, the DMP and Chandigarh plan had a major influence on the planning of these planned neighborhoods in Jaipur. Conspicuous planning features such as predominantly residential land use, liberal allocation of open spaces and parks, and a carefully premeditated mix of diverse populations distinguished these neighborhoods, both spatially and socially, from other parts of Indian cities, including the inner quarters and colonial-era developments.

A simplistic reading of the new neighborhoods' environment may lead one to naively conclude that the planners tried to impose an over-determined lifestyle upon the residents. But the neighborhood unit as a physical planning typology equitably distributed its functions—such as parks, school and convenience shopping—without eliminating or restricting residents' preferences and usage of these facilities. The residents could simply choose not to go to the park or to send their children to a school in another neighborhood. The new neighborhoods did not even require a particular civic sense among the residents, because they could accommodate diverse lifestyles. For instance, the envisaged spatiality could accommodate potential lack of interaction between residents for reasons such as class, caste and religious differences, or if they chose not to socialize with their neighbors. This is an important point because, as described in Chapter 3, the neighborhood residents came from a range of social and economic backgrounds.

Policy makers assumed that mixing diverse populations would address the imperatives of social equity and justice. They also thought it would catalyze a gentle rubbing-off effect, helping lower-income groups, especially those from rural areas and inner-city quarters, adjust to new neighborhoods and gradually learn more "civilized" manners.[5] A nuanced reading of the neighborhood's planning features reveals that the planners were assuming the presence, or at least the initiation and sustenance, of a moral–ethical framework that would reshape the residents' perception and behaviors. Predicated upon high-school civics, the framework would motivate residents to not encroach upon open setbacks, and it would encourage neighbors to either ostracize those who made such appropriations or at the least report the matters to municipal authorities, who would prevent such inappropriate actions. Rooted in a certain perception of what a resident I interviewed called "middle-class sensibilities," planners imagined that the moral–ethical framework would support the spatiality produced by the formal plans.

In making these assumptions, civic officials and public-sector planners did not perceive the built environment of planned neighborhoods as a practical and adaptable composition of spatial elements animated by progressive ideas but rather as an unalterable product of official plans with legal standing. In this line of thinking, once land uses and building footprints were fixed in formal maps, they were inviolable; even small changes were deviations that required paperwork explaining the rationale. Bureaucratic hubris trumped the plans' liberal basis. In line with James Scott's assertion (1998), officials believed that the residents would maintain the envisaged environment for their own welfare and also that a sufficiently powerful state could, through strict enforcement, push the beneficiaries to comply with the official plans. Not surprisingly, Indian municipalities routinely fielded anti-encroachment units staffed by seconded police officers.

Officials failed to account for the fact that societies are complex entities, held together not so much by a state but by shared attributes such as mores, traditions, taboos, reciprocities, sympathies and also an aesthetic sense. In doing so, the officials were claiming a monopoly over the idea of planning, failing to recognize it as an innate human activity. Wouldn't other actors pursue their own plans, especially when their living environment did not meet their requirements and expectations and they discovered the gap between what the postcolonial state promised and delivered? I next explain how neighborhood residents leveraged neighborhood features, quietly adapting the envisaged sociality and spatiality in line with their practical needs and cultural preferences.

Don't Ask, Don't Tell: Leveraging the Planned Features

Adaptations within the planned neighborhoods of Jaipur can broadly be categorized into two types depending upon their focus: dwelling-level changes that involve open setbacks around building footprints, prescribed heights and land use; and changes in the neighborhood infrastructure, such as parks and open spaces. The majority of changes are at the level of dwellings; house footprints have expanded, swallowing setbacks and, in many instances, residents have demolished the original houses to build multigenerational houses and bungalows (Figure 4.1).[6] Foreseeing such possibilities, officials sought to preclude potential changes through regulatory measures and covenants. They also knew that some residents would incrementally add to the rather small built-up areas of the dwellings as and when the families grew and additional funds became available.

In response, in some categories, the house plan contained a provision to build another floor if the extension did not violate building bylaws and the owner sought official permission—which many residents mentioned is not easy to obtain. Some categories of RHB houses also accommodated the possibility of adding more rooms on the ground floor following the predetermined design. Additionally, the property titles contained covenants expressly forbidding sale within a predetermined time period and prohibited the use of property for purposes other than residential. However, given the scope and spread of changes that have taken place, it is evident that controlling measures have not been successful. Interviews with appropriators and extensive photographic documentation of changes reveal three insights regarding residents' interpretation of the built environment at the scale of dwellings.

First, although almost all the appropriators are aware of mandatory setbacks, many simply do not think of the requirement as overly imposing or inviolate. Owners tend to think of the entire lot or the housing unit as their property and believe they should be able to use and build according to their needs and means. In one instance, the owner bought an adjoining lot, demolished the house and converted it into a lawn. Similarly, those living in multifamily units tend to divide the open spaces, including terraces and common areas, among themselves through verbal agreement. Such an arrangement is generally in line with the

FIGURE 4.1 A completely rebuilt bungalow extending into the front setback in Jawahar Nagar. Notice the original house built by the RHB in foreground

established patterns of property use and ownership in the city's historical quarters, where cultural antecedents shape the actors' claims over shared spaces. As a rule of thumb, top-floor apartment owners are entitled to the rooftops, while those on ground floors utilize the street-level open spaces. Many owners construe their claims over open spaces and setbacks as a right and presume their neighbors' consent. The occasional opposition of a neighbor usually ends up in severed social ties and sometimes in life-long rivalries.

The second, and closely related, insight underscores the usually nonchalant attitude of neighbors toward such changes. Owing to social connections and "eyes on the street," residents are generally aware of recent, ongoing and impending changes in their locality, but community networks and mutual acquaintances often restrain them from complaining. Third, more than any other factor, practical and everyday needs often spark change. Interviewees regularly cited growing families and quotidian requirements as reasons for undertaking remodeling and extension of their units, even while expressing satisfaction with the quality of the original construction of RHB houses.

In contrast to individual actions targeting dwellings, neighborhood infrastructure attracts collective action. The transformation of open spaces and parks from spaces offering recreational and environmental value into locations anchoring place-based communities perhaps best exemplifies this phenomenon.[7] At the time of Jawahar Nagar's building, RHB officials thought of harnessing communal sentiments to preserve and maintain open spaces and common areas of the neighborhood.[8] Towards this, the RHB entered into an agreement with homeowners to form a registered cooperative to look after "the use, upkeep and maintenance of common areas and services such as stairs, compound walls and open space … It shall be binding on every allotee (sic) to become a member of this registered agency."[9]

I heard two versions of the fate of resident welfare cooperative associations sponsored by the RHB. On the one hand, the officials asserted that such associations quickly became inactive after their founding.[10] On the other hand, the president of the *Maha Samiti*, the grand coalition of Jawahar Nagar residents' associations, argued that the RHB never created such associations but the residents themselves did. He, however, concurred that many original associations gradually became inactive, rendering the formally conceptualized enterprise ineffectual.

The president of the *Maha Samiti*, a high-ranking government engineer who volunteers his time for community work, believes that the RHB officials did not create residents' associations because to do so would have diminished their control over Jawahar Nagar. When the residents founded welfare associations, the RHB gave them limited responsibilities and resources. He asserts that the associations have been successful in instances where RHB officials cooperated. The president cites the example of three parks, handed over by the RHB after much persuasion, that the *Maha Samiti* has developed successfully. He believes that the residents proactively participate in collective enterprise when their innate interests converge; he cites the popular effort behind the planning and construction of temples in parks and open spaces as an illustrious example (Figure 4.2).[11] The building of temples on open space, not only in Jawahar Nagar and Malviya Nagar but in many parks across the city, is instructive for two reasons: it is an important example of collective action targeting neighborhood infrastructure; and, in accordance with India's secular polity, planned neighborhoods do not provide any sites for religious buildings.

Temple building in planned neighborhoods is a recent phenomenon.[12] Long-term residents pointed out that in the 1970s religiously inclined people used to visit temples in nearby localities. A resident who moved to Jawahar Nagar in 1973 believes that the emergence of temples is partially due to the fact that RHB did not care for the parks and open spaces. Werner Wolff (1990), a German sociologist who studied Jawahar Nagar, documents how the residents repeatedly petitioned the officials to develop the parks and maintain the open spaces during the 1980s. Apparently, enterprising residents with a religious orientation began building small temples in the parks and open spaces around the same time. According to several residents, temple building could also be seen as a preemptive measure against ruling politicians and state officials who may have used these public properties for patronage by allotting them to select businessmen and party loyalists for the building of privately owned public facilities such as for-profit hospitals and schools.[13]

It is interesting to note that the appearance of these temples coincided with the rise of political Hinduism in India during the 1980s. However, I did not find any religious tension arising out of this phenomenon, probably because the temples cater to Hindus and Jains, who comprise the majority of the population in many neighborhoods. At the same time, temple-building activity perhaps benefitted from the rise of political Hinduism, as these focal points not only attracted more people with a similar inclination but also incremental additions such as halls for religious sermons and social gatherings (Figure 4.3). These small and gradual additions transformed the many small temples into multi-facility community complexes that cater to diverse social and age groups.

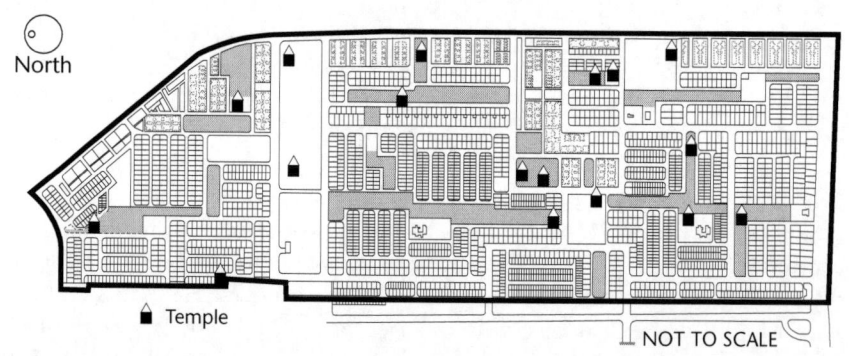

FIGURE 4.2 Map showing 'extra-legal' temples in the parks and open spaces of Jawahar Nagar

Source: Derived from a field survey in the summer of 2006.

FIGURE 4.3   Geeta Mandir Complex in the park of Jawahar Nagar's sector two

Joanne Waghorne (2004) provides a detailed account of how the design of Hindu temples has continually changed since the colonial period in order to keep up with the requirements and lifestyles of devotees. The new temples differ from their historic counterparts in several crucial ways: They house many deities sacred to different sects. They cater to the needs of a variety of communal groups. They offer a flexible combination of spaces, such as big halls and adjacent lawns, which can accommodate diverse functions, including private marriages and religious gatherings. And they increasingly provide a range of services previously not offered in temples, such as yoga classes and traditional Indian Ayurvedic medicine. Thus, it makes sense to visualize these temples not as traditional shrines but cultural institutions that act as a pivot for a range of place-based communities.

These institutions receive community-wide support, including the voluntary donation of monies and effort toward building and maintaining the facilities; patronage of religious ceremonies, communal functions and cultural events; and assistance in obtaining extra-legal electrical, telephone and water connections because civic authorities do not recognize these places. Thus, in a certain way, these multiple-use facilities not only act as a pivot for the place-based associational life of diverse social groups but have also substituted the school as the neighborhood focal point. On the one hand, this phenomenon highlights the significance of cultural preferences in shaping the neighborhoods' adaptation and, on the other hand, shifts the focus onto the planning process by raising the question: How did the various actors work together to produce such a spectacular transformation of parks and open spaces?

I accidentally encountered a different approach to the moral economy in Jawahar Nagar when an interviewee solicited my architectural advice. His neighbor was threatening to invade his privacy by building a bedroom for his soon-to-be married son upon the plot's open setbacks. Although the construction did not pose any threat to the buildings' structural stability or overall safety, it would considerably reduce the gap between the houses, subjecting the interviewee's balcony to intrusion. I encouraged him to lodge a complaint against the encroacher.

The encroacher, instead of apologizing, suggested that the interviewee should also appropriate the balcony in question, because he, too, would soon need space to accommodate his growing family. He also offered to introduce the interviewee to his building contractor, saving him time and effort, and to the pertinent municipal official, who, after expressing that he was unable to help the encroacher in his quest for formal approval, had purportedly promised to turn a blind eye to the unauthorized construction. The interviewee agreed with his neighbor, rejecting what he called my "inflammatory" advice, and built an unauthorized bedroom soon after. The incident highlights the different mode of moral economy that parallels, and often prevails over, the moral–ethical framework anticipated by officials.

Read simply, this kind of spontaneous and reciprocated exchange highlights the fact that neighbors are solicitous of each other's needs in an ethically practical manner. A more nuanced reading reveals that officials could probably never have imagined that the neighborhood culture would be guided by the practice of collaborating with, rather than complaining about, appropriators. In a certain way, the same collaborative spirit underpins the building and patronage of temple complexes, which occupy a central space in the everyday life of many residents. Given the scope and nature of the neighborhood transformations, it is clear that residents have ignored officials' assumptions and largely given up on the difficult-to-navigate channels of postcolonial governance. Instead, they pursue their own plans building off of the official plans, and assembling resources using tacit and informal collaborations with neighbors and acquaintances. I next explain how the service providers and workers of the planned neighborhoods leverage the formal plans in a similarly remarkable manner.

Resourceful Plans: Leveraging Small Opportunities

A robust body of literature documents the litany of harassments, oppressions and exclusions that urban India's poor encounter on a daily basis. It also describes how the relatively better-off actors among marginalized groups utilize the few available resources, such as social connections and political patronage, to obtain basic forms of shelter and economic security.[14] In this section, I explain how service providers and other people working in the neighborhoods—who, unlike the neighborhood residents, were not even considered in the formal plans—pursued their own spatial plans, leveraging the marginal opportunities they found in the wake of planned developments. The phenomenon is perhaps best denoted by the distinctive spread of informal settlements across the city as it grew after independence (Figure 4.4). Figure 4.4 also shows that informal settlements exist in close proximity of the planned neighborhoods, almost as a rule.

It is important to note that many planned neighborhoods and informal settlements are not only adjacent spatially but are also conjoined in development. This is no accident, as the combination of economic opportunity and proximate lands often provided the practical ground for the almost concomitant inception and growth of informal settlements, as explained below.

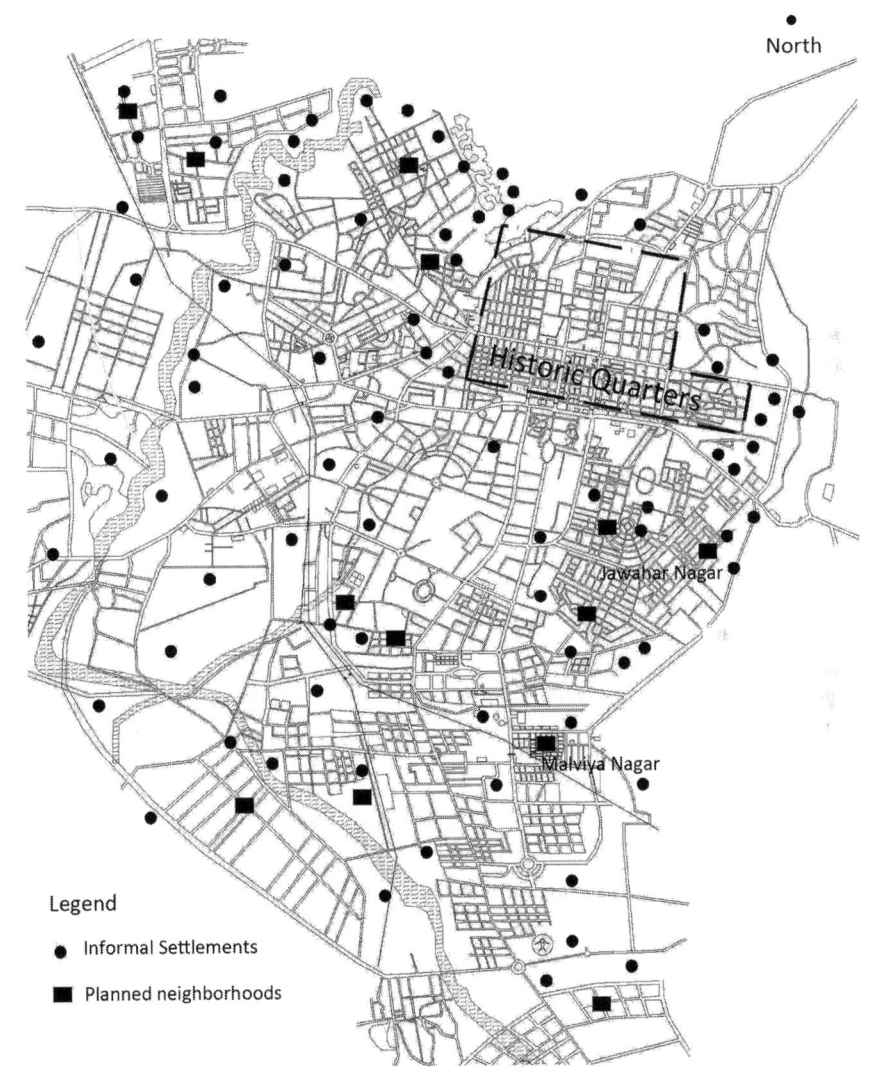

FIGURE 4.4 Map of Jaipur showing the location of informal settlements and planned neighborhoods developed by the public sector between 1950–2000

Source: Derived from civic surveys for *Master Plan of Jaipur City* 1995 and *City Development Plan* 2008.

Large-scale development in Indian cities generally takes place on the urban periphery, employing a large contingent of construction labor.[15] Many workers migrate from nearby rural areas and build temporary huts in the vicinity of building sites, because they are poorly paid, often work overtime and walk to work.[16] The workers in Jaipur utilize two distinct sources of land upon which to build their huts, usually from mud and thatch. First, erstwhile rural settlements encompassed by the growing city are a convenient source of land, as in the case of Malviya Nagar, described later. Second, given that the State is India's biggest landowner, many unoccupied parcels of government land are available on the urban edge. They are especially abundant in marginal locations, such as flood plains and low-lying areas that are deemed unsuitable for planned development.[17] Often the public-sector engineers search for such lands that are located near the project sites and facilitate the building of huts in order to attract labor and expedite the development work.[18] These jerry-built huts frequently form the kernel of future informal settlements, as evident in Figure 4.5, which shows the development over time of an informal settlement called Jawahar Nagar Katchi Basti (JKB) adjoining Jawahar Nagar.[19]

Both Jawahar Nagar and JKB exist on state property, with a road demarcating their extents (Figure 4.6). Jawahar Nagar occupies about 300 acres of land that originally belonged to the state's forest department and was transferred by the government to the RHB in the 1970s. The land was situated on the sandy foothills of Jhalana hills. Well-defined edges delineated the site on three sides, with existing neighborhoods to the west. The southern edge abutted the campus of Rajasthan University, and Jaipur's historic quarters were located on the far north side. The plan envisaged a modest forty-foot-wide road—later upgraded to an arterial bypass for truck traffic in the city's first master plan—delineating the

FIGURE 4.5 Jawahar Nagar and the adjacent informal settlement called Jawahar Nagar Katchi Basti

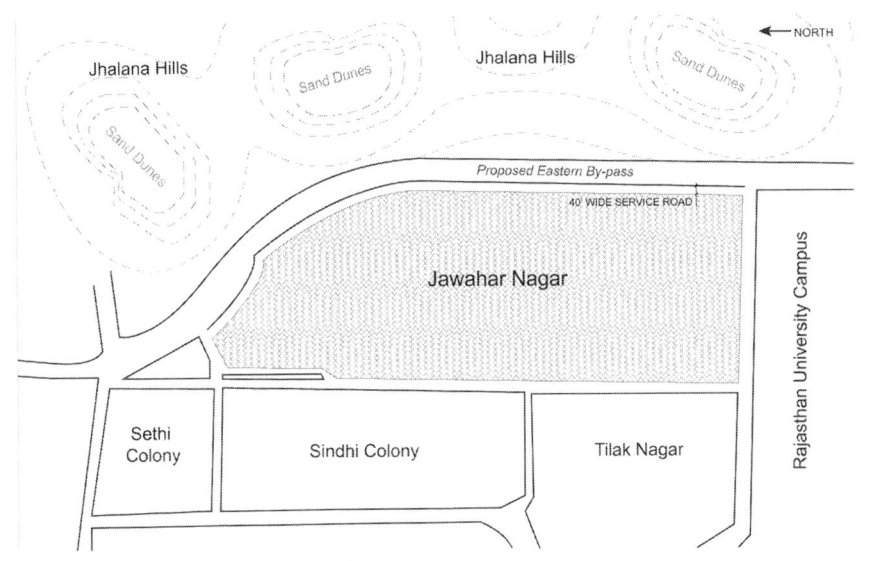

FIGURE 4.6 Location plan: Jawahar Nagar

division between the site's eastern edge and the forest department's remaining land, which comprised sparsely forested dunes and ditches.

Preoccupied with building Jawahar Nagar, RHB did not build the road until 1976. According to anecdotal evidence, as soon as the RHB engineers completed the road, huts began to appear on the land earmarked for the bypass and its right-of-way. During interviews, several planners pointed out that the road, by clearly defining the extent of the forest department's uninhabited land, created opportune conditions for the builders of the informal settlement. A city planner articulated the phenomenon in the following words:

> Do you think it is practically possible for the government to guard all its lands? Officials often do not even know what land belongs to the government and which department owns it unless they check the record and verify the exact position on the site. Big departments like forest, revenue, and railway do not have enough budget to construct boundary walls or post watchmen and ... [that's how] the combination of *khali* [vacant] and *sarkari* [state owned] usually renders urban lands susceptible to the building of informal settlements.[20]

Some planners also described how the incipient core of jerry-built huts gradually spread and changed in nature over time: the dwellings became more permanent, with bricks replacing thatch, and gradually grew in size and number to accommodate families joining the pioneering males. But these were not simple cases of land grabs; a significant cultural impulse supported the development of informal settlements.

First, the mostly middle-class residents of planned neighborhoods, such as Professor and Mrs. Gupta, desired maids, servants, gardeners, handymen, laundry services and dairies supplying fresh milk. Clarence Perry simply could not have imagined that some residents of planned neighborhoods in distant India would want goods and services such as fresh milk ideally produced on their doorstep. Even Jaipur's planners, who were aware of such traditional arrangements, asserted during interviews that they expected modern living to quickly banish outmoded ways of life as the underlying objectives promoted common and greater goods such as public health. Dairy cows belonged to rural or industrial land uses and not inside or adjoining residential areas.

However, the incongruous but tangible requirements of residents meant that a variety of workers and suppliers could use the unguarded and uninhabited government land adjacent to Jawahar Nagar and the rural settlements close to Malviya Nagar to house assorted economic activities. This advanced the incipient informal settlements. Further supporting the development of the informal settlements was the relationship between the neighborhoods' residents and the workers, which was not exclusively shaped by formal terms of employment or monetary exchange but was often marked by social and familial ties; the well-to-do in South Asia are customarily expected to help their helpers in diverse ways. Diligent workers and aspiring individuals could potentially utilize these openings, gradually transforming the informal settlements into productive places servicing not just the adjacent neighborhoods but also those farther away.

Cultural support also arose because many of the informal settlements constituted the original residential quarters of villages and rural hamlets that had been encompassed by the urban expansion. At some level the cultural support signified a larger debate, marked by the competing visions of Prime Minister Nehru and Mahatma Gandhi, about the intellectual position and spatial location of villages in India's urbanization. Gandhi was sympathetic to the villages, perceiving them as the vanguard of India's patrimony, whereas Nehru envisioned India's future in modern cities such as Chandigarh and city-extensions such as Jawahar Nagar and Malviya Nagar. But he wanted to preserve the finest traditions of India's past. Therefore, while introducing the concept of the neighborhood unit to India, pioneering planners such as the German Otto Koenigsberger and the American Albert Mayer had portrayed it as a typology that could preserve and promote the best features of village life, such as face-to-face interaction and physical and non-physical ties between the individual–household–community and place. This assertion had underpinned the putative justification advanced by Section 507 of the Delhi Municipal Act of 1957 that preserving villages provides a glimpse of rural life within cities. In line with this thinking, the influential Delhi Master Plan had preserved the villages within the envisaged urban boundary.[21]

In Jaipur, important historical precedents also lent support to the recognition of residential quarters of villages as human settlements in their own right. Post-independence officials acknowledged these precedents while conceiving and developing city-extensions such as Malviya Nagar. Understanding these precedents requires a short foray into the colonial history of land ownership and organization. The colonial British alienated village commons—such as pastures, forests and wastelands that were traditionally under the care of communities and local chieftains—and formally vested their ownership with the State.[22] After independence, both the central and state governments enacted land reform acts, but, as occurred in other areas of governance, they retained key colonial practices.[23] For instance, all the lands owned by the government of British India and erstwhile princely states such as Jaipur, including the sizable commons of the country's many villages, remained state property, although villagers continued to derive customary benefits, such as grazing privileges for their livestock and wood-cutting.[24]

Public-sector agencies often used such state-owned lands to develop planned neighborhoods. For example, although the agencies acquired a small portion using eminent domain, the major part of Malviya Nagar is sited on government property that historically constituted the communal land of a village called Jhalana Doongar.[25] This village, like many others in this part of the world, comprised a core settlement, or *Gaon*, and a number of satellite settlements, or *Dhanis* that are often inhabited by lower castes or tillers, who need to be close to their fields. Some of the satellite settlements are temporary in nature and find a place in official records only once they reach a certain level of maturity in age and size.[26] One such unrecorded lower-caste settlement—called Raigar Basti, or "leather tanners' settlement"—existed within Malviya Nagar's identified area.

In developing Malviya Nagar, planners did not relocate the residential quarters of the village, or *abadi*, including Raigar Basti. This conformed to the immunity from being uprooted that is traditionally enjoyed by the inhabited land of villages. State agencies move the *abadi* only under extreme circumstances—for instance, to make way for a dam or large factory.[27] Instead, planners demarcated Raigar Basti's extent with a circumferential road that enclosed it within Malviya Nagar (Figure 4.5). As was the case with many other villages encompassed within Indian cities, the planners left the core village outside the formal plan. Neighborhood workers and service providers utilized these rural settlements for housing and, because of their exclusion from plans and the absence of regulation, to set up businesses. This changed the rural character of these settlements. In this respect, Raigar Basti did not begin as an informal settlement. Its incorporation in a planned settlement changed its popular perception, and its official standing due to its unrecorded status, from a rural hamlet to that of a *Katchi Basti*—popular term for an informal settlement in the Indian context.

In interviews, Malviya Nagar's planners emphasized the protracted bureaucratic procedures and potential legal challenges they would have faced should they have opted to relocate Raigar Basti; this highlights why they preferred to develop city-extensions on government-owned land. They also justified their decision by pointing out that they were not acting alone; similar rural settlements exist within Delhi's planned neighborhoods as well.[28] Perceived another way, the official plans generated a few inadvertent and small opportunities, largely owing to the manner and the context in which they were made, that the builders of informal settlements leveraged both ingeniously and successfully. Combining a range of tangible and cultural resources, neighborhood workers and service providers utilized the customarily protected rural settlement of Raigar Basti inside Malviya Nagar and marginal and unoccupied state-owned land to develop JKB alongside Jawahar Nagar. But as is evident in Figure 4.4, which shows the juxtaposition of informal settlements with the planned neighborhood, this was not an isolated event but in fact represented a much larger planning effort by non-state actors to adapt the official plans at the scale of the entire city.

We pick up the development trajectory of these informal settlements again in Chapter 6, where I describe how their growth attracted local politicians, who began to show support for neighborhood workers and service providers to win their votes during the late 1970s.[29] Chapter 6 also describes how popular plans facilitated the incremental legalization of dwellings and provisioning of infrastructure in these informal settlements over time.

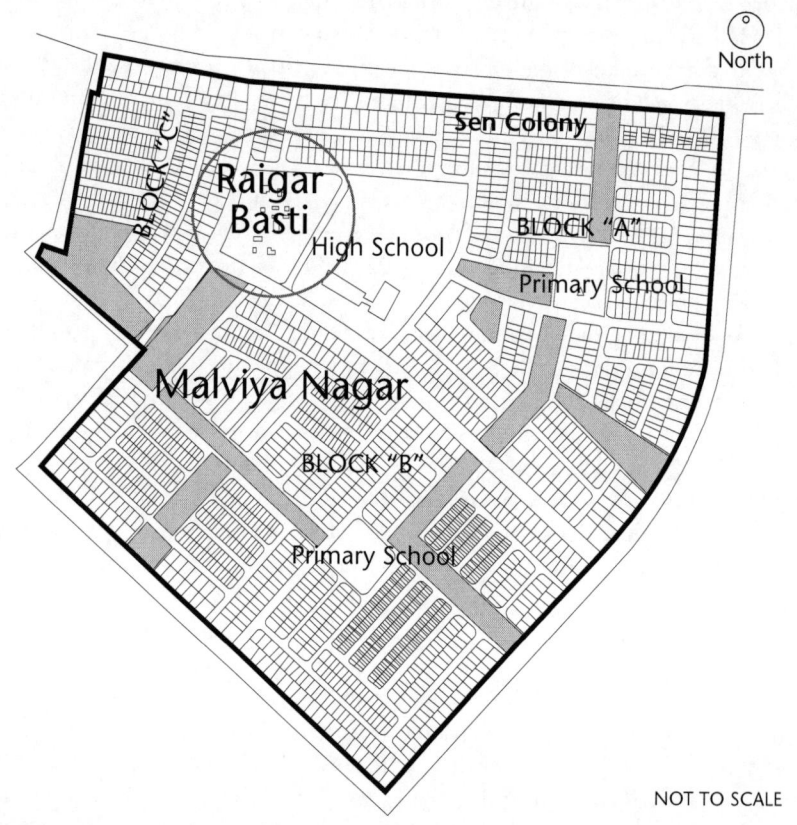

FIGURE 4.7 Map showing Malviya Nagar's layout comprising an erstwhile rural settlement called Raigar Basti

Conclusion

It is clear that the formal plans for the new neighborhoods in Jaipur did not meet with passive compliance or arbitrary opposition. The neighborhood users actively pursued their own plans, ignoring the assumptions and apathy of the postcolonial state and building almost seamlessly with the state-sponsored plans that they did not follow blindly. Unlike those who made the formal planning efforts, the non-state actors had neither professional skills nor the backing of the state. But they had practical needs and firsthand understanding of the cultural context and built environment they inhabited. As I have shown in this chapter, the users cleverly combined diverse resources to transform the planned neighborhoods from within and without by leveraging the (often small) opportunities they found. Their plans were neither pre-formed nor firm in conception or implementation but provisional and tacit. Often conceptualized spontaneously, these purposeful and future-oriented planning efforts developed gradually in response to residents' needs. However, they eventually created no less an impact on the city's urban form and organization than that of the large-scale state-sponsored plans.

It is easy to see that the cause and context shaped the users' actions in fundamental ways. But it is far more crucial to note that a variety of acts—involving resistance, adaptation and appropriation—undertaken by different actors came together, almost magically, as meaningful planning efforts. Such efforts are largely incomprehensible as standalone actions, which are often perceived as unauthorized given India's approach to city planning and development. However, the dramatic cumulative effect of these constituent acts highlights the need to rethink the spatial and temporal scales at which we conceive and examine the impact of plans in cities of the global south. As illustrated in this chapter, it took around thirty years and a sizable amount of urban land for some of these unanticipated kinds of plans to unravel.

However, the professionals, officials, residents, workers and service providers were not the only actors making plans around the idea of planned neighborhoods. Subdividers and real-estate developers also pursued their own plans. These were particularly crucial, because Jaipur, like other Indian cities, began to face massive housing shortages in the 1960s. Public-sector neighborhoods, such as Jawahar Nagar and Malviya Nagar, developed almost twenty-five years after India's independence, came too late and provided too little to address the housing need. In the next chapter, I describe how private subdivision development plans played a major role, almost equaling the planning efforts of the public sector and neighborhood users, in shaping Jaipur's post-independence urban development.

Notes

1 Interview conducted on May 9, 2006.
2 In total, I interviewed thirty-four residents of Jaipur's three neighborhoods in the summer of 2006. The interviewees included respondents from both the planned areas and the adjacent informal settlements.

3 Despite many decades of separation, the situation in Pakistan is apparently not much different. See Hull, *Government of Paper*.

4 Mumford, *The City in History*, 302.

5 To some degree, these concerns reflected the bigger shift in policy toward focusing on urban, rather than rural, communities. For an intellectual genealogy of this shift in India's overall policy, see Glover, "The Troubled Passage from 'Village Communities' to Planned New Town Developments in Mid-twentieth-century South Asia."

6 Employing a longitudinal approach, Rosin has documented similar changes in houses in Jaipur's planned neighborhoods, arguing that these changes to the bungalow typology lead more and more toward the older *haveli* typology. See Rosin, "From Garden Suburb to Olde City Ward."

7 It is important to note that collective action is in line with Arjun Appadurai's notion of "community of sentiments," which he defines as the sentiments that arise when people begin to imagine and feel things together. Appadurai, *Modernity at Large*, 8.

8 Interview with the founding commissioner of the RHB, May 29, 2006.

9 RHB, Brochure for Applicants, 3.

10 Interview with a chief engineer of the RHB, April 28, 2006.

11 Interview with the president of the Jawahar Nagar *Maha Samiti*, May 2, 2006.

12 On the other hand, the spontaneous emergence and development of shrines on public lands is a conspicuous feature of the Indian landscape. See Henn, "Crossroads of Religions." Jaipur's local newspapers routinely report such incidents. See, for instance, *Dainik Bhaskar*, "Zameen kisi ki bhi ho"; and *Rajasthan Patrika*, "Bhagwan bachayain apni zameen."

13 There is some truth to these assertions, as in the early 1990s the authorities allotted part of Jawahar Nagar's open space to local businessmen for building for-profit private schools and hospitals. Although state policy permits the allotment of government-owned land for building public utilities, usually at official discretion and discounted rates, several respondents expressed resentment both at the opaque process of allotment and the reduction of parkland. They believed that the authorities would not dare to allot open spaces and parks containing temples.

14 Many scholars have described how post-liberalization economic activity from the 1990s onward has catalyzed the emergence of new cultural forms and social formations, even as the old patronage politics and deepening of democracy facilitated the rise of earlier disempowered groups. See, for example, Mehta, *The Burden of Democracy*; and Harriss-White, *India Working*.

15 Outward-focused large-scale urban development dominated the official approach to city planning and design in many cities, including Jaipur, during the decades following India's independence. After the liberalization of India's economy in the 1990s, the focus began to shift to project-based development. For a detailed discussion, see Vidyarthi, "Building a 'World Class Heritage City'."

16 The trend has begun to change, and nowadays developers and contractors tend to build temporary housing on construction sites that are often inside the cities. But, apparently the living and working conditions of construction labor in Jaipur have not changed much. See a recent documentation done by a local NGO, accessed at: www.cmfraj.org/Study%20on%20Building%20and%20Construction%20industry.pdf, viewed on March 6, 2013.

17 Most slums in Indian cities are located on government-owned lands, reflecting the bigger issue of inequitable land distribution: the predominant majority, the working class, lives on a fraction of the total urban area. For an overview of the situation in Delhi, see Navlakha, "Urban Pollution."

18 Interview with a senior town planner in Jaipur, February 14, 2006.

19 In the Indian context, the initiation of informal settlements by construction workers hired to build planned developments is not a new phenomenon. Perhaps most famously, it is described in Chandigarh by Sarin, in *Urban Planning in the Third World*.

20 Interview on February 14, 2006.

21 However, the incorporation of rural settlements within planned settings meant that their inhabitants usually maintained their old lifestyles, challenging the modernization of cities, which had motivated Indian planners to adopt the concept of planned neighborhoods in the first place. For a detailed commentary on the similarities between rural and urban India during the early 1970s, about the same time planners incorporated the indigenous settlement of Raigar Basti, described a little later, within Malviya Nagar, see Qadeer, "Do Cities 'Modernize' the Developing Countries?"

22 B. H. Baden-Powell, eminent scholar of the colonial land revenue systems, explains these actions:

> Each village had in those days an indefinite area of waste around it: This was in no sense the joint property of the village landholders, though they had the customary use of it for grazing and wood-cutting … The waste remained the property of the State: and this is evident from the fact that when a grantee of the village appeared, he always took the waste as lawfully his own under the grant, subject, of course, to the customary provision for grazing etc., which was necessary to the welfare of the original holders.
>
> Baden-Powell, "The Permanent Settlement of Bengal," 283.

For a contemporary view, see Brara, *Shifting Landscapes*.

23 Yugandhar and Datta, *Land Reforms in India*.

24 Robbins, "Authority and Environment."

25 In recent years, civil society activists have begun to criticize the manner in which the State has failed to protect village commons from encroachments and have also highlighted the need to preserve them in order to sustain the livelihood of the villagers to whom they rightfully belong. See, for instance, Bhise, *Decolonizing the Commons*. However, I am not aware of any studies that comment on government expropriation of village commons in urban areas, which the development of planned extensions such as Malviya Nagar usually entails.

26 For a detailed discussion of the typology and morphology of Rajasthan's villages and their satellite settlements, see Singh and Khan, "Hindu Cosmology and the Orientation and Segregation of Social Groups in Villages in North Western India."

27 Interview with Mr. S. K. Lahiri on May 22, 2006. A career officer of the Rajasthan Administrative Service, Mr. Lahiri worked in various positions with the state's revenue department, including having a decade-long stint at the government secretariat. Also see Mathur and Mathur, *Land Revenue Law in Rajasthan*.

28 These villages and their satellites, originally on Delhi's outskirts, are commonly identified by the moniker *Lal Dora*, literally "red line," which signifies their status as special planning zones exempt from the legal bindings of the master plan. For their developmental history, see Tyagi, *Urban Growth and Urban Villages*; and for the present status, see Ministry of Urban Development, Government of India, "Report of the Expert Committee on Lal Dora and Extended Lal Dora," accessed at www. urbanindia.nic.in/programme/dd/laldora.pdf, viewed on May 24, 2010.

29 India suffered serious political turbulence during the late 1970s, which resulted in two national and state elections within three years, and the declaration of a national emergency. See Dhar, *Indira Gandhi, the "Emergency," and Indian Democracy*.

PART III

5

DEVELOPER PLANS

Building Subdivisions on the Urban Edge

Largely overlooked, the seemingly mundane act of subdividing peripheral urban land into building lots affects the size and form of human settlements in important ways.[1] It delineates foundational urban tissue on the ground, establishing the lattice for future communities.[2] It also catalyzes development activity, which works as the animating force filling out the lattice in a sporadic and largely unforeseen fashion.[3] As I illustrate in this chapter, Jaipur's post-independence quarters bear testimony to the significance of subdivision development work both in creating a host of new settlements and steering the rapid outward movement of the urban periphery. Sponsored by private builders, this kind of spatial planning deserves our interest for several reasons.

First, developer plans were not driven by official ideology, normative planning concerns, or everyday requirements. They were driven by the potent match between housing demand and easy availability of developable land, and fueled by the promise of profit and prestige associated with property development. In this respect, these entrepreneurial efforts were fundamentally different from the other planning efforts described in this book.

Second, even when faithfully following the official subdivision rules, the developer plans were unauthorized by default, because the princely state had monopolized city expansion since Jaipur's founding, and its successor did not begin establishing a procedure for private subdivision development until the 1980s. Thus, just like the user plans described in the previous chapter, the developer plans originated and progressed in a tacit and provisional manner, typically targeting one farm at a time. The developers' discreet and piecemeal approach centering upon individual farms mean that the layout and street network of many adjacent subdivisions remain disjointed and also that an erratic and uneven urban pattern characterizes large swaths of Jaipur's post-independence growth.[4]

Third, the developers' planning efforts stand out for the magnitude of their effect and the diversity of spatial pattern and development quality they created. Today the subdivisions range from small, well-provisioned enclaves comprising a few spacious lots to sizable communities of several thousand residents connected to utilities and basic infrastructure in varying degrees. This depends upon a combination of factors, such as the size, shape and location of the original parcel; the developer's intention; outreach; and the extent of ensuing development. But when visualized collectively against the backdrop of Jaipur's spatial extent, the significance of developer plans becomes clear in their geographic spread and unanticipated impact on the city's overall urban form. Whereas not a single subdivision existed at the time of princely Jaipur's merger with independent India in 1949, half a century later more than 1,500 subdivisions supplied around 110,000 lots, or approximately one-third of the city's residential land.[5] So, what happened? How did the extra-legal developer plans end up shaping Jaipur in such a significant manner?

This chapter explains how the developer plans constituted a larger shift from the pre-independence mode of land regulation and development administered by Jaipur's state officials and engineers to the post-independence planning approach premised upon comprehensive urban plans prepared by professional planners. The fact that the modes of governance and regulation of the princely period continued to provide the operating framework for post-independence institutions meant that the transition proceeded slowly and strenuously. It also created a unique situation characterized by the old guard's reluctance to relinquish control over land administration, slow development of a supporting framework for the new planning approach and growing housing shortages. These conditions facilitated the emergence of a corps of developers. While some of these new planning actors had worked in the construction sector, they lacked experience in the field of property development or real estate, industries that were neither extensive nor functioned in a formally organized manner in Jaipur. In line with the local business climate shaped by the orthodox and risk-averse ways of the *Bania* castes, which specialized in trading activities, many developers were conservative in orientation and traditional in approach. Thus they planned according to different goals and means than the public-sector agencies.[6]

For example, they were not beholden to development planning's progressive ideals and normative goals rooted in liberal theory, which underpinned the development of planned settlements such as Jawahar Nagar and Malviya Nagar; instead, many developers interpreted the idea of planned neighborhoods rather conservatively. Prioritizing practical business needs and client preferences, they complied with the subdivision rules in a perfunctory manner, while trusting customary practices and conventional patterns in the pursuit of their plans. This line of thinking is evident in the private subdivisions' large lots, which cater to the enduring penchant for the colonial-era bungalow typology, and the developers' widespread use of conventional bazaar-based networks for acquiring farms and marketing lots to diverse social groups.[7] Eschewing publicity and large-scale development activity, the subdividers kept a low profile, quietly using social connections with political intermediaries and petty officials in order to arrange the minimally required paperwork and site development.[8] Cutting corners on the provision of infrastructure and tapping into traditional social networks meant that they could target specific clientele and offer competitive rates and favorable terms of payment, which were crucial considerations, because obtaining a mortgage remained difficult until the liberalization of India's economy in the early 1990s.

Several handicaps encumbered the developer plans, though. The subdivisions lacked the legitimacy of state approval. They also, almost as a rule, were deficient in civic infrastructure and offered few basic amenities. The private subdivisions did offer larger plots, which facilitated the building of customized bungalows and conventional multigenerational and joint-family living near relatives and acquaintances, usually not an easy proposition in the smaller lots and randomly allotted dwellings of the public-sector neighborhoods. However, the developers' strategy of maximizing plotted area also meant that subdivision residents had to frequently forego or, quite like residents of the informal settlements, depend upon nearby public-sector neighborhoods for facilities such as parks, open spaces and schools that set new benchmarks for residential environments.[9] Not surprisingly, the residents of the new private subdivisions soon demanded similar services and legal status.

Chapter 6 takes up that story, describing how the residents used their growing political power to ensure that elected officials paid attention to their concerns. The focus of local electoral politics shifted from party affiliation and corrupt bureaucratic cronyism to pressure from voters and politicians supporting local constituents. As it did so, residents' increasing social confidence centered in the formation of a civic identity that their plans express and cement in a variety of ways including the building of popularly sponsored shrines that, just like their counterparts in the public-sector neighborhoods, offer both religious and secular services and anchor growing place-based communities.

The developer plans described in this chapter are important because they illustrate a critical civic shift central to our understanding of how plan-making contributes to community building and also because they show how private efforts can and do push back against the imposition of misplaced and repressive authority. The following narrative begins by explaining how—despite major changes in the focus and scope of national urban planning policy, explained in the previous chapters—preexisting institutions and practices continued to dictate the organization and use of peripheral urban lands in post-independence Jaipur. I then explain how the slow development of supporting framework for the new planning approach, combined with entrenched legacies and rapid urbanization, shaped the cause and context of developer plans. Tracking the development of one of the earliest, and presently very upscale, subdivisions, which served as the model for later projects, I then illustrate the nature of planning work involved in private subdivision development.

Recasting the Urban Periphery

In order to comprehend the reshaping and regulation of the urban periphery in the post-independence period, it is important to bear in mind that land settlement and administration was one of the most remunerative and, consequently, elaborate state functions in both princely and British India.[10] Jaipur state, for example, derived almost two-thirds of its income from various forms of tax on agriculture land. Colloquially called *lagaan*, or revenue, the tribute's importance for state finances is salient when viewed in the context that Jaipur state, unlike British India, levied hardly any direct charges upon city dwellers, who paid no income, property, or house tax.[11] In other words, the large base of peasant farmers sustained the societal superstructure, and the systematic extraction of revenue comprised a key part of government work and income until India's independence.[12]

Although slight differences abounded, regional revenue systems shared key features that had evolved over centuries, combining elements and practices honed by a long line of rulers. The colonial British introduced a normalized legal system with modern ideas of ownership and created a department of revenue for administering land issues.[13] Jaipur state adopted these practices after entering into a subsidiary alliance with the British East India Company in 1818, later replaced by the direct rule of the government of Great Britain in 1858.[14] Recognizing the varying yield of land tax due to diverse factors such as local cultivation practices and monsoonal variation, the system fielded a dedicated cadre of revenue officials who superintended the entire process of land settlement and tax collection.

Actively generating and exploiting what Bernard Cohn (1996) calls "colonial forms of knowledge," the well-oiled, hierarchically organized bureaucratic machinery aimed to extract the surplus as promptly and efficiently as possible. The revenue officials mapped and classified lands based on soil quality and uses, and utilized detailed records of individual landholdings to document annual productivity and calculate long-term averages for different fields. They also fixed corresponding tax rates, collected cash or in-kind tributes, and resolved and reconciled minor issues and petty disputes—all while seeking to maintain the land's productive usage and wield the state's authority on the ground. Apart from the security apparatus, the revenue service constituted the oldest and largest branch of the government, and it was a powerful one, assuring the predictable flow of revenue from the rural outposts all the way up to the imperial court.

The revenue department classified the ownership of land according to two principal types: *Khalsa*, or state-owned land, administered directly in the name of the King; and *Jagir*, or alienated land, which had been given away to nobles, ministers, priests or courtiers. Some holders of *Jagir* paid fixed annual taxes, while some rendered services. Some lands, such as those given to priests, were *mandir-maafi*, or tax exempt on religious grounds, or were *Inam*—that is, a gift.[15] On the basis of actual possession, irrespective of ownership, the lands were broadly classified into *abadi*, or residential, lands and non-*abadi* lands. This was important because in Jaipur *abadi* lands were exempt from taxes while most non-

abadi lands, such as farms and forests, generated revenue for the feudal system.[16] Non-*abadi* lands were broadly classified as agricultural and non-agricultural lands. Non-agricultural lands—such as forests, pastures (*gochar*) and barren lands—were usually under the care of communities or local feudal lords (*Thakurs*), and the agricultural lands were leased either to cultivators or intermediaries, who paid annual rent in cash or kind.[17] Since agricultural land provided the bulk of revenue, the state carefully controlled its usage and conversion into other uses.[18]

After independence, the central and state governments enacted land reform acts, which awarded land titles and tenancy rights to genuine tillers. These laws abolished the roles of intermediaries and, in many states, forced the big landowners to part with excess lands that they rented; and these lands, along with many state-owned lands, were handed to landless and marginal farmers.[19] As in other areas of governance, the land reform acts retained key colonial practices. For instance, as described in Chapter 4, all the erstwhile state-owned lands, including the sizable community pastures and wastelands, remained government property. The authorities periodically auction these lands to augment public finances, allot them on the grounds of social welfare, or use them for public works, including the development of planned neighborhoods such as Jawahar Nagar and Malviya Nagar.

The government froze the revenue rates at pre-independence levels, effectively making taxation less oppressive. However, the Rajasthan Tenancy Act of 1955, like that of many other states, retained the extensive collection mechanism, maintaining the revenue department's authority over land-related issues. Serving officials of the erstwhile princely states and British India were absorbed into government services and assigned to new organizations. Perhaps of greatest importance, the post-independence governing model extended the scope of revenue officials' duties to include the fast-growing public sector and development programs of the new nation.[20] Superseding all other branches of the preceding imperial administration, including the fairly autonomous engineers of the Public Works Department, the colonial revenue collectors of the national and state Indian Civil Services (ICS) and Provincial Civil Services (PCS) became preeminent general administrators. This was reflected in new nomenclature, the Indian Administrative Service (IAS) and the Rajasthan Administrative Service (RAS).

For the cities, this meant that the revenue officials became much more intimately involved with planning and building issues than in the past. In addition to their continuing jurisdiction over agricultural lands, which comprise the bulk of the urban periphery, the revenue officials (or the new IAS and RAS) now headed most of the government organizations, including those concerned with urban development and housing. Not surprisingly, even when familiar with the new land-use-centered comprehensive urban planning approach, they maintained residual sympathy for their departmental practices, including the customary land classification typology, which retained its historical primacy in the Rajasthan Land Revenue Act of 1959. In everyday planning practice, it meant that even when a land parcel was marked "residential" in the city master plan it remained agricultural until the revenue officials converted it into residential property.

The old guard's persistent hold over peripheral urban lands also meant that their commitment to the official master plans prepared by professional planners was often precarious. A young planner who joined the public sector in the 1960s and rose through the ranks to become the state's chief town planner recounted how higher officials routinely wondered when the "land uses [assigned by the master plan] are of the town planning department, why should we follow it?" He also told me of a district collector who refused to open an exhibition showcasing the city's draft master plan, saying, "This is your master plan. Why should I inaugurate it?"[21]

Since public-sector planners are explicitly subordinate to the RAS and IAS officers, who are located at the bureaucratic apex, the schism between the executive's urban planning and administrative functions does not really matter in organizational terms. In the hierarchy- and rank-conscious postcolonial bureaucracy, state-employed planners are first lesser-ranked civil servants and then subject experts. As in diverse other branches of government service—such as accounts, agriculture and archives—they report to the general administrators. Perceived another way, the long-established cadre of revenue officials ceded little authority to the newly hired urban planners, largely restricting their scope to technical matters such as data analyses and physical planning, while safeguarding their prerogative over land administration in post-independence India. But of more importance, the two vastly incongruous approaches to land planning left open a crucial gap. The old guard did not have a plan beyond the administrative protocol originally designed for extraction of land taxes, while the new planners had a comprehensive land-use plan with progressive goals but no authority to implement it. The emerging land entrepreneurs with a capitalist focus then addressed the gap and the concomitant housing shortages by developing their own approach to spatial planning and property development. This is the focus of the next section.

The Cause and Context of Developer Plans

The slow development of operational procedures matching the new approach to urban planning and rapid urbanization supported by Jaipur's new stature as the state capital influenced the development of private subdivisions in fundamental ways. The slow development of operational procedures resulted in a host of administrative lacunae, described later. Rapid urbanization, among other outcomes, began to produce noticeable housing shortages from the 1960s onward. By this time, city-extensions conceived during the late princely period, such as Bani Park, and the "rehabilitation colonies" developed during the 1950s to house partition refugees, such as Adarsh Nagar, had been largely occupied. Rapid population growth, both within and without the historic quarters, had almost quadrupled the city's population between the 1940s and 1960s.[22]

Although city-specific housing data for the period is not available, there is little doubt that Jaipur's situation roughly reflected the larger trends of underinvestment in the housing sector, rapid population growth and consistent shrinkage urban housing stock across the newly independent nation. Shanti Tangri, studying India's urban housing economy in the late 1960s, documented the grim situation. Public and private investment in housing had increased marginally, from 11.5 to 15.5 billion rupees, in the first three five-year plans (1951–66) of the central government. But when seen as a percentage of total investment in the national economy, in the same period spending on the housing sector had fallen significantly, from 34 percent to 15 percent, signaling that the new nation's attention was shifting away from civic issues. In line with an increasingly urbanized population, the available living space had diminished from an already frugal 113 square feet per capita in 1921 to a paltry 70.61 square feet per capita in 1966.[23]

However, it is important to note that the popular perceptions of housing shortages and urban congestion embodied cultural preferences and biases, such as the predilection for home ownership and independent bungalows, which in turn predicated the nature of developer plans.[24] The director of an early, and eventually very prolific, family-owned real estate enterprise, Mr. Jain, articulated the link between the contemporary climate of opinion and the initiation of his family's subdivision venture: "You know, my elder brother is very clever. He spotted the business opportunity immediately … when we could not find a decent-sized lot to build our own family bungalow [*Kothi*] in the crowded city."[25]

Two interrelated factors behind the slow development of pertinent planning procedures also aided the initiation of developer plans. First, facing pressing concerns on multiple fronts, the newly created Rajasthan state had little focus on urban issues.[26] Thus, many relevant departments were frequently understaffed and underfunded, and the state government was extremely slow to develop regulatory frameworks and oversight mechanisms matching the new approach to urban planning.[27] For example, as described in Chapter 3, public-sector agencies had not undertaken any significant city extension until the development of Jawahar Nagar and Malviya Nagar in the late 1960s. It had certainly not helped that it took the officials fifteen years after the formation of Rajasthan state in 1949 to enact the rules for subdivision (the Rajasthan Urban Areas sub-division, reconstitution and improvement of plot regulation), in 1964. Derived from the neighborhood unit concept, the rules contained several inconsistencies, which were finally ironed out eleven years later, in 1975.

Such tardiness on the part of the authorities obstructed city development in general and private actors in particular, because, unlike the cities of British India, the cities of Rajasthan did not possess much experience and many established procedures for dealing with private involvement in the urban sector.[28] For instance, when the *Thikanedars*—members of the former ruling class who owned large private estates on the city's outskirts and could no longer afford expansive houses—began partitioning and selling their properties during the 1950s, they neither found clearly laid out procedures to follow nor any sympathy on the part of the state officials, who often dilly-dallied and impeded their efforts. Here it is important to note that many officials were not yet comfortable with the new planning approach and thus were resistant to both the ideas about new conceptions of how to use and organize urban land and the shift in authority from the feudal to the modern bureaucracy in a federated system, in which local electoral power shapes administrative behavior.[29]

Second, notwithstanding the limited attention and resources given to the urban sector, a certain power vacuum marked the climate of opinion and decision making at various administrative levels. Perhaps heightened by the swift substitution of a rather firm ruling order with a fledgling political democracy, officialdom's overall approach to urban planning and development issues was marked by hesitance. For example, the town planning organization submitted Jaipur's first master plan in 1971, but concerned officials within the state government vacillated over the draft for five years before approving the final plan in 1976.[30] It then took the development agencies more than two decades to initiate the preparation of downstream sector plans illustrating detailed land uses and road networks in the late 1990s.[31] Such ambiguous administrative practices not only encouraged officials' discretion but also influenced the manner in which emergent developers conceptualized the overall exercise of subdivision design and development.

Diverting their entrepreneurial energy and focus, prospective developers explored feasible routes through a variety of legal loopholes and pay-to-play arenas. In line with their conservative worldview and customary deference to authority, many avoided direct confrontation—"Fools fight the *sarkar* [state]," in the words of Mr. Jain—and sought to work around the many obstacles via obliging patrons and conniving officials.[32] The next section describes the nature of planning work involved in private subdivision development.

Conceiving and Plotting Subdivisions

Against the backdrop of the overall urban planning and policy context and developers' quest for profit and prestige, practical business needs and cultural preferences animated the nature and purpose of subdivision design and development. In this section, I explain how the developers made and pursued their plans, and the manner in which their clients' requirements and predilections influenced the spatial and social configuration of subdivisions.

Frequently, one of the early steps in the subdivision development process was the formation and registration of a so-called "cooperative society" with the state government. Comprehending the underlying logic requires a quick detour. Cooperative societies had arrived in colonial India during the early twentieth century, following their success in the United Kingdom and United States. They were initially popular in the field of agriculture. The main role of early cooperatives was to extend credit to poor farmers, who had no access to regular lines of credit and were often exploited by moneylenders. The concept had gradually spread into the field of housing in British India's largest cities, such as Mumbai where members of an emergent urban white-collar middle class collaborated successfully—often building upon caste, regional and religious affiliations—to develop many garden suburbs and hundreds of apartment buildings.[33]

Nehruvian India further energized and expanded the progressive concept, aiming to supplement the State's development efforts and enhance the collective good by harnessing cooperation among individuals.[34] Thus, apart from ongoing efforts at the level of communities and social groups, state-sponsored large-scale cooperatives had appeared in diverse fields such as the fertilizer, sugar, dairy and banking industries by the 1960s. Despite differences between these industries, they shared general practices of the cooperative sector: members joined by purchasing shares, and the collected capital was used as collateral to raise loans from insurance companies, banks or government agencies in order to pursue business generating common good. In line with national trends, and implicitly acknowledging increasing housing shortages, the state government announced its intention to allow cooperative housing societies. In 1970, it set up a public-sector agency, the Rajasthan State Co-operative Housing Finance Society Limited, with the objective of granting loans and advances to these collective efforts. Many developers used this provision to form phony cooperative societies. Nominally registered with the office of the Registrar of cooperative societies, these fictitious entities served as fronts for private subdivision development that the state of Rajasthan did not otherwise allow.

Another early step in subdivision development was the identifying and procuring of developable land if the developer did not already possess suitable property. In the absence of an organized real-estate market, subdividers routinely relied upon familial and social connections to do so. Reliance upon traditional networks also helped in maintaining business secrecy and negotiating mutually agreeable rates and terms of payment. Identifying suitable land, however, required a certain expertise, because an inept developer could easily violate two distinct sets of statutory requirements.

First, the property should not be located in the incompatible land-use zones of the master plan. The administrative process of "change in land use" was both cumbersome and protracted. Moreover, in the absence of sub-city-level plans showing magnified detail, judging the exact land use for specific parcels was often difficult and prone to divergent interpretations. Disingenuous developers, therefore, could easily create and exploit confusion regarding the situation at hand. For instance, out of the total forty-six subdivisions developed by Mr. Jain's cooperative society, twenty-two were in residential zones, ten partly met this criterion and the rest turned out to be on incompatible land uses such as ecological and institutional.[35] Lacking wherewithal for end-use supervision, the authorities often failed to check the violation of official plans and rules.

Second, the property should have clear and unambiguous title. Much peripheral land comprised state properties such as village commons and pastures, which were often occupied by encroachers. Some peripheral land belonged to lower castes and others were not allowed to buy that land.[36] Finally, record keepers customarily maintained some ambiguity in official documentation, saving a little latitude for future manipulations and small gratifications.[37]

The next step was usually the subdivision of identified land into lots on paper. Normally, this step took place quickly after the "agreement to sale" was signed and the owner had received a token amount as an advance, with promises of more following soon.[38] Base maps for this paper-based exercise were, in turn, derived from two sources. The first source of base maps was a physical survey of the land actually possessed by the owner. The second source was the official *khasra* plan, or a revenue map showing the land parcels and the *abadi* (residential quarters) of a village; along with the separately maintained ownership details, the *khasra* plan forms the revenue record of a village.

Khasra plans are a historical legacy of the colonial British revenue administration. They are usually drawn at a scale of 1 inch to 40 feet upon a piece of cloth by the *Patwari*, a minor revenue official who is in charge of the revenue matters and records of several villages. These cloth maps are often erroneous, because frequent folding and unfolding makes them crinkled, creased and faded over time. Moreover, the fact that these *khasra* maps are generally prepared and updated using the antiquated "chain-survey" method—in which an iron chain, called a *Jareeb,* is used to measure distances—renders these plans vulnerable to a range of vagaries, such as the tautness of the chain, the *Patwari*'s adeptness at measuring inclined distances and, perhaps of greatest importance, his discretion in interpreting these maps (Figure 5.1).[39]

FIGURE 5.1   *Khasra* plan of Jaipur's urban edge showing land parcels

Source: Derived from land revenue map drawn on cloth.

As evident in Figure 5.1, a typical area on the urban edge has few fixed locations, such as the railway track and dug wells, which the *Patwari* employs as "station points," or locations that can be considered immovable over time. From these fixed locations the *Patwari* measures distances in order to ascertain the location and area of a land parcel, or *khasra*, identified as polygons in Figure 5.1. This task is often impeded by factors such as the haphazard shape of *khasras*, as these polygons may have many segments that follow arbitrary angles and natural inclines; and competing interests, as neighboring landowners have frequent disputes over the exact physical demarcation of their parcels. These multi-segmented polygons owe their excruciating shapes to factors such as the terrain's topology and division of property among family members. Thus, the *Patwari*'s disposition as the custodian and interpreter of revenue maps is critical for property owners and developers, inherently invested in intricacies regarding land demarcation and possession—a role that has only continued to grow with incorporation of villages into Jaipur's urban limits.[40]

The second source of base maps is the physical survey undertaken by the developer, usually in the presence of the *Patwari*, to determine the exact extent of a landholding. Such surveys are important, as landholdings on the actual ground often differ from the official revenue records. Such a discrepancy might arise when neighboring owners informally swap land patches to consolidate their holdings, or owners encroach upon adjacent lands belonging to the state or vulnerable neighbors. The physical survey is considered important because the presence of a survey team, a usual precursor to development, brings hidden disputes to the surface. In Mr. Jain's words, "The survey exercise also yields the extent of land that is undisputedly possessed." The presence of a *Patwari* during the physical survey often helps in the resolution of minor disputes, because unhappy neighbors can easily delay the development of a subdivision and create new rivalries for the developer.

Developers then worked with the resultant map that illustrated two types of information: *khasra* boundaries marked with dotted lines and the results of the physical survey, in unbroken lines. On top of this the draughtsman created a draft layout showing the subdivided land. The layout generally comprised two types of lots: those between 150 and 400 square yards, located on inner roads and considered suitable for single-family homes; and larger lots, measuring up to 2,000 square yards, located along the major roads and deemed appropriate for bungalows. The layout was constrained by two factors: First, while public-sector neighborhoods owe their spacious public spaces and regular shapes to the police power of eminent domain and sizable tracts of state-owned land, the combination of small landholdings and haphazard *khasra* shapes restricted private subdivisions to their limited extent and irregular boundaries. Second, the draftsman often had no idea about the status of abutting properties, as developers often failed to buy contiguous parcels. In some situations, competing developers planned adjoining developments without coordination, resulting in disjointed layouts and street networks. Although developers often consulted public-sector planners on layout design, the popular preference for self-owned individual lots, and the constraints described above, meant that the scope for design innovation was at best limited.[41]

Take, for instance, the agricultural land Mr. Jain bought in 1969 to develop Krishna Nagar. Located at a prime location on the then urban edge along Ajmer Road, which is part of the national highway connecting Delhi and Mumbai, Krishna Nagar is among Jaipur's earliest subdivisions. Its plan characterizes the combined influence of irregularly shaped *khasra* boundaries and rather dry-spirited subdivision rules adopted in 1964 (Figure 5.2). Adhering to the minimum standards of the subdivision rules, the layout maximizes the plotted area (66 percent of total land, compared to about 42 percent in the case of Jawahar Nagar) and provides minimum permissible public spaces such as streets, parks and schools. The plan is drawn ingeniously, given the odd shape of the land parcel, but the influence of the neighborhood unit concept is still hard to miss. As evident in Figure 5.2, a hierarchal road network organizes the layout into blocks comprising different-sized lots around a central open space.

However, it is important to keep in mind that, like many other subdivisions in Jaipur, Krishna Nagar does not have a distinctly demarcated boundary on the ground—violating Perry's basic principle about distinct neighborhood boundaries. Different developers subdivided neighboring properties according to their own inward-looking plans, matching, if not slyly exceeding, the maximum permissible plotted area. On the one hand, the dense and disjointed

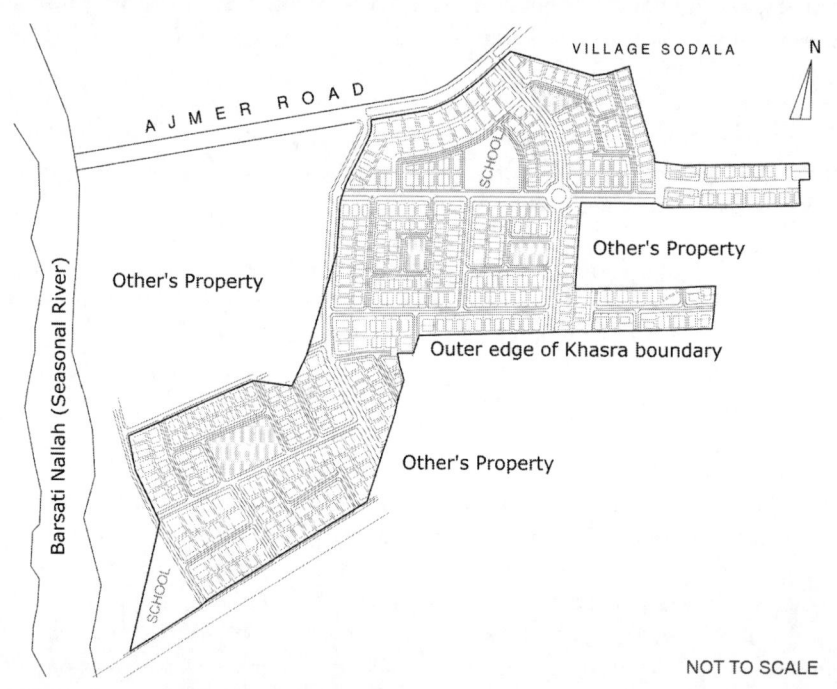

FIGURE 5.2 Layout of Krishna Nagar

spatial organization at the subdivision scale adds up to an intermixed but uneven urban pattern at the sub-city level, with distinct planning and policy implications, which are described in Chapter 6. On the other hand, this spatial form accompanied a distinct type of social configuration mediated by the process of marketing and inhabiting the subdivided land; this is described in the next section.

Selling and Inhabiting Subdivisions

Although important in its own right, the physical layout was ultimately secondary to clients' requirements and preferences, because selling the subdivided land was a major priority for most developers. Private subdivisions were a new phenomenon and many buyers were not yet sure of the outcome. Anxious for inaugural sales, developers routinely made desired changes in the layout to entice well-to-do customers and reputed patrons who preferred a specific lot size, orientation, or neighbor. When bulk buyers and groups of friends and relatives wanted changes, subdividers were not averse to altering the configuration of entire blocks. Similarly, the final price was negotiable, and terms of payment were often tailored to suit clients. The lack of formal regulation and weak government control further enhanced the importance of trustworthy middlemen and shared networks for marketing lots and conducting business. The ability to recast rather firm property lines on the land helped developers and their clients plan the foundational urban tissue and also customize and fine-tune the social form of future communities together.[42]

Subdividers usually followed two parallel lines of action after the draft layout was ready: they began scouting for prospective buyers; and they initiated some form of site development, signifying progress. Mr. Jain's inventive strategy, emulated by many other subdividers, hinged upon attracting a few prominent buyers, who, once invested in the place, encouraged their acquaintances to buy nearby lots and facilitated infrastructure development and the extension of utilities. Each step of basic site development—such as the demarcation of the layout, the leveling of land and earthwork for roads—resulted in the incremental appreciation of land prices. Given that the urban housing economy was driven by housing shortages, the gradual development and periodic selling of subdivided land promised enhanced gains for both the lot-owners and subdividers.[43]

However, such an approach meant that private subdivisions were both slow to develop and relatively homogenous in comparison to public-sector neighborhoods such as Jawahar Nagar and Malviya Nagar, which developed rather quickly (within 5–6 years of ground breaking) and deliberately mixed different economic and social groups. The slow pace of development was in line with the overall planning and policy context, as the pioneering subdividers and homebuilders steadily built up the pressure on decision-makers to establish a procedure for private subdivision development and the legalizing of existing subdivisions through the 1970s and 1980s, which will be described in Chapter 6. On the other hand, the residents' similar socioeconomic profile stemmed from the manner in which developers and initial buyers brought in acquaintances and members of their own networks at the early stages of development.

For instance, the majority of Krishna Nagar's homeowners come from two groups: middle- and high-ranking government officials and traders and businessmen. The government officials were among the original buyers in the early 1970s and helped Mr. Jain with infrastructure development and official approval. The traders and businessmen belonged to two traditionally well-off groups. The first group came from the local business community, which moved from the crowded quarters of the walled city. Many of these extended families had outgrown their ancestral courtyard-based houses and were attracted by the prospect of living on large lots in custom-designed bungalows. Mr. Jain's marketing forays into this tightly knit community were aided by the fact that the prospective buyers did not have many alternatives, as the civic agencies had not developed many neighborhoods, and that Krishna Nagar's "decent-sized" lots were competitively priced, ranging from five to ten rupees per square yard depending upon the lot's location and size.[44]

The second group of traders and businessmen began arriving in the early 1980s, after Mr. Jain had organized basic site development, including a rudimentary road network, and accomplished the conversion of agricultural land into *abadi* land. By this time, land in Krishna Nagar had appreciated by 500 percent and was selling at about 200 rupees per square yard, including a levy of about 30 rupees per square yard for development and other statutory charges. Many of the newly arriving buyers were non-resident Rajasthanis, popularly called *Marwari*, who had migrated to India's northeastern states, such as Assam and Manipur. Troubled by militancy there, they wanted to buy lots in Jaipur in order to construct houses that could be used during their periodic visits to Rajasthan and also as back-up residences for reverse migration should militancy make it impossible for them to continue living in northeast India. The influx of these wealthy residents and the consequent building of diversely ostentatious bungalows (Figures 5.3 and 5.4) established Krishna Nagar's reputation as an upscale locality and boosted the trajectory of its real-estate prices.[45]

In terms of caste and religious affiliations, the majority of Krishna Nagar's inhabitants are higher caste Hindus and Jains, even though other sections of society are not intentionally excluded. Although religion does not play any noticeable role in the everyday life of the community, a pious faction, as in Jawahar Nagar and Malviya Nagar, has organized the building of temple complexes offering a range of facilities such as meeting halls and services such as yoga classes. While the imposing Sri Hari Har Hindu temple was built in the public park, wealthy members of the Jain community donated land for two temples belonging to different sects, which were built incrementally.[46] They serve steady congregations for the morning and evening ritual of *Pratikraman*, usually a two-hour-long religious service. During *Chaumasa*—the four-month-long rainy season, when *bhikshus* and *sadhvis*, or male and female preachers, camp in one place—these facilities attract more visitors than usual, and they spend long

FIGURE 5.3 A bungalow modelled after an imagined 'Victorian villa' in Krishna Nagar

FIGURE 5.4 A bungalow modelled after an imagined traditional Haveli in Krishna Nagar

hours listening to sermons and sharing communal meals. In this respect, these focal points anchor a sizable and growing place-based community of Jain households in Krishna Nagar and nearby subdivisions.[47]

However, it is important to note that while many subdivisions tend to house similar populations, they do not necessarily share the demography of neighboring localities. This is due to several reasons. First, subdividers developing nearby properties often catered to clients belonging to different backgrounds. Many developers targeted specific groups, which is evident in the names of subdivisions that identify with particular professions (for example, Doctor's Colony and Gems Enclave) or specific religions (for example, Muslim majority Kidwai Nagar and Jain dominated Mahavir Nagar).[48] Second, the price of interior parcels was generally less than the farms fronting major roads. This meant that subdividers could develop adjacent properties for different income groups, tapping a larger clientele. For instance, the subdivision called "Krishna Nagar extension" houses a distinctly less-affluent population than the adjoining Krishna Nagar. Third, even though many original buyers sold their properties and numerous lots changed hands several times, the community profile and popular perception are often slow to change. When seen through this lens, the socioeconomic texture of private subdivisions is relatively more granular than that of the deliberately mixed populations of public-sector neighborhoods, but it is more fine-grained than Jaipur's historical quarters, where caste and religious identities often dictate a neighborhood's composition.

The success of early subdivisions such as Krishna Nagar in attracting buyers enticed a diverse range of developers, with more than 170 cooperative societies operating in Jaipur by the mid-1970s.[49] An important administrative precedent had been established by Krishna Nagar's land-use conversion from agricultural to *abadi*, through Mr. Jain's connections with state officials and clever use of an archaic revenue department procedure meant for villages rather than urban areas. Nevertheless, private subdivisions in Jaipur lacked the legitimacy of state approval. The UIT could not approve subdivision developments because it did not have the authority to convert lands into residential properties. Nor could it easily acquire the lands, because the developers could take legal action, delaying and effectively stalling the proceedings. The cooperative societies were officially registered with the state government for the explicit purpose of providing lots to their members and therefore had a certain legal and administrative standing in the eyes of the executive and judiciary. However, the office of the collector, who is in charge of revenue matters at the district level, had no specific policy or directive from the state government to convert their agricultural lands into residential properties. In the city's master plan, the UIT had colored some of these lands yellow to denote their residential land use, but this was at best tokenism, because it did not actually have the jurisdiction to convert and subsequently permit these subdivisions.[50]

From this perspective, it is clear that the subdividers addressed the transition of authority from the old system to the new by making plans that not only fostered place-based local communities but also contributed to larger-scale civic building.[51] The cooperatives were essentially a public institution, which, when combined with the private capital of developers, generated the overall institutional structure to sustain new developments, despite the impediment of the old state institutions.

However, as private subdivision development work gathered pace and the number of lot owners continued to grow through the late 1970s and early 1980s, the climate of opinion began to change. Some developers had encroached upon state lands and beguiled buyers, typically from lower-income groups, by offering cheaper rates than nearby developments. Several developers had vanished, while many had undertaken little or no site development. The lack of even rudimentary services such as electricity and water supply in many subdivisions was notable when compared with the amenities and infrastructure of public-sector neighborhoods. As the early settlers took possession of their lots and started building homes in private subdivisions, they began to demand similar legal status and civic amenities. The next chapter describes how a range of populist plans arose to address the situation.

Conclusion

It is clear that the transition from the princely mode of city building to the post-independence approach to urban planning and development was both difficult and protracted. It also framed the conception and advancement of developer plans in crucial ways. As illustrated in this chapter, a combination of powerful factors—such as unresponsive government, growing urban population and housing shortages—helped set the stage for developer plans. In aiming to tap the economic energy of urbanization, developers' entrepreneurial efforts were little different from their counterparts' who were proactively building and shaping human settlements in many other parts of the world. However, the dearth of established procedures, along with official tardiness and bureaucratic turf wars in post-independence Jaipur, meant that the subdivision development work largely proceeded in an unregulated manner and that developers of many stripes pursued their own plans, generating unforeseen cumulative effects.

Yet the pursuit of profit did not trump residents' cultural preferences, which played an important role in shaping the spatial design and social organization of private subdivisions. As explained, the enduring predilection for single-family homes and large bungalows influenced the layout plans, even though the inhabitants desired the progressive features of public-sector neighborhoods, such as parks, open spaces and schools. Similarly, many residents patronized temples and encouraged their relatives and acquaintances to live nearby, while not minding that members of diverse socioeconomic groups lived in close proximity. The developers apparently understood and acknowledged the larger interplay of society's conservative and liberal impulses by positioning the private subdivisions as a sort of halfway settlement between the comparatively traditional living of

Jaipur's historical quarters and Rajasthan's vast spread of rural areas, and the relatively progressive public-sector neighborhoods of Nehruvian India. The next chapter explains how this notion played out at the sub-city scale.

Notes

1 There is little scholarly work explaining subdivision design and development and its effect on urban form and growth in different parts of the world. In the U.S. context, some notable exceptions include: Warner, *Streetcar Suburbs*; and Rybczynski, *Last Harvest.*

2 The importance of foundational urban tissue cannot be understated. It establishes rather difficult-to-change property lines and determines supportable building type. See Scheer, *The Evolution of Urban Form*, 27–60.

3 Primarily driven by local factors, the dynamic phenomenon is ubiquitous in diverse contexts. In the United States, for instance, the practice of home rule puts planning power in the weakest farming communities at the urban periphery, where the strong influence of developers, combined with lax county regulation, allows for the disjointed purchasing of farmland for subdivision development. See Holway et al., "Combating Zombie Subdivisions."

4 This pattern is commonly recognized as sprawl in the United States. However, a higher density often marks the haphazard pattern of development in urban India. See, for instance, Pucher et al., "Urban Transport Trends and Policies in China and India."

5 JDA, *Jaipur Master Development Plan 2025*, Vol. 1, 228–230.

6 Although not all subdividers came from a mercantile background or the *Bania* castes, most employed traditional routines and customary ways of doing business. See Laidlaw, *Riches and Renunciation*; and Babb, *Emerald City*, for a description of Jaipur's business climate and practices.

7 It is important to keep in mind that the local bazaars were not only places of exchange but also constituted larger networks of commerce, culture and political power. For the organization and significance of the traditional bazaar-based networks, see Yang, *Bazaar India*; and Bayly, *Rulers, Townsmen, and Bazaars.*

8 Gupta, *Land Assembly in the Indian Metropolis.*

9 Interview with two retired chief town planners on March 7, 2007 and February 16, 2006. Both retired in the early 2000s and were closely involved with the approval of private subdivisions through the 1980s and 1990s.

10 The State had historically enumerated and classified people, land and production in various regions of India. See Bayly, *Empire and Information.* After the British Crown's takeover in 1858, the trend apparently intensified and expanded to include the nationalization of forests; confiscation of commons; and massive investment in roads, railways and canals. See Goswami, *Producing India.*

11 See *Imperial Gazetteer of India*, Vol. XIII, 395–6.

12 Hira Singh has described in detail the various forms of extra-economic coercion employed by the landlord class for extracting taxes such as *hasil, bigori, lag-bag* and *begar* from the peasants. See Singh, *Colonial Hegemony and Popular Resistance*, 106.

13 Baden-Powell, *The Land Systems of British India.*

14 British colonial officials developed and disseminated a range of technologies and tools, such as the cadastral survey, for land settlement and land tenure, and titling programs that have continued to influence postcolonial developments across the empire. See, for instance, Home, "Scientific Survey and Land Settlement in British Colonialism."

15 *Imperial Gazetteer of India.* Vol. XIII, 396.

16 Mathur and Mathur, *Land Revenue Law in Rajasthan.*

17 The cultivators were tenants-at-will and had no hereditary rights to land. However, the right to cultivation descended from father to son, and this was recognized by Jaipur state. Ibid., 395.

18 Interview with S. K. Lahiri on May 22, 2006. The impact of the shift in the land-use regime after India's independence is not well documented. For a careful study describing the impact upon state forests and nature preserves, see Gold and Gujar, *In the Time of Trees and Sorrows.*
19 Yugandhar and Datta, *Land Reforms in India, Vol. 2: Rajasthan—Feudalism and Change.*
20 Buch, *Planning the Indian City*; and Buch, *Of Man and His Settlements.*
21 Interview conducted on May 3, 2006.
22 See Figure 5.5.

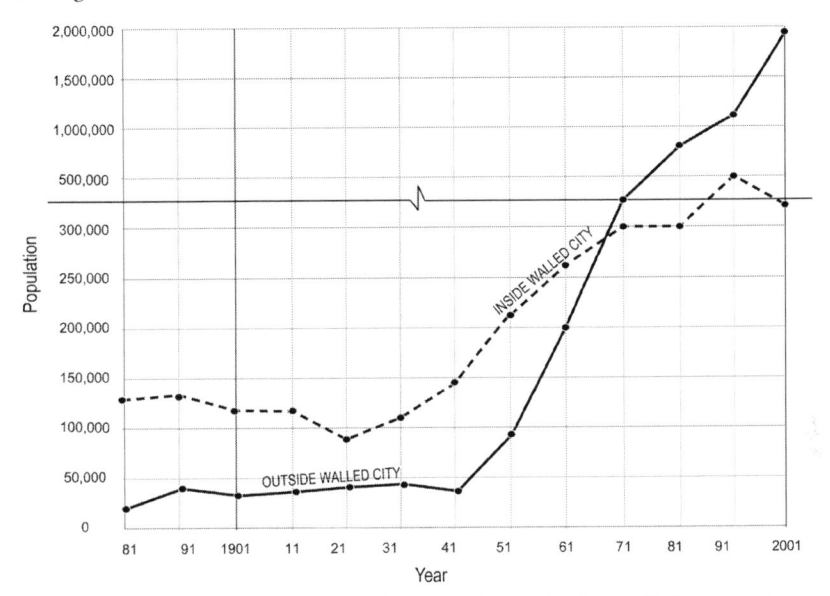

FIGURE 5.5   Growth of population inside and outside the walled city in Jaipur (1881–2001)

Source: Derived from Master Plan for Jaipur (1971–1991), India. Government of Rajasthan (2005). *Preparation of City Development Plan for Jaipur, 2005.* India. JDA (1998). *Master Development Plan – 2011, Jaipur Region.* Vol. 1 & 2. India. JDA (2011). *Master Development Plan – 2025, Jaipur Region.* Vol. 1–4. India.

23 Tangri, "Urban Growth, Housing, and Economic Development."
24 For a discussion of the importance of bungalow typology in India's building traditions, see Lang et al., *The Bungalow in Twentieth-Century India.*
25 Interview on June 6, 2006. The bungalow typology has long occupied center stage in the Indian popular imagination. A senior town planner highlighted the underlying sentiment captured by a popular song from the late 1930s.

TABLE 5.1 Popular song about residential imagery

Song from Hindi movie President (1937), performed by K.L. Saigal	English translation by author
Ek bangala bane nyara rahe kunba jis mein saara	I long for an incomparable bungalow In which the extended family can live
Sone ka bangala, chandan ka jangalaa	A bungalow of gold with sandalwood fencing

TABLE 5.1 continued

Song from Hindi movie President (1937), performed by K.L. Saigal	English translation by author
vishvakarma ke dware	Designed by Vishwakarma (the architect of gods)
ati sundar pyara pyara	Extremely beautiful and charming
ek bangala bane nyara	I long for an incomparable bungalow
Itana uncha bangala ho ye	The bungalow should be so tall
maano gagan ka tara	That it appears like a star in the sky
jispe chadh ke indradhanush par	Our kid should be able to straddle the rainbow
jhulaa jhule chand hamara	And swing on it from the bungalow's rooftop
bhanda rahe lachami ke haathon mei sara	Finances be in Laxmi's (goddess of wealth) hands
paye ab jee bhar ke sub kuch jisne bipat uthaye	The deprived deserve plentiful now
Ek bangala bane nyara	I long for an incomparable bungalow
rahe kumba jis mein saara	In which the extended family can live

Source: Translated by author.

26 For an account of changing political organization and the role of cosmopolitan elites, see Sisson, "Institutionalization and Style in Rajasthan Politics." For the shift in the domain of urban public affairs, see Singh, *Urban Planning in India.*
27 The situation was not unique to Rajasthan and reflected similar phenomena in many other parts of India. See Wilcox, "Politicians, Bureaucrats and Development in India."
28 Whereas the colonial officials actively promoted private investment in the development of urban extensions in British Indian cities such as Ahmedabad and Bombay through modalities such as town-planning schemes and land-pooling, similar work in Rajasthan's cities, many of which were seats of long-ruling dynasties, was almost exclusively within the state's purview. Arguably, state power passed on quickly to the new leadership in the post-independence period, but the ruling elites continued to have a firmer control over urban affairs in Rajasthan than in other parts of the country. See, for instance, Sharma, *Urban Community Power Structure*, which documents the trend in Udaipur.
29 *Thikanedars* were hereditary feudal lords governing regions and villages within princely states. They were often quite powerful, with independent standing and status. See Singh, *Colonial Hegemony and Popular Resistance.* Jaipur's rulers had granted them city estates on a freehold basis, but state officials did not permit the subdivision of their lands after Jaipur's merger with independent India. Interviews with G. S. Nandiwal on March 30, 2006; April 10, 2006; and May 11, 2006. He described in detail how if the officials had wanted to facilitate subdivisions, they could have easily used the Revenue Act's provision allowing land-use conversion from agricultural to residential land use upon paying twenty times the yearly rent, but they did not.
30 Interview with N. Rajbanshi, February 14, 2006. During the early 1970s, Mr. Rajbanshi was a young planner deputed by the chief town planner, Mr. Kambo, to follow up on Jaipur's Master Plan with state officials. He recounted how, due to the absence of precedence and unknown outcomes, officials were hesitant to notify the otherwise complete plan.

31 Evidently, the post-independence shift in the focus and scope of planning policy has not fully percolated through the system as yet. For instance, even the current master plan (2009–25), which is Jaipur's third, concludes the review of preceding master plans by noting that they "lacked follow up actions such as preparation of functional plans, zonal development and zoning regulation after the finalization of the master plan." JDA, *Jaipur Master Development Plan 2025*, Volume 1, 5–6.

32 Gupta, *Land Assembly in the Indian Metropolis*.

33 Rao, *House, But No Garden*.

34 India's experience and some notable successes with cooperative societies have been studied in detail. For the cooperative movement's linkages with national polity and its significance to the formation of the modern Indian state and civil society, see Frankel, *India's Political Economy 1947–2004*.

35 According to the list of schemes submitted to JDA until May 31, 1994, released into the public domain in 1996.

36 *The Rajasthan Lands (Restrictions of Transfer) Ordinance of 1976* seeks to safeguard the properties owned by lower castes by preventing their sale.

37 For a detailed discussion on the manipulation of official property records and associated documents in South Asia, see Hull, "Ruled by Records."

38 Often, the subdividers did not purchase the land officially but signed an *Ikrarnama*, or an agreement to sale, with the owner. This helped subdividers save the registration fee and also enabled them to buy the land of lower-caste people, if the situation so warranted, as the records continued to vest the ownership with the original landholder. For instance, out of the forty-six subdivisions developed by Mr. Jain, only one subdivision's land was registered in the name of his cooperative society; the rest were subdivided on the basis of agreement to sale.

39 For a comprehensive description of the *Patwari*'s everyday modalities and influence, see Gupta, "Blurred Boundaries."

40 Authorities have continued to enlarge Jaipur's urban region by incorporating outlying villages (Figure 5.6). Thus, instead of decreasing, urbanization has ironically enhanced the importance of the *Patwari*'s role on the vastly expanded urban edge.

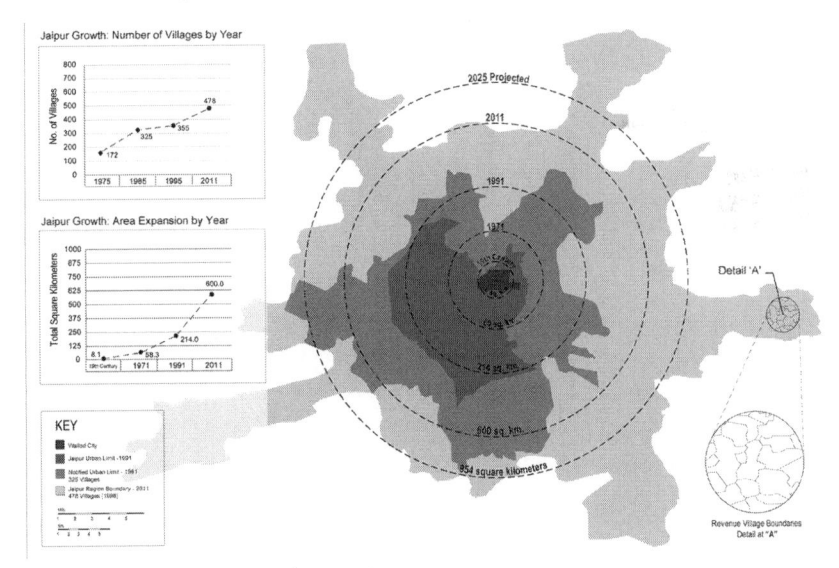

FIGURE 5.6 Jaipur's growth over time

Source: Derived from JDA (1998). *Master Development Plan – 2011, Jaipur Region.* Vol. 1 and 2. JDA (2011) *Master Development Plan – 2025, Jaipur Region.* Vol. 1–4.

41 Interview with a retired chief town planner on March 7, 2007. Mutual acquaintances often facilitated such consultations in informal settings. Some public-sector town planners also helped the developers with the approval process and, it is said, obtained lots in lieu at discounted prices.

42 Interview with Mr. Jain on June 6, 2006.

43 A peculiar combination of local conditions, rather than neoliberal modalities of profiteering, supported the appreciation of real-estate prices in private subdivisions such as Krishna Nagar. While many buyers were genuine homebuilders, private subdivisions attracted two distinct sets of investors. The first group was relatively smaller and comprised speculators, usually operating on a short-term basis (0–3 years) because real-estate investment promised a better rate of return than other options, such as bank deposits, gold, or the stock market. The second and larger set of investors visualized vacant lots as a form of insurance for an uncertain future and as a secure form of investment, since land was tangible. They parked their savings on a long-term basis with specific goals, such as their future retirement or their children's education or marriage. Sometimes subdividers also kept lots using *benami*, or fake, identities and registered them as lot-owners in the records they submitted to the authorities. Apparently, assembling a *benami* identity was not a very complicated process, as one simply needed a name, a photograph and a signature that might have belonged to a person. Since only the subdivider knew these details, he could reassemble the three constituents of an identity when the lot was sold. Creation of such fake identities helped circumvent the national legislation, the Urban Land (Ceiling and Regulation) Act of 1976, which imposed a ceiling on vacant land in cities. The purpose of the Act was to increase the supply of urban land available to meet housing shortages and it enabled the state to acquire such vacant lands. Finally, since a major portion of land transactions were usually conducted using "black," or untaxed, money, outside the formally accounted economy, real-estate investment often suited tax-evading businessmen, corrupt officials and politicians. Subdividers preferred and obliged the latter in particular, because they could pass on insider's knowledge, help with official approvals and shape overall public policy regarding real-estate development. In this respect, the phenomenon was not unique to Jaipur. For a description of land speculation around Delhi's first master plan, see Lahiri, "A Capital Century."

44 Interview with a reputed property dealer who was one of the first to operate in the Krishna Nagar area, on June 6, 2007.

45 The building of impressive mansions in native places by expatriate members of the merchant classes is a well-established custom in India. See Hardgrove, "Merchant Houses as Spectacle of Modernity in Rajasthan and Tamil Nadu." Krishna Nagar's land price (Figure 5.7 opposite) has continued to increase in an impressive manner.

46 The patronage of neighborhood-based religious buildings and rituals by wealthy merchants and successful businessmen is a long-standing practice in the Indian tradition. See Mines, "Temples and Charity."

47 Interview with Prem Mama Ji, a resident of Krishna Nagar and member of the managing committee of the Shewtambar Jain temple, on June 15, 2011. He reported that approximately 650 households had an affiliation with the temple, a number that has consistently increased since the temple's founding in the late 1990s.

48 Apparently, the phenomenon has a certain lineage in the South Asian tradition. Qadeer, writing about Lahore in the late nineteenth century, reports the development of new settlements along occupational and religious lines. See Qadeer, *Lahore*, 83. And Rathore describes spatial segregation based on religious lines in the aftermath of communal riots that took place in Jaipur, and many other Indian cities, in 1989. Rathore, "Ramganj, Jaipur."

49 Arora et al., *Jaipur*.

50 Interview with a retired chief town planner on May 3, 2006.

51 In this respect, many subdividers were not mere real-estate developers but could be called "community builders." See Weiss, *The Rise of the Community Builders.*

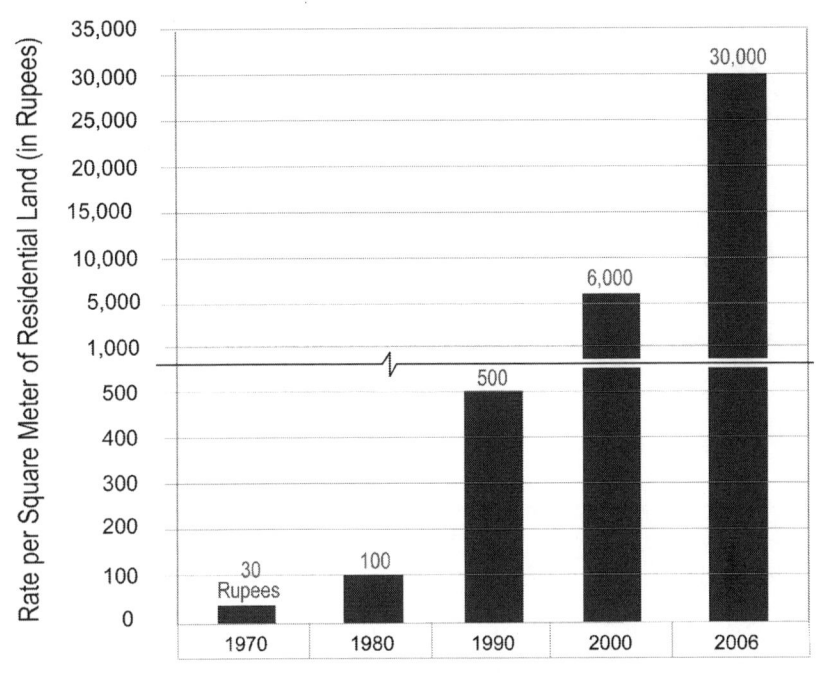

FIGURE 5.7   Rate per square meter of residential land in Krishna Nagar

Source: Derived from interviews with local real-estate dealers in 2006.

6

POPULAR PLANS
Reconciling Diverse Efforts

"Every civilization gets the monument it deserves," according to César Daly, nineteenth-century urban thinker and perceptive observer of Paris's modern makeover.[1] Elaborating on this notion in his seminal book *Bourgeois Utopias*, Robert Fishman describes how suburbia's domestic architecture, shaped by mostly open and single-family residential land uses, cleverly reconciled the paradox of community building based on private property. Tracking the typology from its origin in eighteenth-century London, through its ostensible zenith in the postwar United States, to its purported quick demise in sprawling Los Angeles, he illustrates how the suburban ideal embodied middle-class culture, which celebrated family life and newfound affluence shaped by the workings of modern capitalism.

The temptation to extend the elegant metaphor to late twentieth-century Jaipur is hard to resist, simply because the city's seemingly chaotic urban form seems to epitomize India's ongoing process of social and political change, framed by the deepening of popular democracy, so well.[2] Within a few decades of princely Jaipur's merger with the rest of the country, the city had changed dramatically. Most of the built-up area comprised distinctly planned post-independence quarters, where planning actors pursued their own plans, leveraging different opportunities. Not surprisingly, and often to the abject horror of the local elites, large parts of the once architecturally unique city had become indistinguishable from largely nondescript urban India, with politician-led popular plans playing a key role in that transformation. While many plans worked in isolation and several at cross-purposes, popular plans targeted wider support. Consequentially, they sought to reconcile varying aims, multiple perspectives and parochial interests—fostering, even if inadvertently, a unique form of urbanism.

The undertaking of this kind of spatial planning entailed actors thinking and acting across different plan purposes and scales. Take, for instance, the user and developer plans discussed in the previous chapters. Popular plans not only acknowledged their divergent goals but also, unlike the other efforts described in this book, addressed the often-overlooked intermediate spatial and policy scales where these plans came together. Straddling the space between the top-down official planning approach and bottom-up adaptation efforts of neighborhood residents, and the city-level master plans and settlement-level layouts, these plans rendered Jaipur's post-independence quarters like a patchwork quilt of differently planned areas juxtaposing each other, characteristic of much of urban India. Here, many rural and informal settlements abutted their formally planned conjoined twins, which had considerably changed from within, while a jumble of private subdivisions surrounded them all.

Such a settlement pattern meant that electoral districts rarely comprised similarly planned areas, obliging political aspirants to address diverse constituencies and competing interests.[3] The pattern's substantial spatial spread also ensured that different electorates remained politically relevant across the geographically nested voting districts electing local, state and national representatives.[4] As the settlements grew in size and influence, their voters attracted increasing attention in the competitive realm of local politics. Relying upon nearby public-sector neighborhoods for facilities such as parks, open spaces and schools, which set new benchmarks for residential environments, the residents of informal settlements and private subdivisions demanded civic amenities, security and propriety. The subsequent emergence of popular plans signified that the urban poor and marginalized sections of society had rightly become powerful pressure groups within a few decades of India's independence.

While the nature and focus of the city's electoral politics changed in line with pressure from constituents and local patronage, residents' increasing social confidence centered on the formation of place-based communities and civic infrastructure. Gradually, and frequently in sync with election cycles, residents' demands garnered a slew of popular measures, including the extension of utilities, development of facilities, piecemeal regularization of unauthorized subdivisions and incremental legalization of many informal settlements; this process continues today.[5]

This chapter begins by outlining the emergence of populism in India's post-independence polity and moves on to illustrate the development of sector plans and the regularization of unauthorized settlements. I then explain the nature of the planning work involved in populist efforts, which produced both beneficial and harmful effects, such as tenure security and social mobility in an unequal society, and the development of housing in unsafe lands such as floodplains. I then conclude with some final thoughts.

The Lead-Up to the Making of Popular Plans

The rise of popular plans shaping Jaipur's post-independence quarters cannot be understood in isolation from larger shifts in national and state public policies. In brief, with direct and tangible benefits failing to materialize, public faith in the ability of adopted economic policies to deliver widespread welfare improvements had begun wavering by the 1960s.[6] The rhetoric of development abounded, and ruling elites continued to pay lip service to the notion of nation building. However, the insignificant trickle-down effects and scanty returns on investments in industry and large-scale infrastructure projects made a mockery of that rhetoric, as society's basic needs—such as for food, clothing and shelter—went unmet. Unforeseen difficulties—such as wars with China in 1962 and Pakistan in 1965, Nehru's death in 1964 and the failed monsoons of 1966 and 1967—resulted in food shortages, a balance of payments crisis, the devaluation of the rupee and runaway inflation. In a rare acknowledgement of failure, circumspect policy-makers declared a "plan holiday" for three years and suspended the impending fourth five-year plan from 1966–69. A critical review sponsored by the Ford Foundation created national awareness about the extent of absolute poverty.[7] Meanwhile, the political climate was dominated by infighting and a split in the ruling Congress Party.

Playing the "politics of poverty," a commonly used term at the time, Mrs. Indira Gandhi, who was Prime Minister Nehru's daughter, moved to position herself as the savior of the poor and oppressed. Riding high on a populist slogan, "*Garibi Hatao,*" or "Abolish Poverty," she led her faction to power in the 1971 general election. She then consolidated her power by placing personal loyalists in various official and party positions. A debate about the failure of national economic planning to reduce poverty and alternate approaches required to help the poor played out during the fourth five-year plan period (1969–74), as populist measures began to emerge at the state level. The state governments were closer to the people, especially when compared to the long-term policy orientation of the Delhi-based planning commission; and state-subsidized tangible goods, such as rations and clothing, provided direct and immediate benefits to potential voters.[8]

Spreading quickly across a number of states, including Tamil Nadu, Maharashtra and West Bengal, populist schemes providing direct state subsidies and goods to the poor became a conspicuous feature of the public policy landscape during the 1970s. Political turbulence following the declaration of a national emergency in 1975 and successive national and state elections between 1977 and 1980 further strengthened their electoral purchase.[9] Notwithstanding regional and thematic differences, many populist schemes exhibited the ability to delineate a range of distinctions between the patrician and the plebian.[10] Mobilizing people based on diverse characteristics such as language, caste and status, these efforts aimed to tap the growing political participation and ambitions of the lower and intermediate social strata. In this respect, these efforts promoted social welfare and symbolized positive political development in an unequal and non-egalitarian society, where goods, growth and gains tended to flow toward already better-off actors.

However, it is important to note that populist measures evoked a range of reactions. To many businessmen and bureaucrats, they were cheap political stunts that wasted scarce national resources. Leftists derided them as well, but typically characterized them as open political bribery impeding the oncoming revolution. Closer to the purpose at hand, urban planners abhorred them almost as an article of faith.[11] Any acknowledgement of the various unauthorized actions undertaken by non-state actors, such as private developers and neighborhood residents, could only undermine the official plans. Indian planners posited these plans as the only game in town, and this was affirmed by the law of the land. Because the growing presence of self-interest pressure groups in urban areas held out the promise of the formation of influential coalitions—which was a major, if unstated, aim of many populist efforts—planners tended to see them as a particularly pernicious pivot of a potential collective assault on their professional expertise and occupational turf.

It certainly mattered that, on a parallel but uncoordinated level, the official planning approach in many Indian cities had begun to unravel by the 1970s.[12] This was especially evident in the housing sector, which takes up the bulk of city land. While Madhu Sarin (1982) was describing the development of informal settlements by workers hired to build Chandigarh, whom the comprehensive plan had notoriously overlooked, Jaipur's post-independence quarters were undergoing similar changes, as described in the previous chapters. Driven by housing shortages and the government's tardy response, unanticipated settlements such as JKB and Krishna Nagar began to spread. The settlements started appropriating locations that the city's master plan had set aside for other uses and began to block most of the projected future developments, jeopardizing the very project of Nehruvian modernist planning.[13] The rise of populist measures in the domains of city development in general and housing policy in particular provided a way out of the tricky situation. Reaching out to powerful interest groups, such as the residents of informal settlements and private subdivisions, popular measures aimed to reconcile a range of divergent planning efforts. The next section explains how planning craft helped decision-makers visualize varying plans and their effects. Howsoever reluctantly, like professional bureaucrats elsewhere, Jaipur planners did help make popular plans, but they claimed duress and passed the responsibility, in the words of a senior planner, on to "unprincipled politicians," who only seemed eager to take all the credit.[14]

Visualizing Diverse Plans

Before the transformation of computing from a tool primarily for analysis to a tool for synthesis, and the advent of computer-aided visualization and Geographical Information Systems, the mapping of spatial phenomena and the presentation of planning analyses were onerous tasks. Although planners and officials possessed anecdotal knowledge about the building of subdivisions and informal settlements on the urban edge, they did not know the exact nature of spatial change. A significant push came from the residents and influential patrons of Krishna Nagar, who began to press for state approval and land titles in the late 1970s, following the conversion of agricultural land into residential use.

Obtaining the relevant drawings and revenue maps, planners plotted the layouts of Krishna Nagar and adjacent developments on the area plan. A senior planner explained the process in the following words:

> We did a small exercise and pasted together the plans of several contiguous subdivisions in the Krishna Nagar area. It was a big poster, about 20 feet by 10 feet, and showed an alarming situation. The road network was in total disarray, as most roads were narrow and ended in cul-de-sacs. We presented it to the chief minister and asked him if we wanted to create such a Jaipur. We also pleaded that such piecemeal approvals must not be given. We need to take into account the overall area and its requirements.[15]

The planners' clever use of graphic aids helped decision-makers see how the various settlements comprised a haphazard spatial structure. Planners described how randomly developing subdivisions, peripheral rural hamlets that were turning into urban villages, and incipient informal settlements were deficient in open spaces and civic infrastructure. They noted that they also constituted a disorganized road network that would impede the flow of people, vehicles and commodities, jeopardizing the city's foreseeable future. While state leaders and their trusted bureaucrats deliberated about feasible options and the political fallout of potential judgments, planners proposed that an overall "sector plan" should guide the development of local places.[16] According to this method, the city would be divided into sectors and a road network plan delineating major roads would be devised for each area. Operating at the intermediate scale, between the city-level master plan and individual settlements of various kinds, the functional road network would serve the interiors of each area and provide basic connectivity. Figure 6.1 shows the sector plan for the Shyam Nagar area, which was prepared in 1982. The first in the series of many, it signified a subtle but significant change in planning practice.

The sector plan began by outlining the hierarchal road network comprising all the national and state highways, such as Ajmer road; master plan roads, such as the Gopalpura Bypass; and sector roads, such as "Janpath," or people's street, which traverses the middle of Figure 6.1. Once the spatial structure of a sector had been demarcated using the existing and proposed major roads, individual settlements fitted within it, like pieces of a jigsaw puzzle, as and when they developed. Their location and names were incrementally added to the sector plan, as were the forty- and thirty-feet-wide internal roads, as evident in Figure 6.1.

The introduction of sector plans for guiding the development of the urban periphery was important for two reasons. First, it shows that by the early 1980s the authorities had realized that future city extensions would not be sponsored solely by the public sector. Accordingly, sector plans aimed to create a spatial framework. By using roads as the main structuring element, the sector plans not only turned the development agencies' attention toward the building of road-related infrastructure but also made room for settlements developed by non-state actors.

FIGURE 6.1 Sector 6: Shyam Nagar area

Source: Derived from sector plan for Shyam Nagar area prepared by the Jaipur Development Authority, 1982.

Second, the preparation and implementation of sector plans quietly shifted public attention from the adopted planning approach, which envisioned a comprehensively designed city comprising self-contained neighborhoods, toward a utilitarian road network that would, even if successfully pursued, shape the city's spatial structure and urban future in a flexible and rather open-ended manner. Analyzed carefully, the move not only signified the winnowing of the state's ambitions to control urban form and organization but also revealed the silent yet significant shift in its approach to unforeseen spatial changes, pursued by many urban actors, that had shadowed the formal plans.[17] The next section explains how the practical needs and cultural preferences of different planning actors shaped the ensuing popular efforts. Aware of pertinent factors such as the bureaucratic turf wars and colonial revenue practices, sponsors cleverly employed popular measures to mediate between divergent plan purposes and thematic focuses.

Recognizing Diverse Planning Efforts

While the sector plans aimed at accommodating aggregate spatial change into the city's overall physical structure, specific initiatives targeted unauthorized settlements occupying interstitial spaces. In this section, I explain the planning and policy work involved in the legalization of informal settlements and private subdivisions. I sketch out a broad outline of the two leading popular efforts, consistently supported by the state's top leadership since the late 1970s.[18] By this time, Jaipur's extra-legal neighborhoods, comprising informal settlements and many subdivisions developed by the cooperatives, supplied a sizable part of the housing stock (Figure 6.2) and also had some of the largest self-interest residents' groups active in the city's electoral politics.

Following considerable political turbulence, marked by the infamous state of emergency in 1975, general elections in 1977 and intervening presidential rule, a new government came to power in Rajasthan state in 1980. Within a few months, under relentless pressure from the developers and residents of private subdivisions, it revised the procedure of land conversion by enacting new rules for the "Allotment, conversion & regulation of agricultural land for residential, commercial and public utility purposes in urban areas." These rules allowed significant relaxation of existing regulations and laid down a procedure for regularizing the unauthorized subdivisions.[19] In a nod to the difference of opinion between the revenue officials and urban planners over land-use administration, the conversion rules required subdividers to obtain two separate but interlinked approvals from the office of the district collector, who had jurisdiction over land-revenue matters, and an approval of the physical layout from the UIT.

First, the UIT's town-planning wing examined the subdivision's technical aspects. This process entailed verifying land-use compatibility with the function assigned by the master plan, and checking the layout's compliance with the subdivision rules prescribing development parameters such as the ratio of plotted

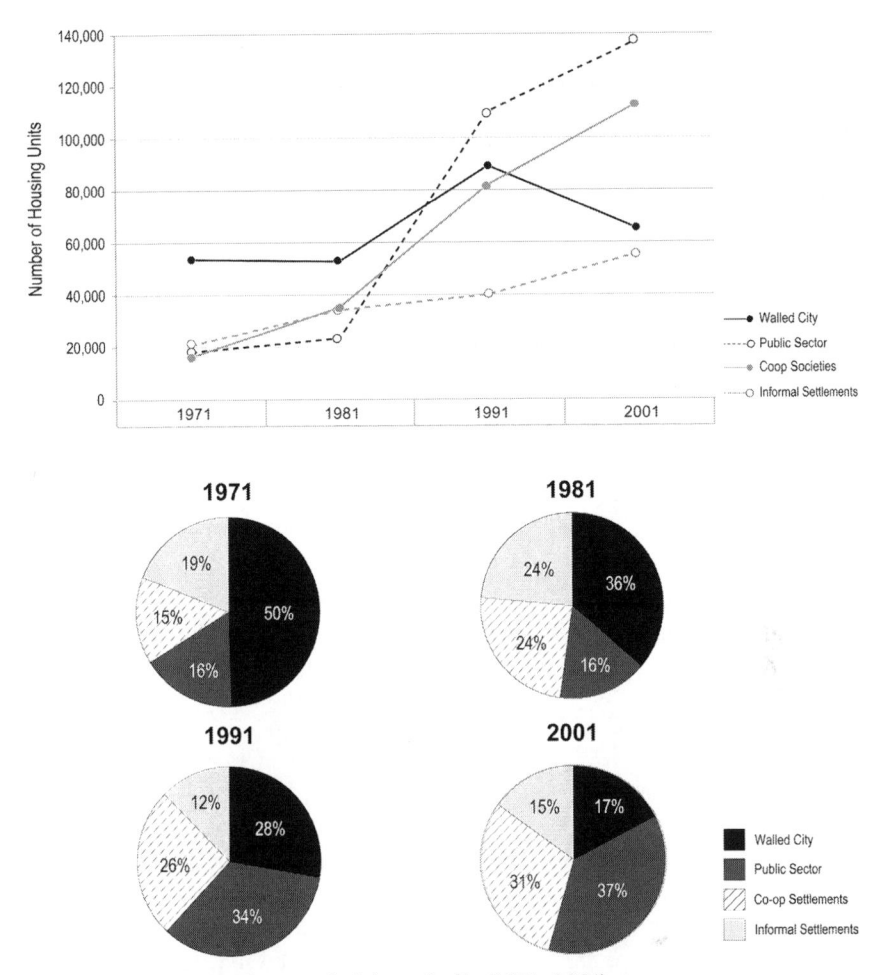

FIGURE 6.2 Housing by type in Jaipur, India (1971–2001)

Source: Derived from Government of Rajasthan, Department of Urban Development & Housing (1976) *Master Plan for Jaipur (1971–1991).* India. Government of Rajasthan (2005) *Preparation of City Development Plan for Jaipur, 2005.* India. JDA (1998) *Master Development Plan – 2011, Jaipur Region.* Vol. 1 & 2. India. JDA (2011) *Master Development Plan – 2025 Jaipur,* Vol. 1–4. India. JDA (1995) *Civic Surveys for Masterplan of Jaipur City: Household Sector.* India.

to open spaces, road widths, plot sizes and mandatory building setbacks. As explained in Chapter 5, many subdividers had maximized plotted area by providing little open space, few parks and narrow roads, and had paid little attention to statutory requirements. Moreover, many owners had taken possession and secured their lots with boundary walls. In many instances, people had already constructed houses and started living in undeveloped subdivisions. Thus, drastic measures such as the large-scale demolition of existing properties could prove politically contentious and legally time-consuming. The situation forced planners to rethink their own expectations.[20] Shortly afterward, practical requirements trumped planning parameters.

A senior planner with the UIT described the situation in the following words: "What could we do except ensure that the subdivision had some open space and civic facilities? We had to have some objective measure to ensure this."[21] Coming up with an "objective measure" entailed working out a compromise, which sought to ensure that the layout provided at least thirty-foot-wide roads; a minimum of 40 percent open space, including roads and parks; and a maximum of 60 percent plotted area. However, in special cases, such as small subdivisions and places where more than 80 percent of the houses had already been built, up to 66 percent plotted area would be permissible. Moreover, the land surrendered for access and sector plan roads could be counted toward the open area. Thus, although in maps and documents their layouts could potentially meet the criterion of 60:40, many settlements would actually have little open space and no schools to cater to their populations, and they would continue to be a "civic-infrastructure parasite" on the nearby public-sector neighborhoods.[22]

On the one hand, the idea of 60:40 represented the ultimate reduction of Perry's progressive concept to a technical banality. On the other hand, it represented the immense political pressure on the state government and urban planners to reconcile the developer plans with the formal planning efforts. Since many subdivisions contravened even the liberalized land conversion rules of 1980, the planners, revenue officials and developers negotiated. The planners insisted that the subdivisions must have adequate open spaces, a predominant residential character and roads at least thirty feet wide. After a series of meetings, the deal was settled on the ratio of 60:40.[23] Since many subdivisions already existed on the ground, the approval process worked retrospectively and did not change the physical situation drastically. However, some subdividers ceded vacant lots to the UIT or converted them into open spaces, exceeding the ratio of 60:40.

Once the town-planning wing was satisfied with a subdivision's technical aspects, it stamped "technically approved" on the layout and forwarded the case to the collector's office. The relevant officials then checked the ownership details and compared the physical area with revenue records in order to check if the subdivision encroached upon contiguous lands. They also visited the site to corroborate the layout with actual ground conditions. After the subdivision's ownership and physical extent had been verified, the collector's office converted the agricultural land to *abadi* in its records, stamped "administratively approved" on the subdivision plan and sent it back to the UIT. The UIT then calculated official fees, such as the regularization charges to be paid by each lot-owner; development charges—that is, a levy for the provision of basic utilities and civic infrastructure; and other assorted costs, such as the lease money and registration fee. After paying the outstanding dues, homeowners got a set of papers, including the coveted *Patta*—the official title to land—and celebrated the legal ownership of the lot on which, in several instances, they had been living "illegally" for more than a decade.

Perceived electoral gains created strong votaries for regularization in both the main political parties. Steady streams of tax revenue and development work enticed government officials and engineers to hasten the regularization of private subdivisions.[24] The development of sector plans and the organization of regularization drives quickly became a major preoccupation for the newly created JDA, which replaced the UIT in 1982.[25] Ironically, the normalizing of the regularization process catalyzed the development of new unauthorized subdivisions. Apparently, working in a complementary manner, the two phenomena boosted the supply of house lots developed by the cooperative sector (see Figure 6.2) during the 1980s. But even as the policy shift promoting regularization facilitated land ownership and tenure security among a growing section of the city's population, its populist orientation generated unwarranted outcomes and harmful effects.

In Krishna Nagar, for instance, ensuing development and rising land values energized real-estate developers and property dealers, who, often in collusion with petty politicians and low-level officials, explored new avenues of profit. Exploiting a variety of administrative loopholes and lacunae, such as the impreciseness of the revenue map, these actors promoted the development of housing on the floodplains of the adjoining seasonal river (see left side of Figure 5.2). This gradually reduced the width of the water channel from an average of 500 feet to a minuscule 40 feet.[26] Arguably, the contrast between the salutary and perverse effects of popular planning efforts emerged even more sharply in the informal settlements, which, unlike the private subdivisions, housed vulnerable populations and occupied marginal locations. I next pick up this thread in relation to JKB, offering a window into the complex realms where popular plans played out on the ground.

In comparison with the relatively smooth regularization of private subdivisions described above, informal settlements had to go through an incremental and often contentious regularization process.[27] For instance, JKB did not even exist in the official records until it was devastated by Jaipur's famous floods of 1980. Alteration of the natural topography, due to the building of a road separating JKB and Jawahar Nagar, had rendered the low-lying spots between sand dunes remarkably vulnerable to the accumulation of storm water. Images of an inundated settlement and destitute, distraught households made good copy for the local newspapers and put JKB on the official radar.[28] The UIT, the organization in charge of Jaipur's development and civic maintenance at the time, proposed to rehabilitate the entire settlement and move it to a safer but distant location at public expense. The UIT consequently conducted a survey, which documented around 3,000 households.

Following the announcement of the rehabilitation scheme in 1981, several families moved to the new location, but many remained in their huts on the original site. In the official version of the narrative, JKB is next mentioned in reference to a lawsuit filed by Jawahar Nagar residents against the state and RHB. The lawsuit challenged JKB's presence; its encroachment on the right-of-way of the proposed Eastern bypass; and the inconvenience caused by the incessant truck traffic on the forty-foot-wide road. Over the next decade and a half there were reports of several attempts by the authorities to forcibly remove JKB; street protests, some resulting in "stone pelting," a "baton charge," and "light skirmishes"; the legal passage of the case; and various court orders to stay the proceedings. However, during that period, the electrical utility provided connections and the municipal corporation installed hand pumps, or public stand posts, to supply drinking water. Finally, in 2004, India's Supreme Court settled the dispute by prohibiting truck traffic, which had plied the forty-foot-wide road for almost eighteen years, creating a nuisance for the residents. It directed JKB's regularization in line with the state's overall rehabilitation policy for informal settlements.[29] This time around the JMC conducted a fresh survey and recorded about 6,500 households.[30]

A parallel account, offered by RHB officials and Jawahar Nagar residents, illustrates how social networks and political patronage not only contributed to JKB's development but also worked against its popular depiction as a slum. During interviews, Jawahar Nagar residents frequently portray JKB residents as freeloaders and thieves, who, for example, use Jawahar Nagar's parks and steal electricity. Evidence to the contrary, such as the fact that many JKB kids play on the roadside and many JKB residents have legal electricity connections, are usually glossed over. In "othering" JKB residents, Jawahar Nagar residents tend to underscore that they are legal and law-abiding residents while JKB residents are not. As anthropologists frequently remind us, the classical phenomenon of "othering" is marked by a love–hate relationship and central to define self in comparison with the other.

Thus, the ire of Jawahar Nagar residents becomes especially pronounced when they describe JKB's residents as astute clients of rival politicians, who, in the words of a RHB official, "blatantly nurtured this nuisance for reaping electoral advantage." One frequently mentioned political contender, the minister of urban development and housing at the time of the flash floods, reportedly announced the rehabilitation scheme in official settings, then turned around and surreptitiously issued a famous verbal directive to officials, which several repeated: "Rehabilitate them on the original site only." The ostensible clarification, according to common wisdom among RHB officials and well-connected residents of Jawahar Nagar, not only explains why the rehabilitation drive failed in 1981 but also illuminates the reasons for the extension of utilities during the 1980s.

Jawahar Nagar residents' often candid disdain for JKB and its inhabitants swiftly gives way to reluctant confessions when quizzed about their maids, servants and vegetable vendors. For instance, the same person who called the JKB residents "thieves and freeloaders" said: "Our maid—she has been working for us close to fifteen years now—lives there and so does the person who irons our clothes. We often help them get health care through our acquaintances." Similarly, many residents of Jawahar Nagar mention using JKB's conveniences, such as repair shops and handymen, and helping JKB residents on a regular basis. When seen from this perspective, popular measures helped moderate the apparently conflictive aspects of local cultural particularities, such as the "othering" of informal settlements by the residents of planned neighborhoods.

However, the regularization of JKB's dwellings exemplifies the ultimate impact of popular plans. In line with John Turner's observation (1972), the process of regularization recognized the existence of the settlement and legitimized its ongoing development. Step-by-step utilitarian functions, such as the extension of water and electricity supply lines, and formalization, which gradually extended tenure rights to homeowners, comprised the act of regularization. It is important to note that resident intermediaries often mediated the set of material practices that operationalized the popular efforts. Thomas Hansen (2001) has suggested that the extension of democracy to many groups, secluded earlier, in urban India has given rise to multi-dimensional intermediaries, such as the part-time realtor and weekend political worker whose day job is facilitating bureaucratic dealings such as utility connections, ration cards and birth certificates. These men of local eminence frequently act as mediators between ordinary people and authorities, and work through networks of local patronage, providing key instrumentalities in Indian cities' vast informal areas such as JKB.

One such JKB character, Ram Ji Gurjar, exemplifies the ongoing social change in several dimensions. Simultaneously straddling several realms, Mr. Gurjar claims a "mastery" over key bureaucratic procedures, delivering direct and tangible benefits to his "clients." His main business is running a dairy, which operates from a sludgy barn adjacent to his two-storied, solidly built house in JKB. He supplies fresh milk twice daily to his longstanding clients on their doorsteps in Jawahar Nagar. He also rents out several shops built upon the right-of-way of the forty-foot-road that separates JKB and Jawahar Nagar. Most of these shops cater to the needs of JKB's residents, but some, such as the flourmill, also service Jawahar Nagar residents. He is also an active part-time *pramukh karya-karta*, or chief-worker, of a political party, which was in power both in the state and JMC during my study. Mr. Gurjar bragged of his ability to mobilize 200 votes.[31]

Mr. Gurjar embodies many contradictions that show up often as mutually exclusive social and moral claims in arguments about social order and planning protocols. He is part of a larger group of middle-class people that both supports and exploits the popular planning by the urban poor. Not surprisingly, JKB residents count on him for a number of reasons, including the following: he is seen as a fellow resident; he is perceived as well connected; he has the right set of tools, such as communication skills, to enable him to comprehend and use official idiom; and he has intimate knowledge of legal procedures and documentation regarding ownership of land and property transactions. Mr. Gurjar benefits from his intimate knowledge of JKB's municipal surveys and land records. His explanation of the situation in JKB is as good as, and sometimes even better than, the information handed out by municipal officials: some parts of JKB have been fully regularized following the 1981 survey, and consequently have a *Patta*, or legal title to land, while others have been partly regularized. Huts built on the partly regularized land have survey numbers, allotted following the municipal survey in 2004.[32] These survey numbers are used for everyday purposes, such as postal addresses, and are also admissible as official records in courts of law, a fact Mr. Gurjar is keenly aware of. In his own words: "Possession (*Kabja*) and [supporting] official documents (*Kagaz*) eventually lead to property title (*Patta*)."

This knowledge is a crucial prerequisite for Mr. Gurjar's real-estate business, because extralegal huts cannot be bought or sold through formal channels, such as a registered sale deed. Therefore, Mr. Gurjar employs alternate instrumentalities, such as the power of attorney, in which the owner entrusts legal rights to the buyer for living in, maintaining and even further selling the property. He also employs the modality of a gift deed, through which the owner gives the property in perpetuity to the buyer, and an irrevocable will, in which the owner declares the buyer to be the property's legal heir. These instruments, though not originally intended for transferring immovable property, meet the barest obligatory requirements of law and are easily prepared through Mr. Gurjar's acquaintances who are deed writers, stamp paper vendors and public notaries.[33] He correctly points out that Jawahar Nagar residents have employed similar approaches for selling, buying and amalgamating adjoining lots, and for demolishing readymade dwellings and building bigger houses—all of which are explicitly prohibited, in order to prevent speculation in public-sector housing. Mr. Gurjar justifies his activities by drawing a parallel with extra-legal acts in the planned settlements, described in Chapter 4, where lot-level open setbacks have been reduced or even disappeared, floors beyond legally permissible height have been added and residential houses have been converted into shops and offices.

Mr. Gurjar's contributions to the development of JKB are not limited to the real-estate sector, as he played an active role in organizing street protests against the Eastern bypass. The ending of relentless truck traffic not only made life easier for JKB's residents but also triggered an increase in the settlement's property values. Mr. Gurjar believes that his rented shops fronting the road are now worth a hundred thousand dollars and rival the real estate on the other side of the road. "How much difference could be in the price on this or the other side of the same road?" he said. "Now the properties on our side, too, are being built solidly." This is especially true for properties fronting the road, which have begun to blur the distinction between JKB and Jawahar Nagar. Despite the fact that residents on the eastern edge of Jawahar Nagar lament the diminishing of their property values, they resignedly agree with the changes in the JKB houses fronting the road:

> You know that homeowners of Jawahar Nagar opposite JKB have had a horrid time. First, the *Katchi Basti* made their lives hell, and on the top of it their property values did not appreciate much. Ironically, my milkman

tells me that property values have increased in JKB … [Smirking] … Maybe in a few years, those JKB houses might even become better than Jawahar Nagar houses. You know, parts of it are quite good now … they already have a number of schools and even a college in the JKB.[34]

Although JKB's solidly built houses are still a work in progress, with many fronting the separating road (see Figure 4.5 on page 78), they are emblematic of deeper, long-term implications of popular efforts. These changes show how the formality of Jawahar Nagar has begun to gnaw at the edges of JKB, if formality means what a JKB resident described as a "cemented" house, with legal documents and utility connections, facing houses of almost similar appearance on the other side of the road. Buoyed by newfound confidence and self-assurance, many JKB residents now perceive their locality as a part of upscale Jawahar Nagar and not simply as a *Katchi Basti*. This is especially true of the younger generation. Moreover, ongoing welfare programs support the development of place-based community—including the provision of physical amenities, such as paved pathways and streetlights, and augmentation of social infrastructure, such as community health services and midday meals in the elementary schools.[35]

In this respect, one fact about the nature of popular plans becomes clear: despite many unwarranted outcomes, such as the building of settlements on floodplains and the public right-of-way, politician-led popular plans have done a rather fair job of involving urban populations.[36] Such ability should not be underestimated in a democracy. It is difficult enough to involve people even after delivering on the promise of crucial public goods such as secure and well-designed neighborhoods. To do so given the scale and complexity of urban India is remarkable. Although the majority of JKB's residents remain troubled by deeply structural inequalities, the path to a better settlement is clear to many. Like their counterparts elsewhere, they want a secure, healthy and pleasing environment. Sick of development rhetoric, they quietly exercise electoral rights and implicitly demonstrate purposeful future-oriented thinking by making their own spatial plans. Toward this end, popular plans provide crucial help. They are, therefore, a fitting conclusion to the tale of the neighborhood unit's travels and travails in independent India. Popular plans sought to reconcile the efforts of diverse planning actors and, in doing so, helped create a unique form of urbanism that is justly deserved by the deepening of popular democracy across a sharply unequal part of the world.

Thinking with Spatial Plans

What does this story mean for planners? Practitioners generally ignore the notion that many actors make plans, presumably because they make a profession out of the activity. Those working in the global south tend to agree with local authorities, which typically perceive unanticipated spatial developments as unauthorized and planning largely as an expert-driven, rational technique. Not surprisingly, many conflate the scope and nature of spatial plans with the issues of governance and administration, paying little attention to the practical priorities and cultural preferences of urban actors. Lacking sensitivity to local histories, many professionals are also not certain about the relevance of different kinds of planning efforts. This is important because not all plans are documented, much less understood, and they become comprehensible only when examined minutely and tracked over time.

As I have shown, Indian city planning in the second half of the twentieth century was not exclusively a state-sponsored enterprise, and the planning efforts of non-state actors were not aimless subversions. Many of these acts were small but added up to significant change at the neighborhood and city scales, where they affected much more than individual needs and values. When they are examined carefully, it is clear that spontaneous spatial plans made among many actors generated meaningful community improvements as they transformed and enriched the formal urban plans. The development of Jaipur's post-independence quarters provides support for the view that the gap between informal and formal systems of social order is more of a continuum, and that plan-making practices, depending upon the context, may prove to be a resource or an impediment across the continuum. Indeed, once practitioners begin to appreciate the worth of these spatial forms of democratic expression, they have sufficient ingredients at hand to design rich, lively and diverse places.

On the other hand, scholars of colonial, postcolonial and neoliberal conceptions of planning usually tell the story of city planning and development by referring to two sides of the same coin: how the indigenous elite import and impose planning ideas from the West and the manner in which excluded actors and the urban poor contest and sabotage their efforts through informal means.[37] By tracking the long-term trajectory of a global planning idea in a local context, I have shown how the concept of planned neighborhoods gradually changed the way Indian actors perceived city living, even as they simultaneously transformed the prototypical model in significant ways. At a certain level, it did not really matter where the idea originated but what the people did with it.

In this respect, paying attention to people's plans and actions is important, because we are beginning to witness a growing number of concepts such as Smart Growth and New Urbanism being employed in an increasingly interconnected world. For future urban planners, the message is clear: despite major advancements in many aspects of human life, numerous places have failed to anticipate and prepare for social inequalities, environmental externalities and physical hardships. Perceptive observers of the field, such as Patsy Healey (2010), have highlighted the need for a better kind of planning in the twenty-first century. Planners can and should tap into the energy and enthusiasm of an increasingly urbanized population seeking civic amenities, security and propriety in different parts of the world.

Working with Spatial Plans

The trend to regularize extra-legal developments on an ex post facto basis is increasingly popular across urban India. Implicitly acknowledging the diversity of spatial plans at work, legalization of the built reality also marks the culmination of the Nehruvian project of modernist urban transformation. Knowledgeable players and government insiders confide, even if only privately, that urban India's ubiquitous features, such as informal settlements and mixed land use, are impossible to wish away in the foreseeable future. Thanks to India's vigilante civil society, large-scale demolitions and slum clearances are increasingly difficult to execute.

However, the planned neighborhood ideal, just like many other Western cultural forms—such as the English language, representative democracy and the sport of cricket—continues to have a powerful influence in India. Well-to-do households have begun to patronize privately organized gated developments promising security, well-maintained parks and open spaces, utilities and civic amenities—key concerns of the neighborhood unit concept. Others want these goods as well, and rightly so.

So, what can the planners and officials do? Perhaps a judicious beginning would be to legitimize and support emergent public-led initiatives such as the development and upkeep of parks and open spaces in built-up areas. The process should rightly start with marginalized localities. While the residents of public-sector neighborhoods such as Jawahar Nagar can access many resources, including government support, informal and erstwhile rural settlements incorporated into cities desperately need more open spaces and play areas. By giving up its self-imposed solitary burden and sharing civic responsibility with the public, the state can pave the way for thinking through the next steps, such as the careful replanning of existing urban areas, the identification of appropriate planning parameters and the devising of meaningful ways to involve residents and users in the designing of neighborhoods.

While planning actors deliberate upon their future course of action, it might help to take a longer view. For example, it is increasingly clear that many post-independence city-extensions have begun to share characteristics—such as diversity of land use, tightly woven spatial fabric and relatively higher density than the originally planned urban form—with the historical quarters of Indian cities. From this perspective, places such as Jaipur offer established templates for city planning and development. As city planning moves away from the Nehruvian approach, while local people rediscover their rich urban heritage (Vidyarthi 2014), perhaps it is feasible to design a few experimental neighborhoods employing features such as courtyard-based buildings, parameter blocks with zero setbacks and commercial activity along main thoroughfares. Studies of user response and transformations over time can then be used to reimagine neighborhood design and planning features.

However, perhaps the biggest challenge facing Indian planners and urban officials involves land planning and development. As discussed, the pre-independence bureaucracy was organized to squeeze the indigenous population and the thin middle class under colonialism had consisted of those who worked for or contracted with the State. Urban planning came into the post-independence picture as part of the reforms that Nehru and others hoped would foster a new middle class and address more efficiently the demands of urbanization. The master plans, therefore, adopted conceptions of place that completely displaced the colonial hierarchy linking land revenue and land use. Today, enhanced economic activity fuels the rise of emergent economic and social groups, comprising a spectrum of entirely new occupations ranging from office-park-based high-tech workers to informal-settlement-based trash recyclers, for whom the old state fails to work. So the bureaucracy resists, as the old elite recognize the ascendancy of these new groups, often using corruption rather than reform to assure their position. This is inefficient and expensive. This situation not only calls for a rethinking of the land ownership and organization systems but also behooves us to make better plans.

As I have shown throughout this book, plan-making works in different ways. In particular, plan-making for places can transform how the State does its work. The complex adaptation supported and sustained by the spatial plans of diverse urban actors does not deny the inequalities that persist, but shows how plans work to help people create places that articulate new forms of civic community combining old and new; and places that contribute to improved political and administrative practices, even as these coexist with the legacies of corruption and repression.

Notes

1   Quoted in Fishman, *Bourgeois Utopias*, 3. For Daly's interpretation of Baron Haussmann's renovation of Paris that cast a formative influence on urban planning, see Papayanis, "César Daly, Paris and the Emergence of Modern Urban Planning."

2   The changing nature and scope of India's political democracy, given crucial shifts in other aspects of life, has attracted wide scholarly interest. See, for example, Corbridge and Harriss, *Reinventing India*; Briggs, *Democracy as Problem Solving*; and Appadurai, "Deep Democracy."

3   The spatial proximity of different social and economic groups is a conspicuous, but not extensively documented, feature of urban India's political landscape. For a notable exception, see the following study, which describes the phenomenon among various dimensions of poverty in Delhi: Baud, Sridharan, and Pfeffer, "Mapping Urban Poverty for Local Governance in an Indian Mega City."

4   Here it is important to note that, due to constitutional safeguards, there have been few or no reports in India of gerrymandering—that is, the manipulation of constituency boundaries to create partisan advantaged districts. For a quick overview, see Singh, "A Century of Constituency Delimitation in India."

5   Scholars have noted the positive effect of local political competition on the provision of infrastructure across different sectors and regions. See, for instance, Crost and Kambhampati, "Political Market Characteristics and the Provision of Educational Infrastructure in North India."

6 Frankel, *India's Political Economy 1947–2004*.
7 Pune-based economists V. N. Dandekar and Nilakantha Rath authored the report, titled *Poverty in India*. It was widely disseminated at the beginning of 1971, after its publication in the *Economic and Political Weekly*.
8 Frankel, *India's Political Economy 1947–2004*.
9 India suffered serious political turbulence during the late 1970s. This resulted in two national and state elections within three years and the declaration of a national emergency, which had serious implications for public life and electoral politics. See Dhar, *Indira Gandhi, the "Emergency," and Indian Democracy*. Also see Tarlo, *Unsettling Memories*.
10 Subramanian, "Populism in India."
11 See, for instance, Verma, *Slumming India*.
12 Not surprisingly, some of the earliest studies came from newly planned cities. See Prakash, *New Towns in India*; and Grenell, "Planning for Invisible People."
13 See Jaipur's second and third master plans, adopted in 1998 and 2011 respectively, which acknowledge the massive subversion of the preceding plans.
14 It is important to note that, without exception, interviewed planners and officials blamed career politicians for the ills of urban India.
15 Interview on May 3, 2006.
16 Interview with two retired chief town planners on February 16, 2006, and March 7, 2007.
17 John Harriss describes the change in the following words:

> And so it has turned out, anthropologists are well equipped to study the "everyday state," and our collective gaze shows how banal, mundane and routinized—how unexotic—so much of the state now is in contemporary India. The idea of the state and the myth of its sublime qualities are still extant, as we have seen, but the everyday structures and institutions of the nation-state, in most political and administrative contexts, are now very prosaically at the center of modern India's imagination.
>
> Harriss, *Power Matters*, 210.

18 It is important to note that the regularization of various types of unauthorized urban settlements is generally an ongoing phenomenon in many parts of India. For a detailed description of the official procedure concerning the rehabilitation of informal settlements in other cities, see Baken-Jan, *Plotting, Squatting, Public Purpose and Politics*.
19 See Risbud, *Government Policies and Illegal Land Supply by Housing Cooperatives, Jaipur*.
20 Interview with a retired chief town planner on February 16, 2006.
21 Interview on May 3, 2006.
22 Gupta, *Land Assembly in the Indian Metropolis*.
23 Interview with N. Rajbanshi, February 14, 2006. Also see the minutes of the Building Plan Committee's 23rd meeting, held on April 12, 1984.
24 Neelima Risbud, a professor at the School of Planning and Architecture, New Delhi, described the political popularity and speed of regularization at Jaipur in the following words:

> It ought to be admitted that the Government has never acted in a positive manner but always regularized unauthorized sales, conversions, subdivisions, and construction. There are more approvals than rejections. This has created a feeling that all illegal development will be regularized one day ... The planning staff of the JDA is so preoccupied with the preparation of sector plans for accommodating regularized schemes of cooperative societies that it is left with very little time to devote to the planning of new schemes.
>
> Risbud, *Government Policies and Illegal Land Supply by Housing Cooperatives, Jaipur*, 19.

25 Gupta, *Land Assembly in the Indian Metropolis*.

26 These encroachments have continued to grow over time, while the authorities and courts take intermittent action. See, for instance, *The Times of India*, "Finally nine-story structure razed."

27 Difficulties associated with the regularization of informal settlements in different parts of the world are well documented. See, for instance, Durand-Lasserve and Royston, *Holding Their Ground*.

28 Interview with a retired chief town planner on May 3, 2006.

29 See the official *Katchi Basti Niyaman Niti* 2005, or Informal Settlements' Regularization Policy. Accessed at www.rajasthan.gov.in/rajgovresources/actnpolicies/Kachhibasti_Niti.pdf, viewed on May 6, 2010.

30 Following the court decision in 2004, parts of JKB were surveyed, along with 81 other informal settlements housing around 120,000 people. According to the official census conducted in 2001, in total, Jaipur comprises 174 identified *Katchi Bastis* (including the 82 surveyed) with a population of around 370,000 people (approximately 15 percent of the city's total population). (Data compiled by the author from the lists of *Katchi Bastis* and surveyed households up to 2004 in JMC and JDA's jurisdiction.)

31 Several of these voters belong to Gurjar's own caste, which the authorities classify as an "other backward class," placing him somewhere in the middle of the pecking order. His standing and status are derived from both personal relations—including the network of people from his native place in a nearby rural region, who, like him, have migrated to the city—and the professional contacts that he has made in Jaipur. For theoretical and analytical perspectives on the phenomenon, see Jeffery, "A Fist is Stronger than Five Fingers: Caste and Dominance in Rural North India"; Jaffrelot, "The Rise of the Other Backward Classes in the Hindi Belt"; and Krishna, "What Is Happening to Caste?"

32 Not all residents have taken advantage of the amnesty scheme and obtained land titles, though. Apparently, some residents are too poor to pay the regularization charges, and some feel intimidated dealing with the authorities. Fatima Wajahat has documented the phenomenon in lucid detail. See Wajahat, "Perceptions of Tenure Security in a Squatter Settlement in Lahore, Pakistan."

33 See Hull, *Government of Paper*.

34 Interview with a Jawahar Nagar resident, June 15, 2006.

35 In addition, the government of Rajasthan, like that of many other states, routinely announces blanket regularization of all types of unauthorized settlements, barring those on floodplains and ecological land uses, developed before the cutoff date. For informal settlements and private subdivisions, the cutoff date is presently August 2009 and June 1999 respectively. See *Rajasthan Patrika*, "Batengi Patton ki Rewadyian—Cabinet ka mahtvyapurna faisla [State cabinet announces the freebie of land titles]."

36 The beneficiaries of populist plans include a range of social groups, such as small traders that run mom-and-pop stores and other small business owners in residential areas. See Mehra, "Protesting Publics in Indian Cities."

37 There are, of course, a few notable exceptions. See, for instance, Glover, *Making Lahore Modern*.

BIBLIOGRAPHY

Abu-Lughod, J. 1987. *Rabat: Urban Apartheid in Morocco*. Princeton: Princeton University Press.

Al Sayyad, Nezar. 2001. *Hybrid Urbanism*. New York: Praeger Publications.

Alcock, A.E.S. 1955. "A New Town in the Gold Coast." *Town and Country Planning,* **23**, 52–61.

Aldhous, W., S. Groak, B. Mumtaz and M. Safir. (Eds). 1983. "Otto Koenigsberger." *Festschrift, Habitat International,* **7** (5/6), 337–346. Oxford: Pergamon Press.

Anand, Mulk Raj. 1977. "An Epistle Dedicatory to the Master-builder Sawai Jai Singh." *Marg,* **30** (4), 9–24.

Anderson, Benedict. 1991. *Imagined Communities: Reflections on the Origins and Spread of Nationalism*. New York: Verso.

Anderton, Frances. 1989. "Learning from Jaipur." *Journal of Architectural Education,* **42** (4), 15–24.

Ansari, Jamal H. 1977. "Evolution of Town Planning Practice and System of Urban Government in India." *Urban and Rural Planning Thought,* **XX** (1), 9–23.

Appadurai, Arjun. 1996. *Modernity at Large: Cultural Dimensions of Globalization*. Minneapolis: University of Minnesota Press.

——2002. "Deep Democracy. Urban Governmentality and the Horizon of Politics." *Environment and Urbanisation,* **13** (2), 23–43.

Archer, John. 1996. "Colonial Suburbs in South Asia, 1700–1850, and the Spaces of Modernity." In *Visions of Suburbia*. Edited by Roger Silverstone. New York: Routledge.

Arnold, David. 2000. "Gramsci and Peasant Subalternity in India." In *Mapping Subaltern Studies and the Postcolonial*. Edited by Vinayak Chaturvedi. London: Verso.

Arnold, E. 1886. *India Revisited*. London: Ballantyne Press.

Arora, Ramesh K., Rakesh Hooja and Shashi Mathur. 1977. *Jaipur: Profile of a Changing City*. Jaipur: Indian Institute of Public Administration.

Ashcroft, Bill, Gareth Griffiths and Helen Tiffin. 1998. *Post-Colonial Studies: The Key Concepts*. New York: Routledge.

Axinn, William G., Jennifer S. Barber and Ghimire Dirgha J. 1997. "The Neighborhood History Calendar: A Data Collection Method Designed for Dynamic Multilevel Modeling." *Sociological Methodology,* **27**, 355–392.

Babb, Lawrence A. 2014. *Emerald City: The Birth and Evolution of an Indian Gemstone Industry*. Albany: The State University of New York Press.

Baden-Powell, B.H. 1892. *The Land Systems of British India*. 3 vols. Oxford: Clarendon Press.

——1895. "The Permanent Settlement of Bengal." *The English Historical Review*, **10** (38), 276–292.

Baken-Jan, R. 2003. *Plotting, Squatting, Public Purpose and Politics: Land Market Development, Low Income Housing and Public Intervention in India*. Surrey: Ashgate.

Banerjee, Tridib. 1993. "Transnational Urbanism Reconsidered: Post-colonial Development of Calcutta and Shanghai." In *Urban Anthropology in China*. Edited by G. Guldin and A. Southall. Leiden: E.J. Brill.

——2005. "Understanding Planning Cultures: The Kolkata Paradox." In *Comparative Planning Cultures*. Edited by Bishwapriya Sanyal. New York: Routledge.

——2009. "US Planning Expeditions to Postcolonial India: From Ideology to Innovation in Technical Assistance." *Journal of American Planning Association*, **75** (2), 193–208.

——and William Baer. 1984. *Beyond the Neighborhood Unit*. New York: Plenum Press.

Bansal, A.K. 1964. *The Aspect of Urban Design for a State Capital in India*. Unpublished Diploma Course in Town and Country Planning thesis, New Delhi: School of Planning and Architecture.

Bapat, M. 1983. "Hutments and City Planning." *Economic and Political Weekly*, **18** (11), 399–406.

Bardhan, P. 1984. *The Political Economy of Development in India*. New Delhi: Oxford University Press.

Baud, I., N. Sridharan and K. Pfeffer. 2008. "Mapping Urban Poverty for Local Governance in an Indian Mega City." *Urban Studies*, **45** (7), 1385–1412.

Bauer, Catherine. 1934. *Modern Housing*. Boston: Houghton Mifflin.

Bauman, Zygmunt. 1991. *Modernity and Ambivalence*. Oxford: Polity Press.

Baviskar, Amita. 2003. "Between Violence and Desire: Space, Power, and Identity in the Making of Metropolitan Delhi." *International Social Science Journal*, **55** (175), 89–98.

Bayly, C.A. 1988. *Rulers, Townsmen, and Bazaars: North Indian Society in the Age of British Expansion 1770–1870*. Cambridge: Cambridge University Press.

——1996. *Empire and Information: Intelligence Gathering and Social Communication in India 1780–1870*. Cambridge: Cambridge University Press.

——2011. *Recovering Liberties: Indian Thought in the Age of Liberalism and Empire*. Cambridge: Cambridge University Press.

Benjamin, S. 2008. "Occupancy Urbanism: Radicalizing Politics and Economy beyond Policy and Programs." *International Journal of Urban and Regional Research*, **32** (3), 719–729.

Beverley, Eric Lewis. 2011. "Colonial Urbanism and South Asian Cities." *Social History*, **36** (4), 482–497.

Bhabha, Homi K. 1994. *The Location of Culture*. New York: Routledge.

Bhatia, Gautam. 2001. "Building an Ugly India." *Seminar*. Available at www.india-seminar.com/2001/501/501%20gautam%20bhatia.htm, accessed on April 15, 2004.

Bhise, S.N. 2004. *Decolonizing the Commons*. New Delhi: National Foundation for India.

Bijlani, H.U. 1988. "Urban Social Facilities." In *South Asian Urban Experience*. Edited by R.C. Sharma. New Delhi: Criterion Publications, 57–74.

Birch, E.L. 1980. "Radburn and the American Planning Movement: The Persistence of an Idea." *Journal of the American Planning Association*, **46** (4), 424–439.

Bowles, Chester. 1971. *Promises to Keep: My Years in Public Life*. New York: Harper and Row.

Boyer, Christine M. 1983. *Dreaming the Rational City*. Cambridge: The MIT Press.

Brara, R. 2006. *Shifting Landscapes: The Making and Remaking of Village Commons in India*. New Delhi: Oxford University Press.

Breese, Gerald. 1974. *Urban and Regional Planning for the Delhi-New Delhi Area: Capital for Conquerors and Country*. Princeton: Princeton University Press.

Briggs, Xavier de Souza. 2008. *Democracy as Problem Solving: Civic Capacity in Communities Across the Globe*. Cambridge: The MIT Press.

Brooks, Michael. 2002. *Planning Theory for Practitioners*. Chicago: Planners Press.

Brugemann, Robert. 2005. *Sprawl: A Compact History*. Chicago: University of Chicago Press.

Buch, Mahesh N. 1987. *Planning the Indian City*. New Delhi: Vikas Publishing House Pvt. Ltd.

——1991. *Of Man and His Settlements*. New Delhi: Sanchar Publishing House.

Burra, N. 1998. "Exploitation of Children in Jaipur Gem Industry: Structure of Industry." *Economic and Political Weekly*, **23** (3), 75–79.

Cahnman, Werner J. (Ed.). 1973. *Ferdinand Tonnies: A New Evaluation*. Leiden: E.J. Brill.

Caine, W.S. 1891. *Picturesque India*. London: George Routledge and Sons Ltd.

Calthorpe, Peter and William Fulton. 2001. *The Regional City: Planning for the End of Sprawl*. Washington D.C: Island Press.

Campbell, Scott and Susan Fainstein (Eds). 2003. *Readings in Planning Theory*. Cambridge: Blackwell.

Chakrabarti, Vibhuti. 1998. *Indian Architectural Theory: Contemporary Usage of Vastu Vidya*. Surrey: Curzon Press.

Chakrabarty, Dipesh. 1989. *Rethinking Working-Class History: Bengal 1890–1940*. Princeton: Princeton University Press.

——1992. "Postcoloniality and the Artifice of History: Who Speaks for 'Indian' Pasts?" *Representations*, **37**, 1–26.

——2002. *Habitations of Modernity: Essays in the Wake of Subaltern Studies*. Chicago: University of Chicago Press.

Chase, John, Margaret Crawford and John Kaliski. 1999. *Everyday Urbanism*. New York: Monacelli Press.

Chatterjee, Partha. 1993. *The Nation and its Fragments: Colonial and Postcolonial Histories*. Princeton: Princeton University Press.

——2004. *The Politics of the Governed: Reflection on Popular Politics in Most of the World*. New York: Columbia University Press.

Chaturvedi, Vinayak. 2000. *Mapping Subaltern Studies and the Postcolonial*. London: Verso.

Chicago Plan Commission. 1943. *Building New Neighborhoods: Subdivision Design and Standards*. Chicago: The Plan Commission.

Chief Town Planner and Architectural Advisor. 1976. *Master Plan for Jaipur*. Jaipur: Government Press.

Chopra, Preeti. 2011. *A Joint Enterprise: Indian Elites and the Making of British Bombay*. Minneapolis: University of Minnesota Press.

Clinard, Marshall and B. Chatterjee. 1962. "Urban Community Development." In *India's Urban Future*. Edited by K. Davis and R. Turner. Berkeley: University of California Press.

Cohn, Bernard. 1996. *Colonialism and its Forms of Knowledge*. Princeton: Princeton University Press.

——2004. *The Bernard Cohn Omnibus*. New York: Oxford University Press.

Cooley, Charles. 1909. *Social Organization: A Study of the Larger Mind*. New York: Charles Scribner's Sons.

Corbridge, Stuart and J. Harriss. 2000. *Reinventing India: Liberalization, Hindu Nationalism and Popular Democracy*. Cambridge: Polity.

Crewe, Q. 1985. *The Last Maharaja: Biography of Sawai Man Singhji II, Maharaja of Jaipur*. London: Michael Joseph Ltd.

Crost, B. and Uma Kambhampati. 2010. "Political Market Characteristics and the Provision of Educational Infrastructure in North India." *World Development*, **38** (2), 195–204.

Dahir, James. 1947. *The Neighborhood Unit Plan: Its Spread and Acceptance: A Selected Bibliography with Interpretive Comments*. New York: Russell Sage Foundation.

Dainik Bhaskar. 2013. "Zameen kisi ki bhi ho: Pujari ki Nazar padte hi Mandir tayyar" [Does not matter who owns the land: Priests are quick to build temples], Jaipur edition, October 17.

Dalton, Linda C. 1986. "Why the Rational Paradigm Persists—The Resistance of Professional Education and Practice to Alternative Forms of Planning." *Journal of Planning Education and Research*, **5** (3), 147–153.

Davar, Satish. 1977. "A Filigree City Spun out of Nothingness." *Marg*, **30** (4), 35–58.

De Certeau, Michel. 1984. *The Practice of Everyday Life*. Berkeley: University of California Press.

Delhi Development Authority (DDA). 1962. *Master Plan for Delhi*. Delhi: Delhi Development Authority.

Dhar, P.N. 2001. *Indira Gandhi, the "Emergency," and Indian Democracy*. New York: Oxford University Press.

Dick, H.W and H.J. Rimmer. 1998. "Beyond the Third World City: The New Urban Geography of South-east Asia." *Urban Studies*, **35** (12), 2303–2321.

DNA (Daily News and Analysis) 2011. "Government wants to Regularize PR Nagar: Cabinet confirms plan to de-acquire land in Controversial Scheme," Jaipur edition, September 30.

Durand-Lasserve, Alain and Lauren Royston. 2002. *Holding Their Ground: Secure Land Tenure for the Urban Poor in Developing Countries*. New York: Routledge.

Dutt, Ashok K. 1993. "Cities of South Asia." In *Cities of the World—World Regional Urban Development*. Edited by Stanley D. Brunn and Jack F. William. New York: HarperCollins.

Echeverri-Gent, John. 1993. *The State and the Poor: Public Policy and Political Development in India and the United States*. Berkeley: University of California Press.

Evenson, Norma. 1989. *The Indian Metropolis: A View Toward The West*. New Haven: Yale University Press.

Fahim, M. 2009. *Local Government in India Still Carries Characteristics of its Colonial Heritage*. Available at www.citymayors.com/government/india_government.html, accessed May 24, 2009.

Faludi, A. 1973. *Planning Theory*. Oxford: Pergamon Press.

Federal Housing Administration (FHA). 1936. *Planning Neighborhoods for Small Houses*. Technical Bulletin 1 (July), Washington DC: FHA.

——1947. *Neighborhoods Built for Rental Housing*. Washington DC: U.S. Government Printing Office.

Ferguson, James. 1994. *The Anti Politics Machine: "Development," Depoliticization, and Bureaucratic Power in Lesotho*. Minnesota: University of Minnesota Press.

Fernandes, L. 2006. *India's New Middle Class: Democratic Politics in an Era of Economic Reform*. Minneapolis: University of Minnesota Press.

Fisher, Robert and Peter Romanofsky (Eds). 1981. *Community Organizations for Urban Social Change*. Westport: Greenwood Press.

Fishman, Robert. 1982. *Urban Utopias in the Twentieth Century: Ebenezer Howard, Frank Lloyd Wright, Le Corbusier*. Cambridge: The MIT Press.

——1987. *Bourgeois Utopias: The Rise and Fall of Suburbia*. New York: Basic Books.

——(Ed.) 2000. *The American Planning Tradition: Culture and Policy*. Washington D.C.: Woodrow Wilson Centre Press.

Fludernik, Monika (Ed.). 1998. *Hybridity and Postcolonialism*. Warsaw: Stauffenburg Verlag.

Flusty, Steven. 2004. *De-Coca-Colonization: Making the Globe from the Inside Out*. New York: Routledge.

Forgacs, David (Ed.). 1988. *A Gramsci Reader: Selected Writings, 1916–1935*. London: Lawrence and Wishart.

Forsyth, Ann. 2005. *Reforming Suburbia: The Planned Communities of Irvine, Columbia, and The Woodlands*. Berkeley: University of California Press.

Foucault, Michel. 1972. *Archeology of Knowledge*. New York: Pantheon Books.

——1991. "Governmentality." In *The Foucault Effect: Studies in Governmentality*. Edited by Graham Burchell, Collin Gordon and Peter Miller. London: Harvester Wheatsheaf.

Frankel, Francine R. 2009. *India's Political Economy 1947–2004*. Second edition, New Delhi: Oxford University Press.

Friedman, Avi. 2002. *Planning the new Suburbia: Flexibility by Design*. Vancouver: UBC Press.

Friedmann, John. 1987. *Planning in the Public Domain*. Princeton: Princeton University Press.

——2003. "Why do Planning Theory?" *Planning Theory,* **2** (1), 7–10.

Gans, Herbert J. 1968. *People and Plans*. New York: Basic Books.

Garde, Ajay M. 2008. "Innovations in Urban Design and Urban Form: The Making of Paradigms and its Implications for Public Policy." *Journal of Planning Education and Research,* **28** (1), 61–72.

Gayatri Devi. 1996. *A Princess Remembers: The Memoirs of the Maharani of Jaipur*. Delhi: Rupa and Co.

Geddes, Patrick. 1919. *Barra Bazaar Improvement – A Report to the Corporation of Calcutta*. Calcutta: Corporation Press.

Gillette, Howard, Jr. 1983. "The Evolution of Neighborhood Planning: From the Progressive Era to the 1949 Housing Act." *Journal of Urban History,* **9** (4), 421–444.

Gilmour, David. 2007. *The Ruling Caste: Imperial Lives in the Victorian Raj*. New York: Farrar Straus Giroux.

Glover, William. 2008. *Making Lahore Modern: Constructing and Imagining a Colonial City*. Minneapolis: University of Minnesota Press.

——2012. "The Troubled Passage from 'Village Communities' to Planned New Town Developments in Mid-twentieth-century South Asia." *Urban History,* **39** (1), 108–127.

——2013. "A Place of One's Own." *Tanqeed*. Available at www.tanqeed.org/2013/08/a-place-of-ones-own/#sthash.UP00pyDR.dpbs, accessed on November 15, 2013.

Gold, A.G. and B.R. Gujar 2002. *In the Time of Trees and Sorrows: Nature, Power, and Memory in Rajasthan*. Durham: Duke University Press.

Goodfriend, Douglas E. 1979. "Nagar Yoga: The Culturally Informed Town Planning of Patrick Geddes in India 1914–1924." *Human Organization,* **38** (4), 343–355.

Goswami, Manu. 2004. *Producing India: From Colonial Economy to National Space*. Chicago: University of Chicago Press.

Government of India. 1963. *Report of the Committee on Urban Land Policy*. Delhi: Ministry of Health.

Gowda, Thope C. 1962. *Planning Proposal for Mangalore*. Unpublished Diploma Course in Town and Country Planning thesis, New Delhi: School of Planning and Architecture.

Grenell, Peter. 1972. "Planning for Invisible People: Some Consequences of Bureaucratic Values and Practices." In *Freedom to Build*. Edited by John Turner and Robert Fichter. New York: Macmillan, 95–121.

Guha, Ranajit. 1982. *Subaltern Studies: Writings on South Asian History and Society*. London: Oxford University Press.

——and Gayatri Chakravorty Spivak (Eds.). 1988. *Selected Subaltern Studies*. New York: Oxford University Press.

Gupta, Akhil. 1995. "Blurred Boundaries: The Discourse of Corruption, the Culture of Politics, and the Imagined State." *American Ethnologist,* **22** (2), 375–402.

Gupta, R.C. 1992. *Land Assembly in the Indian Metropolis*. New Delhi: Uppal Publishing House.

Gusfield, Joseph. 1965. "Political Community and Group Interests in Modern India." *Pacific Affairs,* **38** (2), 123–141.

Hansen, Thomas Blom. 2001. *Wages of Violence: Naming and Identity in Postcolonial Bombay*. Princeton: Princeton University Press.

Harris, R. 2008. "Development and Hybridity Made Concrete in Colonies." *Environment and Planning A,* **40**, 15–36.

Harriss, John. 2006. *Power Matters: Essays on Institutions, Politics and Society in India*. New Delhi: Oxford University Press.

Harriss-White, B. 2002. *India Working: Essays on Society and Economy*. Cambridge: Cambridge University Press.

Hardgrove, Anna. 2002. "Merchant Houses as Spectacle of Modernity in Rajasthan and Tamil Nadu." *Contributions to Indian Sociology*, **36** (1), 323–363.

Harvey, David. 1985. *The Urbanization of Capital: Studies in the History and Theory of Capitalist Urbanization*. Baltimore: John Hopkins University Press.

Havell, E.B. 1913. *Indian Architecture*. London: John Murray.

Haynes, Douglas E. 1991. *Rhetoric and Ritual in Colonial India: The Shaping of a Public Culture in Surat City 1852–1928*. Berkeley: University of California Press.

——and Gyan Prakash (Eds). 1991. *Contesting Power: Resistance and Everyday Social Relations in South Asia*. Berkeley: University of California Press.

Healey, Patsy. 1997. *Collaborative Planning. Shaping Places in Fragmented Societies*. London: Macmillan.

——2010. *Making Better Places: The Planning Project in the Twenty-First Century*. London: Palgrave Macmillan.

Health Survey and Development (Bhore) Committee. 1946. *Final Report*. Volumes 1–4. Delhi: Publications Division, Government of India.

Henderson, C. and M. Weisgrau (Eds) 2007. *Raj Rhapsodies: Tourism, Heritage and the Seduction of History*. Hampshire: Ashgate.

Henn, Alexandar. 2008. "Crossroads of Religions: Shrines, Mobility and Urban Space in Goa." *International Journal of Urban and Regional Research*, **32** (3), 658–670.

Hicks, D. T. 1967 "Rebuilt Agadir." *Architectural Review*, **848**, 293–300.

Hirschman, Albert. 1967. *Development Projects Observed*. Washington D.C.: The Brookings Institution.

Hobsbawm, E.J. 1987. *The Age of Empires, 1875–1914*. New York: Pantheon Books.

Hoch, C. 2007. "Making Plans: Representation and Intention." *Planning Theory*, **6**, 15–35.

Holquist, Michael and Katerina Clark. 1984. *Michael Bahktin*. Cambridge: Harvard University Press.

Holway, J., D. Elliott and A. Trentadue. 2014. "Combating Zombie Subdivisions: How Three Communities Redressed Excess Development Entitlements." *Land Lines*, **1**, 4–13.

Home, Robert. 1997. *Of Planting and Planning: The Making of British Colonial Cities*. London: Spon.

——2006. "Scientific Survey and Land Settlement in British Colonialism, with Particular Reference to Land Tenure Reform in the Middle East." *Planning Perspective*, **21** (1), 1–22.

Hosagrahar, Jyoti. 2001. "Mansions to Margins: Modernity and the Domestic Landscapes of Historic Delhi." *The Journal of the Society of Architectural Historians*, **60** (1), 26–45.

——2005. *Indigenous Modernities*. New York: Routledge.

Hoselitz, Bert F. 1954. "Problems of Adapting and Communicating Modern Techniques to Less Developed Areas." *Economic Development and Cultural Change*, **2** (4), 249–268.

——1955. "Generative and Parasitic Cities." *Economic Development and Cultural Change*, **3** (3), 278–294.

——1956. "Nationalism, Economic Development, and Democracy." *Annals of the American Academy of Political and Social Science*, **305**, 1–11.

——1957. "Urbanization and Economic Growth in Asia." *Economic Development and Cultural Change*, **6** (1), 42–54.

Hull, Matthew. 2008. "Ruled by Records: The Expropriation of Lands and the Misappropriation of Lands in Islamabad." *American Ethnologist*, **35** (4), 501–518.

——2012. *Government of Paper: The Materiality of Bureaucracy in Pakistan*. Berkeley: University of California Press.

Huntington, Samuel. 1987. "The Goals of Development." In *Understanding Political Development*. Edited by Myron Weiner and Samuel Huntington. Boston: Little Brown.

Imperial Gazetteer of India. 1908. *Vol. XIII: Gyaraspur to Jais*. New Edition published under the Authority of His Majesty's Secretary of State for India in Council. Oxford: Clarendon Press.

Institute of Town Planners, India (ITPI). 1955. "Autumn Planning Seminar and State Planning Officials' Conference at Lucknow." *Journal of the Institute of Town Planners, India,* (November), 8–28.

——1958. "Autumn Planning Seminar and State Planning Officials' Conference at Jaipur." *Journal of the Institute of Town Planners, India.* (October), 1–25.

——1976. *Silver Jubilee Year Book.* New Delhi: ITPI.

Isaacs, Reginald R. 1948. "The Neighborhood Theory." *Journal of the AIP,* Spring, **14** (2), 15–23.

——1948. "The 'Neighborhood Unit' is an Instrument for Segregation." *Journal of the National Association of Housing Officials,* **5** (8), 215–219.

Jackson, John Brinckerhoff. 1984. *Discovering the Vernacular Landscape.* New Haven: Yale University Press.

Jacobs, Jane. 1961. *The Death and Life of Great American Cities.* New York: Vintage Books.

Jaffrelot, Christophe. 2000. "The Rise of the Other Backward Classes in the Hindi Belt." *The Journal of Asian Studies,* **59** (1), 86–108.

Jain, M.S. 1992. *Surplus to Subsistence.* New Delhi: Vishwa Prakashan.

——1993. *A Concise History of Modern Rajasthan.* New Delhi: Vishwa Prakashan.

Jaipur City Municipal Council. 1946. *Building Bye Laws.* Jaipur: Government of Jaipur.

Jaipur Development Authority (JDA). 1995. *Civic Surveys for Master Plan of Jaipur City.* Jaipur: Jaipur Development Authority.

——1996. *List of Schemes as on 31.05.1994 submitted by The New Pink City Griha-Nirman Co-operative Society Limited.* Jaipur: Print "O" Land.

——1998. *Jaipur Master Development Plan 2011.* Jaipur: Jaipur Development Authority.

——2011. *Jaipur Master Development Plan 2025.* Jaipur: Jaipur Development Authority.

Jeffrey, Craig. 2001. "A Fist is Stronger than Five Fingers: Caste and Dominance in Rural North India." *Transactions of the Institute of British Geographers,* **26** (2), 217–236.

——2002. "Caste, Class and Clientelism: A Political Economy of Everyday Corruption in Rural North India." *Economic Geography,* **78** (1), 21–41.

——2010. *Timepass: Youth, Class, and the Politics of Waiting in India.* Stanford: University of Stanford Press.

Jiménez-Domínguez, Bernardo. 2007. "Urban Appropriations and Loose Spaces in the Guadalajara Cityscape." In *Loose Space.* Edited by Karen A. Frank and Quentin Stevens. New York: Routledge.

Johnson, D.L. 2002. "Origin of the Neighborhood Unit." *Planning Perspectives,* **17**, 227–245.

Kadakia, P.O. 1964. *Gandhidham – A Planning Study.* Unpublished Diploma Course in Town and Country Planning thesis. New Delhi: School of Planning and Architecture.

Kalia, Ravi. 1987. *Chandigarh: In Search of an Identity.* Carbondale: Southern Illinois University Press.

——1995. *Bhubaneswar: From a Temple Town to a Capital City.* Carbondale: Southern Illinois University Press.

——2004. *Gandhi Nagar: Building National Identity in Postcolonial India.* Columbia: University of South Carolina Press.

——2006. "Modernism, Modernization and Postcolonial India: A Reflective Essay." *Planning Perspectives,* **21** (2), 133–156.

Kamilia, A. K. 1964. *A Study of Bhubaneswar.* Unpublished Diploma Course in Town and Country Planning thesis. New Delhi: School of Planning and Architecture.

Karatchkova, E. 2007. "Ghost Towns and Bustling Cities: Constructing a Master Narrative in Nineteenth Century Jaipur." In *Raj Rhapsodies: Tourism, Heritage and the Seduction of History.* Edited by C. Henderson and M. Weisgrau. Hampshire: Ashgate.

Keeble, Lewis. 1959. *Principles and Practice of Town and Country Planning.* London: The Estates Gazette Ltd.

Keller, Suzanne. 1968. *The Urban Neighborhood.* New York: Random House.

Khambatta, R.S. 1960. "Master Plan of Township at Vikroli." *Journal of Institute of Town Planners, India,* (July), 45–48.

Khan, Masood. 1994. "Cultural Transfers: The Repossession of Architectural Form." *Environmental Design: Journal of the Islamic Environmental Design Research Centre*, **1–2**, 84–103.

Khilnani, Sunil. 1999. *The Idea of India*. New York: Farrar Straus Giroux.

King, Anthony D. 1976. *Colonial Urban Development: Culture, Social Power, and Environment*. New York: Routledge and Kegan Paul.

——1984. *The Bungalow: The Production of a Global Culture*. London: Routledge and Kegan Paul.

——2004. *Spaces of Global Cultures: Architecture, Urbanism, Identity*. New York: Routledge.

Kipling, R. 1895. *Out of India*. New York: G.W. Dillingham.

Kirchherr, E.C. 1968. "Tema 1951–1962: The Evolution of a Planned City in West Africa." *Urban Studies*, **5** (2), 207–217.

Klemek, Christopher. 2011. *The Transatlantic Collapse of the Urban Renewal: Postwar Urbanism from New York to Berlin*. Chicago: University of Chicago Press.

Koenigsberger, Otto H. 1952. "New Towns in India." *Town Planning Review*, **23** (2), 94–131.

Kopardekar, H.D. and G.R. Diwan. 1994. *Urban and Regional Planning: Principles, Practice and the Law*. Talegaon-dabhade: Sudhanwa H. Kopardekar.

Kostof, Spiro. 1992. *The City Assembled*. New York: Bulfinch Press.

Krishna, Anirudh. 2003. "What Is Happening to Caste? A View from Some North Indian Villages." *The Journal of Asian Studies*, **62** (4), 1171–1193.

Kulshreshtha, Naveen. 1993. *History of Formal Housing in Delhi (1930–1982)*. Unpublished Master of Architecture in Human Settlements thesis. Leuven: Post Graduate Center of Human Settlements, K.U. Leuven.

Kumar, Arun. 1995. "Colonial Requirements and Engineering Education: The Public Works Department, 1847–1947." In *Technology and the Raj: Western Technology and Technical Transfers to India, 1700–1947*. Edited by Roy MacLeod and Deepak Kumar. New Delhi: Sage Publications, 216–232.

Kusno, Abidin. 2000. *Behind the Postcolonial: Architecture, Urban Space and Political Cultures in Indonesia*. London: Routledge.

Lahiri, Nayanjot. 2011. "A Capital Century." *The Caravan Magazine* (January). Also available online, accessed at www.caravanmagazine.in/archive/January-2011 viewed on May 6, 2013.

Laidlaw, J. 1996. *Riches and Renunciation: Religion, Economy, and Society among Jains*. New York: Oxford University Press.

Lanchester, H.V. 1914. "Calcutta Improvement Trust: Precis of Mr. E. P. Richards' Report on the City of Calcutta." *Town Planning Review*, **5**: 115–130 and 214–224.

Lang, Jon, Madhavi Desai and Micky Desai. 2012. *The Bungalow in Twentieth-Century India*. Surrey: Ashgate.

Lawhon, Larry L. 2009. "The Neighborhood Unit: Physical Design or Physical Determinism." *Journal of Planning History*, **8** (2), 111–132.

Lewis, John P. 1962. *Quiet Crisis in India*. Washington D.C.: Brookings Institution.

Liechty, M. 2003. *Suitably Modern: Making Middle-Class Culture in a New Consumer Society*. Princeton: Princeton University Press.

Liscombe, Rhodri Windsor. 2006. "In-dependence: Otto Koenigsberger and Modernist Urban Resettlement in India." *Planning Perspectives*, **21** (2), 157–178.

Logan, John R. and Harvey L. Molotch. 1987. *Urban Fortunes: The Political Economy of Place*. Berkeley: The University of California Press.

Loomba, Ania. 1998. *Colonialism: Postcolonialism*. New York: Routledge.

Lu, Duanfang. 2006. "Traveling Urban Form: The Neighborhood Unit in China." *Planning Perspectives*, **21** (3), 369–392.

Lynch, Kevin. 1981. *Good City Form*. Cambridge: The MIT Press.

Mathur, S.C. and P.K. Mathur. 1992. *Land Revenue Law in Rajasthan: Act with Statutory Rules and Notifications*. Jaipur: Unique Press.

Mayer, Albert. 1950. "The New Capital of Punjab." *Journal of American Institute of Architects*, **14**, 166–175.

——and Matthew Nowicki. 1950. "Supplementary Notes to the Architectural Study of Superblock L-37." *Albert Mayer Papers on India*, The University of Chicago Library. Box: 18, folders 30–33.

Mazzarella, William. 2003. *Shoveling Smoke*. Durham: Duke University Press.

Mehra, Diya. 2012. "Protesting Publics in Indian Cities: The 2006 Sealing Drive and Delhi's Traders." *Economic & Political Weekly*, **47** (30), 79–88.

——2013. "Planning Delhi ca. 1936–1959." *South Asia: Journal of South Asian Studies*, **36** (3), 354–374.

Mehrotra, Rahul (Ed.). 2005. *Everyday Urbanism: Margaret Crawford vs. Michael Speaks*. Ann Arbor: Taubman College of Architecture and Urban Planning, University of Michigan.

Mehta, C.S. 1963. *Udaipur: A Planning Study*, Unpublished Diploma Course in Town and Country Planning thesis. New Delhi: School of Planning and Architecture.

Mehta, Pratap Bhanu. 2003. *The Burden of Democracy*. New Delhi: Penguin Books.

Menon, A.G.K. 2000. "The Contemporary Architecture of Delhi: The Role of the State as Middleman." In *Delhi: Urban Space and Human Destinies*. Edited by Veronique Dupont, Emma Tarlo and Denis Vidal. New Delhi: Manohar.

Merrill, Dennis. 1990. *Bread and the Ballot: The United States and India's Economic Development 1947–1963*. Durham: The University of North Carolina Press.

Metcalf, T.R. 1989. *An Imperial Vision: Indian Architecture and Britain's Raj*. Berkeley: University of California Press.

Mewada, H.K. 1960. "Master Plan for Gauhati." *Journal of the Institute of Town Planners, India,* (Jan-April), 94–96.

Miller, Zane L. 1981. "The Role and Concept of Neighborhoods in American Cities." In *Community Organizations for Urban Social Change*. Edited by Robert Fisher and Peter Romanofsky. Westport: Greenwood Press, 3–32.

Mines, Mattison. 2006. "Temples and Charity: The Neighborhood Styles of the Komati and Beeri Chettiar Merchants of the Madras City." In *The Meaning of the Local: Politics of Place in Urban India*. Edited by Geert De Neve and Henrike Donner. Oxon: UCL Press, 89–115.

Mirza, Ismail. 1954. *My Public Life: Recollections and Reflections*. London: Allen & Unwin.

Mishra, K.N. 1958. *The Development of Allahabad: A Master Plan*. Allahabad: Kitabistan.

Mitchell, Tim. 2002. *Rule of Experts*. Berkeley: University of California Press.

Mumford, Lewis. 1933. "The Planned Community." *Architectural Forum,* **58**, 253–254.

——1954. "The Neighborhood and the Neighborhood Unit." *Town Planning Review*, **24**, 256–270.

——1961. *The City in History*. New York: Harvest Books.

Nagpur Improvement Trust. 1953. *Nagpur Master Plan*. Nagpur.

Nair, Janaki. 2011. *Mysore Modern: Rethinking the Region under Princely Rule*. Minneapolis: University of Minnesota Press.

Nandy, Ashis. 1983. *The Intimate Enemy: Loss and Recovery of Self under Colonialism*. New Delhi: Oxford University Press.

Nasr, Joseph and Volait Mercedes (Eds) 2003. *Urbanism: Imported or Exported?* West Sussex: Wiley-Academy.

Nath, V. 1995. "Planning For Delhi and National Capital Region." *Economic and Political Weekly,* **30** (35), 2191–2202.

National Institute of Urban Affairs (NIUA). 1991. *Jawahar Lal Nehru on Building a New India*. New Delhi: NIUA.

Navlakha, Gautam. 2000. "Urban Pollution: Driving Workers to Desperation." *Economic & Political Weekly*, **35** (51), 4469–4471.

Nehru, Jawahar Lal. 1960. *The Discovery of India*. New York: Anchor Books.

Neuman, Michael. 2005. "The Compact City Fallacy." *Journal of Planning Education and Research,* **25**, 11–26.

Oldenburg, Veena Talwar. 1984. *The Making of Colonial Lucknow, 1856–1877*. Princeton: Princeton University Press.

Pandey, Gyanendra (Ed.). 1993. *Hindus and Others: The Question of Identity in India Today.* New Delhi: Viking.

Papayanis, Nicholas. 2006. "César Daly, Paris and the Emergence of Modern Urban Planning." *Planning Perspectives,* **26** (3), 325–346.

Patricios, Nicholas N. 2002. "The Neighborhood Concept: A Retrospective of Physical Design and Social Interaction." *Journal of Architecture and Planning Research,* **19** (1), 70–90.

Peace, Adrian. 1980. "Structured Inequalities in a North Indian City." *Contributions to Indian Sociology,* **14** (2), 239–260.

Perera, Nihal. 2002. "Indigenizing the Colonial City: Late 19th Century Colombo and its Landscape." *Urban Studies,* **39** (9), 1703–1721.

——2004. "Contesting Visions: Hybridity, Liminality, and Authorship of the Chandigarh Plan." *Planning Perspectives,* **19** (2), 175–199.

Perry, Clarence A. 1924. "Planning a City Neighborhood from the Social Point of View." *Proceedings of the National Conference of Social Work* (Chicago), p. 421.

——1929. *The Neighborhood Unit, A Scheme for Arrangement for the Family-Life Community.* Monograph One in Neighborhood and Community Planning, Regional Survey of New York And its Environs. New York: Regional Plan of New York and its Environs.

——1933. *The Rebuilding of Blighted Areas: A Study of the Neighborhood Unit in Re-planning and Plot Assemblage.* New York: New York Regional Planning Association.

——1939. *Housing for the Machine Age.* New York: Russell Sage Foundation.

Pizarro, Rafael E., Liang Wei and Tridib Banerjee. 2003. "Agencies of Globalization and Third World Urban Form: A Review." *Journal of Planning Literature,* **18** (2), 111–130.

Prakash, Gyan. 1990. "Writing Post-Orientalist Histories of the Third World: Perspectives from Indian Historiography." *Comparative Studies in Society and History,* **32** (2), 383–408.

——1999. *Another Reason: Science and the Imagination of Modern India.* Princeton: University of Princeton Press.

Prakash, Ved. 1969. *New Towns in India.* Durham: Program in Comparative Studies on Southern Asia, Duke University.

Prakash, Vikramaditya. 2001. "Between Objectivity and Illusion: Architectural Photography in the Colonial Frame." *Journal of Architectural Education,* **55** (1), 13–20.

Pratt, Mary Louise. 1992. *Imperial Eyes: Travel Writing and Transculturation.* New York: Routledge.

Pucher, J., Z. Peng, N. Mittal, Y. Zhu and N. Korattyswaroopam, 2007. "Urban Transport Trends and Policies in China and India: Impact of Rapid Economic Growth." *Transport Reviews,* **27** (4), 379–410.

Purdom, Charles B. 1949. *The Building of Satellite Towns: A Contribution to the Study of Town Development and Regional Planning.* London: Dent.

Qadeer, Muhammad A. 1974. "Do Cities 'Modernize' the Developing Countries? An Examination of the South Asian Experience." *Comparative Studies in Society and History,* **16** (3), 266–283.

——1983. *Lahore: Urban Development in the Third World.* Lahore: Vanguard Books.

——2000. "Ruralopolises: The Spatial Organisation and Residential Land Economy of High-density Rural Regions in South Asia." *Urban Studies,* **37** (9), 1583–1603.

Rajasthan Housing Board (RHB). 1981. *Brochure for Applicants: Jawahar Nagar.* Jaipur: Rajasthan Housing Board.

Rajasthan Patrika. 2009. "Bhagwan bachayain apni zameen" [May God save his own land] Jaipur edition, December 29.

——2012. "Batengi Patton ki Rewadyian – Cabinet ka Mahtvyapurna Faisla" [State cabinet announces the Freebie of Land Titles] Jaipur edition, October 4.

Rand, Christopher. 1956. "Letter From Jaipur." *The New Yorker* (September 15 issue).

Rao, Nikhil. 2013. *House, But No Garden: Apartment Living in Bombay's Suburbs, 1898–1964.* Minneapolis: University of Minnesota Press.

Rathore, Gayatri Jai Singh. 2012. "Ramganj, Jaipur: From Occupation-based to 'Communal' Neighborhood?" In *Muslims in Indian Cities: Trajectories of Marginalization.*

Edited by Laurent Gayer and Christophe Jaffrelot. New York: Columbia University Press, 81–104.

Raychaudhuri, Siddhartha. 2001. "Colonialism, Indigenous Elites and the Transformation of Cities in the Non-Western World: Ahmedabad (Western India), 1890–1947." *Modern Asian Studies,* **35** (3), 677–726.

Reiner, Thomas A. 1963. *The Place of the Ideal Community in Urban Planning.* Philadelphia: University of Pennsylvania Press.

Reps, John W. 1992. *The Making of Urban America: A History of City Planning in the United States.* Princeton: University of Princeton Press.

Risbud, Neelima. 2000. *Government Policies and Illegal Land Supply by Housing Cooperatives, Jaipur.* New Delhi: Research report number 23, Human Settlement Management Institute.

Robbins, Paul. 1998. "Authority and Environment: Institutional Landscapes in Rajasthan, India." *Annals of the Association of American Geographers,* **88** (3), 410–435.

Rohe, William. M. 2009. "From Local to Global: One Hundred Years of Neighborhood Planning." *Journal of the American Planning Association,* **75** (2), 209–230.

Rosin, Thomas. 2001. "From Garden Suburb to Olde City Ward – A Longitudinal Study of Social Processes and Incremental Architecture in Jaipur, India." *Journal of Material Culture,* **6** (2), 165–192.

Rosser, Colin. 1972. *Urbanization in India. An International Urbanization Survey Report to the Ford Foundation.* New Delhi: Ford Foundation.

Rossi, Aldo. 1984. *The Architecture of the City.* Cambridge: The MIT Press.

Rostow, W.W. 1952. *The Process of Economic Growth.* New York: W. W. Norton & Co.

Roy, A. 2009. "Why India Cannot Plan its Cities: Informality, Insurgence, and the Idiom of Urbanization." *Planning Theory,* **8** (1), 76–87.

Roy, Ashim Kumar. 1977. "Architecture: The Dream and the Plan." *Marg,* **30** (4), 25–26.

——1978. *History of the Jaipur City.* New Delhi: Manohar.

Rudolph, S. and L. Rudolph. 1984. *Essays on Rajputana.* New Delhi: Concept Publishing Company.

——1987. *In Pursuit of Lakshmi: The Political Economy of the Indian State.* Chicago: University of Chicago Press.

Rybczynski, Witold. 2007. *Last Harvest.* New York: Scribner.

Sable, Scott. 1980. "Indian Education: A View from the Bottom Up." In *The Transformation of A Scared Town: Bhubaneswar, India.* Edited by Susan Seymour. Boulder: Westview Press, 157–184.

Sachdev, Vibhuti and Giles Tillotson. 2002. *Building Jaipur: The Making of an Indian City.* London: Reaktion Books.

Said, E. 1978. *Orientalism.* New York: Vintage.

Sandercock, Leonie. 1998. *Towards Cosmopolis: Planning for Multicultural Cities.* New York: John Wiley.

Sanyal, Bishwapriya. 2002. "Globalization, Ethical Compromise and Planning Theory." *Planning Theory,* **1** (2), 116–123.

——(Ed.). 2005. *Comparative Planning Cultures.* New York: Routledge.

——, Lawrence Vale and Christina Rosan. 2012. *Planning Ideas that Matter: Livability, Territoriality, and Reflective Practice.* Cambridge: The MIT Press.

Sarin, M. 1982. *Urban Planning in the Third World: The Chandigarh Experience.* London: Mansell Publishing.

Sarkar, Jadunath. 1984. *A History of Jaipur.* Delhi: Manohar Publications.

Scheer, Brenda. 2010. *The Evolution of Urban Form: Typology for Planners and Architects.* Chicago: APA Planners Press.

Schubert, Dirk. 1995. "Origins of the Neighborhood Units Idea in Great Britain and Germany: Examples from London and Hamburg." *Planning History,* **17** (3), 32–40.

Scott, James C. 1985. *Weapons of the Weak: Everyday Forms of Peasant Resistance.* New Haven: Yale University Press.

——1998. *Seeing like a State.* New Haven: Yale University Press.

Scriver, Peter. 1994. *Rationalization, Standardization, and Control in Design: A Cognitive Historical Study of Architectural Design and Planning in the Public Works Department of British India, 1855–1901.* Delft, Netherlands: Publicatiebureau Bouwkunde of the Delft University of Technology.

——2007. "Empire-building and Thinking in the Public Works Department of British India." In *Colonial Modernities: Building, Dwelling and Architecture in British India and Ceylon.* Edited by Peter Scriver and Vikramaditya Prakash. New York: Routledge/Architext, 69–92.

Sealey, Neil E. 1982. *Planned Cities in India.* London: Extramural Division, School of Oriental and African Studies, University of London.

Seymour, Susan (Ed.). 1980. *The Transformation of A Scared Town: Bhubaneswar, India.* Boulder: Westview Press.

Sharma, C.L. 1992. *Urban Community Power Structure: An Empirical Study of Local Elites.* Udaipur: Shiva Publishers.

Showers, H.L. 1916. *Notes on Jaipur.* Jaipur: Rai Bahadur Seth Nauranga Rai Khaitan.

Silver, Christopher. 1985. "Neighborhood Planning in Historical Perspective." *Journal of American Planning Association,* **51** (2), 161–174.

——2006. "New Urbanism and Planning History: Back to the Future." In *Culture, Urbanism and Planning.* Edited by Javier Monclus and Manuel Guardia. Hampshire: Ashgate.

Singh, C.P. 2000. "A Century of Constituency Delimitation in India." *Political Geography,* **19**, 517–532.

Singh, Hira. 1998. *Colonial Hegemony and Popular Resistance: Princess, Peasants and Paramount Power.* Toronto: Canadian Scholars Press.

Singh, J.P. and M. Khan. 1991. "Hindu Cosmology and the Orientation and Segregation of Social Groups in Villages in North Western India." *Geografiska Annaler,* **81** (B), 19–39.

Singh, S.R. 1979. *Urban Planning in India: A Case Study of Urban Improvement Trusts.* New Delhi: Ashish Publishing House.

Sisson, Richard. 1966. "Institutionalization and Style in Rajasthan Politics." *Asian Survey,* **6** (11), 605–613.

Sivaramakrishnan, K. and Arun Agrawal. (Eds). 2003. *Regional Modernities: The Cultural Politics of Development in India.* Stanford: Stanford University Press.

Smith, C. 2006. *The Plan of Chicago: Daniel Burnham and the Remaking of the American City.* Chicago: University of Chicago Press.

Soja, Edward. 1996. *Thirdspace: Journeys to Los Angeles and other Real-and-imagined Places.* Cambridge: Blackwell.

Solow, A.A., C.E. Ham and E.O. Donnelly. 1969. "The Concept of Neighborhood Unit: Its Emergence and Influence on Residential Environment Planning and Development." In *Final Report on Planning, Designing and Managing the Residential Environment: Stage One.* Edited by I.M. Robinson. Los Angeles: Graduate Program of Urban and Regional Planning, University of Southern California.

Spivak, Gayatri Chakravorty. 1988. "Can the Subaltern Speak?" In *Marxism and the Interpretation of Culture.* Edited by Carry Nelson and Lawrence Grossberg. Urbana: The University of Illinois Press.

Srinivas, S. 2001. *Landscapes of Urban Memory: The Sacred and the Civic in India's High-tech City.* Minneapolis: University of Minnesota Press.

——2012. *Market Menagerie: Health and Development in Late Industrial States.* Stanford: Stanford University Press.

Staples, Eugene L. 1992. *Forty Years: A Learning Curve.* New Delhi: The Ford Foundation.

STEM. 1992. *An Objective Review on Implementation of Master plan in Selected Class I Cities and Other Towns.* Bangalore: Centre for Symbiosis of Technology, Environment and Management.

Stern, Robert. 1988. *The Cat and the Lion: Jaipur State in the British Raj.* Leiden: E.J. Brill.

Steuteville, Robert. 2000. *New Urbanism and Traditional Neighborhood Development.* Ithaca: New Urban News.

——and Philip Langdon. 2003. *New Urbanism: Comprehensive Report & Best Practices Guide*. Ithaca: New Urban News.

Subramanian, Narendra. 2007. "Populism in India." *SAIS Review*, **XXVII** (1), 81–91.

Subramanian, T.S.R. 2004. *Journeys through Babudom and Netaland: Governance in India*. New Delhi: Rupa & Co.

Sundaram, Ravi. 2011. *Pirate Modernity: Delhi's Media Urbanism*. New York: Routledge.

Sutton, David. 2001. *Remembrance of Repasts: An Anthropology of Food and Memory*. Oxford: Berg Publishers.

Swamy, M.C. Krishna. 1966. "New Towns in India." *Journal of the Institute of Town Planners, India*, **49–50**, 40–51.

Tafuri, Manfredo. 1980. *Theories and History of Architecture*. New York: Icon (Harpe).

Talen, Emily. 2000. "The Problem with Community in Planning." *Journal of Planning Literature*, **15** (2), 171–183.

——2002. "Social Goals of New Urbanism." *Housing Policy Debate*, **13** (1), 165–188.

——2005. *New Urbanism and American Planning: The Conflict of Cultures*. New York: Routledge.

Tangri, Shanti. 1968. "Urban Growth, Housing, and Economic Development: The Case of India." *Asian Survey*, **8** (7), 519–538.

Tarlo, Emma. 2003. *Unsettling Memories: Narratives of the Emergency in Delhi*. Berkeley: University of California Press.

Taylor, Charles. 2004. *Modern Social Imaginaries*. Durham: Duke University Press.

Taylor, Nigel. 1998. *Urban Planning Theory since 1945*. London: Sage Publications.

The Housing Team. 1965. *India's Urban Housing: A Report to the Ford Foundation*. New Delhi: Ford Foundation.

The Times of India. 2012. "Finally, Nine-story Structure Razed," Jaipur edition, 17 September.

Throgmorton, James A. 2003. "Planning as Persuasive Storytelling in a Global-scale Web of Relationships." *Planning Theory*, **2** (2), 125–151.

Tillotson, G.H.R. 1989. *The Tradition of Indian Architecture: Continuity, Change and the Politics of Style since 1850*. New Heaven: Yale University Press.

——2008. "CG Blomfield Last Architect of the Raj." *South Asian Studies*, **24**, 133–139.

Tipple, Graham. (Ed.). 2000. *Extending Themselves: User Initiated Transformations of Government-built Housing in Developing Countries*. Chicago: University of Chicago Press.

Tod, J. 1920. *Annals and Antiquities of Rajasthan*. Vols 1–3. London: Humphrey Milford, Oxford University Press.

Town and Country Planning Organization (TCPO). 1962. *Town and Country Planning in India*. New Delhi: TCPO, Ministry of Health, Government of India.

——1996. *Urban and Regional Planning and Development in India*. New Delhi: TCPO, Ministry of Urban Affairs and Employment, Government of India.

Town Planning Organization (TPO). 1956. *Interim General Plan for Greater Delhi*. New Delhi: Ministry of Health, Government of India.

Tsing, Anna Lowenhaupt. 1993. *In the Realm of the Diamond Queen*. Princeton: Princeton University Press.

Turner, John F.C. 1972. *Freedom to Build: Dweller Control of the Housing Process*. New York: Macmillan Publishing Company.

Tyagi, V.K. 1982. *Urban Growth and Urban Villages: A Case Study of Delhi*. Delhi: Kalyani Press.

Tyrwhitt, J. (Ed.) 1947. *Patrick Geddes in India*. London: Lund Humphries.

Uttar Pradesh Town Planning Organization (UPTPO). 1952. *Progressive Uttar Pradesh: Town Planning*. Lucknow: New Government Press.

Vagale, L.R., B.M. Buta and M.S.V. Rao. 1959. "Faridabad—A Critical Study." *Planning Thought*, **2** (3), 85–108.

Venturi, Robert, Dennis Scott Brown and Steven Izenour. 1972. *Learning from Las Vegas*. Cambridge: The MIT Press.

Verma, Gita Dewan. 2003. *Slumming India: A Chronicle of Slums and Their Saviours*. Delhi: Penguin Books.

Vidyarthi, Sanjeev. 2014. "Building a 'World Class Heritage City': Jaipur's Emergent Elites and New Approach to Spatial Planning." In *Contesting the Indian City*. Edited by Gavin Shatkin. West Sussex: Wiley-Blackwell.

Volwahsen, Andreas. 1968. *Architecture of the World: India*. Lausanne: Hennessey & Ingalls.

Waghorne, Joanne P. 2004. *Diaspora of the Gods: Modern Hindu Temples in an Urban Middle-Class World*. New York: Oxford University Press.

Wajahat, Fatima. 2014. "Perceptions of Tenure Security in a Squatter Settlement in Lahore, Pakistan." In *Transforming Asian Cities*. Edited by Nihal Perera and Wing-Shing Tang. New York: Routledge.

Ward, Stephen V. 2002. *Planning the Twentieth-Century City*. Chichester: John Wiley.

Warner Jr., Sam Bass. 1962. *Streetcar Suburbs: The Processes of Growth in Boston 1870–1900*. Cambridge: Harvard University Press.

Weiss, Mark A. 1987. *The Rise of the Community Builders: The American Real Estate Industry and Urban Land Planning*. New York: Columbia University Press.

White, M. and L. White. 1962. *The Intellectual Versus the City*. New York: Mentor Books.

Wilcox, Wayne. 1965. "Politicians, Bureaucrats and Development in India." *The Annals of the American Academy of Political and Social Science*, **358** (1), 114–122.

Wirth, Louis. 1938. "Urbanism as a Way of Life." *American Journal of Sociology*, **44** (1), 1–24.

Wolff, Werner Y. 1990. *Open Space Planning in India*. Bern: Peter Lang Publishers.

Yang, Anand. 1998. *Bazaar India: Markets, Society and the Colonial State in Bihar*. Berkeley: University of California Press.

Yin, Robert K. 1994. *Case Study Research: Design and Methods*. New York: Thousand Oaks, Sage Publications.

Young, Robert J.C. 1995. *Colonial Desire: Hybridity in Theory, Culture, and Race*. New York: Routledge.

Yugandhar, B.N. and P.S. Datta (Eds). 1995. *Land Reforms in India, Vol. 2: Rajasthan—Feudalism and Change*. New Delhi: Sage Publications.

INDEX

eBooks
from Taylor & Francis

Helping you to choose the right eBooks for your Library

Add to your library's digital collection today with Taylor & Francis eBooks. We have over 50,000 eBooks in the Humanities, Social Sciences, Behavioural Sciences, Built Environment and Law, from leading imprints, including Routledge, Focal Press and Psychology Press.

Free Trials Available

We offer free trials to qualifying academic, corporate and government customers.

Choose from a range of subject packages or create your own!

Benefits for you
- Free MARC records
- COUNTER-compliant usage statistics
- Flexible purchase and pricing options
- 70% approx of our eBooks are now DRM-free.

Benefits for your user
- Off-site, anytime access via Athens or referring URL
- Print or copy pages or chapters
- Full content search
- Bookmark, highlight and annotate text
- Access to thousands of pages of quality research at the click of a button.

eCollections

Choose from 20 different subject eCollections, including:

- Asian Studies
- Economics
- Health Studies
- Law
- Middle East Studies

eFocus

We have 16 cutting-edge interdisciplinary collections, including:

- Development Studies
- The Environment
- Islam
- Korea
- Urban Studies

For more information, pricing enquiries or to order a free trial, please contact your local sales team:

UK/Rest of World: **online.sales@tandf.co.uk**
USA/Canada/Latin America: **e-reference@taylorandfrancis.com**
East/Southeast Asia: **martin.jack@tandf.com.sg**
India: **journalsales@tandfindia.com**

www.tandfebooks.com